God Bless You

Dream Big

Love

LITA

BRIG & LITA HART

For years Brig Hart has inspired thousands of people to live life abundantly and to succeed in business. Many prominent business leaders, thought leaders, church leaders, and even a few politicians have either joined Brig on stage at one of his events or enjoyed his company.

A few of these occasions are reflected below...

The Beach Boys
American Rock Band

Terry Bradshaw
Co-Host of Fox NFL Sunday &
Former NFL Quarterback

Dr. Joyce Brothers
American Psychologist & Advice Columnist

Ray Charles
American Musician

Jerry Clower
Country Comedian

Phil Driscoll
World-Class Trumpet Player, Singer & Composer

Art Linkletter
Radio & Television Personality

Oliver North
Political Commentator & Former USMC Officer

Jack Eckerd
Founder of Eckerds Drug Stores & Philanthropist

Joe Theismann
*Sportscaster on NFL Network &
Former NFL Quarterback*

Newt Gingrich
American Politician

Ed Hearn
World Series Champion & Motivational Speaker

Jack Kemp
American Politician & Former AFL Quarterback

Tommy Lasorda
Former Major League Baseball Pitcher & Manager

Mylon LeFevre
Former Christian Rock Singer

Louise Mandrell
Country Music Singer

Clebe & Deanna McClary
Marine & Motivational Speaker

Warren Moon
Former CFL & NFL Quarterback

Dr. & Mrs. Myles Munroe
Senior Pastor of BFMI & Author

Sandi Patty
Christian Music Singer

Kyle Petty
NASCAR Driver

Ronald Reagan
40th President of the United States

Mary Lou Retton
American Gymnast & Olympic Gold Medalist

Alan Thicke
Actor, Songwriter & Game Show Host

Heather Whitestone
Miss America 1995

Zig Ziglar
Motivational Speaker & Author

WHY NOT YOU? WHY NOT NOW?
PUBLISHED BY FRANKLIN GREEN PUBLISHING
500 Wilson Pike Circle, Suite 100
Brentwood, Tennessee 37027
www.franklingreenpublishing.com

Cover design by R3Global and Marc Pewitt

ISBN 978-0-982638-729

Printed in the United States of America

2 3 4 5 6 7 8 9 10—15 14 13 12 11

WHY NOT YOU? WHY NOT NOW?

The Brig Hart Story

BRIG HART

WITH KEN ABRAHAM

FRANKLIN GREEN
PUBLISHING

Brentwood, Tennessee

My partner for life and
best friend, Lita

To the people who mean the most to me: My best friend and partner for life, Miss Lo-Lita, my loving wife. She so lets me be me and keeps me grounded. Thanks a heap. To my three precious children: Brittany, Daniel, and Paul. You are my flesh and blood. I learn more every day just how special it

My precious offspring:
Daniel, Brittany, and Paul

is to have the privilege to raise you guys. I see in each one of you the power and potential God has endowed in you. Look out, world! Here come the Harts to make a difference for the better.
I'm so proud of you!

✦ ✦ ✦

In loving memory of my mom and dad, Cornelia H. Hart (1931–2010) and Robert L. Hart (1930–1997). I choose to honor you because you will forever have a wonderful influence on me and on all the people with whom you ever interacted. I so miss you and the great wisdom you imparted to me and your precious grandchildren. I will see you in heaven.

✦ ✦ ✦

To all the pioneers and mavericks out there who choose to live life to the fullest through the industry that has been such a blessing to me and my life. Relationships with family and friends are invaluable. So here's to all those who choose to take the path less traveled, because that makes all the difference. Onward and upward!

CONTENTS

"Anyway"

The Paradoxical Commandments

By Kent M. Keith

People are often illogical, unreasonable, and self-centered.
Love them anyway.
If you do good, people will accuse you of selfish, ulterior motives.
Do good anyway.
If you are successful, you will win some false friends and true enemies.
Succeed anyway.
Honesty and frankness make you vulnerable.
Be honest and frank anyway.
The biggest men and women with the biggest ideas can be shot down by
the smallest men and women with the smallest minds.
Think big anyway.
People favor underdogs but follow only top dogs.
Fight for a few underdogs anyway.
What you spend years building may be destroyed overnight.
Build anyway.
People really need help but may attack you if you do help them.
Help people anyway.
Give the world the best you have, and it may never be enough.
Give the world the best you have anyway.

A PERSONAL WORD FROM BRIG BEFORE YOU BEGIN

OBEDIENCE, DILIGENCE, and faithfulness are key ingredients to success. If I can learn and apply these attributes in my life, so can you. I have no special gifting or exceptional talent, but I live an extraordinarily blessed life. Through everyday life experiences, I have somehow been able to identify and act upon ordinary circumstances and create extraordinary results from just desiring to do so.

Do you want more out of life? Are you willing to do something about it? If so, this book is for you. What one person can do, another can do as well. Although this book shares my life's story, read on and you will see that it is really all about you. I am writing to encourage you, just as I have been encouraged by others through the stories of their life experiences. I've heard that encouragement is "oxygen to the soul." I like that. And I want you to be encouraged as you see that the failures I faced were never fatal. A person can get knocked down and, with God's help, get back up again and win!

The Bible says that "a live dog is better off than a dead lion."[1] If you are breathing, God is not done with you yet! If you've been knocked down in life, get yourself up, dust yourself off, and get going again. Dare to dream a big dream, and then muster the faith you need to pursue it. God created everyone with a dream and a purpose in life. You just have to step out and live with positive expectation. I have gone from zero to hero in life, from

Oh yeah, fifty-five
(the new forty)—Brig

the pits to the palace, simply by taking advantage of the opportunities that came my way. Yes, it's a real-life rags-to-riches story without any one special deal that came my way. In every situation I've faced, there were people I came into relationship with who held a key to the next door of opportunity that opened up to me. If you can learn to identify and take advantage of those divine appointments, life can get exciting for you. The success you desire just may be in the situation you are in now and with the people who are within your sphere of influence at this very moment. You can do the same. You are a winner, and the world is waiting to hear your story. Don't deny yourself—or us—the privilege of experiencing that dream worked out in and through you.

In the pages ahead, I'll show you how Lita and I did it. If I can overcome and become, so can you. You just have to decide for yourself. *Why not me? Why not now?*

CHAPTER **1**

If I Can Do It, So Can You!

'VE BEEN POOR AND I've been rich. Rich is better!

I wasn't born poor, nor did anyone rob me of my wealth. Neither did lack of opportunity force me into poverty. No, I made myself poor. I was so broke at one point, in fact, that I couldn't pay an eighteen-dollar electric bill despite having owned several successful businesses in Jacksonville, Florida.

How did I get to be so destitute? It's easy. Anyone can be broke if you do what I did. I continually believed the wrong ideas and invested my time and energy in activities that not only kept me on a treadmill to nowhere but also produced a life characterized by foolish, irresponsible, unwise decisions.

Being poor, broke, and in debt was by no means my goal, but I accomplished that goal because of my state of mind. I really wanted to be rich just once before I died, but I didn't want money to dictate every decision I ever made. In the years since, I have declared war on poverty.

How did I grow rich? That was amazingly simple too. I grew rich, or wealthy, in the truest sense of the word—physically, financially, emotionally, and spiritually—by changing what I believed, what I thought, what I spoke, and how I acted. Transforming the way I saw others and myself opened a world of possibilities for me. God made us free moral agents; we get to choose which way we believe. You can trust this: you'll never get what you want, but you will always get what you picture. You can change your circumstances simply by changing the way you see and think about yourself.

If I can do it, you can too!

Are you satisfied with where you are in your life? Me neither. I don't want much; I just want *more*. Everyone wants more than what he or she currently has. Every person in your workplace, in your sphere of influence, in your town, in your church—everyone you see around you— wants more of life's best. Why? Because God put a mandate within you and me to take authority over the earth: "Be fruitful and multiply; fill the earth and subdue it; have domin- ion over the fish of the sea, over the birds of the air, and over every living thing that moves on the earth." Although we've not always handled our world with care, that God- given responsibility has never been rescinded. God wants you to have more, do more, and be more than you have yet imagined. His dream for you is far greater than your own dreams for yourself!

Everyone wants more.

God wants you to be blessed so you can be a blessing to others. But how can you be a blessing to others if you are not blessed yourself?

I've found a way that you can have more for your family and how you can have more to share with others. In the pages ahead, I'll not only tell you how I broke out of the perils of poverty and became a person of prosperity (some say successful, but I believe that success is a journey, not a destination, so I am still on my way), but I'll show you how you can do the same and more!

It's time for *you* to move into a whole new way of living. "Oh, Brig, I don't know," I hear you saying. "Times are tough." No time is a good time to take that first tenuous step to start something new. But as the old saying reminds us, "The journey of a thousand miles begins with the first step." If

BRIGISM

I don't want much, I just want more. How much more? Just a little bit.

you wait until all things are perfect and in place before you launch out on your journey, you will never begin. For example, if you wait until you have all the equipment you need to exercise (new jogging shirts, shorts, and shoes), for the weather to be perfect, and for you to have nothing else to do, you will never begin, much less maintain, a healthy exercise regimen. You simply have to make a quality decision to start and to start *now!* The results will follow. The same is true in business. No time is a good time, so now is as good a time as any.

Think about it: will there ever be a better time for you to step out of your comfort zone, to dare to believe for something more or something better, to discover what could actually happen if you succeed? The answer, whether you realize it or not, is "no." Now is the time. Today is the day to begin a new way of doing things, especially if what you have been doing is not working or is not bringing you the results you expected. If you wait another week, month, or year before risking that tenuous first step, you will gain nothing, and you will have lost more time—time that you could have used to pursue your dreams, time that you could have enjoyed with your family or friends, time that you could have been investing in making a difference in your world. So why wait? Do something, and do it now. Making a quality decision is the key to starting you on your journey to success.

No time is a good time, so now is as good a time as any.

Life is too short to spend most of your time doing things you don't fully enjoy doing. If you are sick and tired of being sick and tired, don't blow this off. Do something about it, and do it now! An ancient adage advises, "To thine own self be true." In other words, be honest about your situation. I also like the popular motto: "Life is short; eat dessert first!" Learn from my mistakes, be encouraged and inspired by my progress and successes, and start now to build toward your new and exciting future.

Why not you? Why not now? Those are the questions I want you to keep in mind as you read how a long-haired, hippie-type, beer-drinking, dope-smoking surfer who was lost, broke, and mad at the world and himself could have his life turned inside out, then totally renovated and redirected on an incredible journey I didn't even know was possible. As you read, I won't mind if you think to yourself, *That Brig Hart is just an ordinary person like me. He's not a brilliant intellect or a financial genius, yet he went on to become one of the most successful network marketers in history. It's my turn.*

B R I G I S M

Experience is the best teacher as long as it is someone else's experience. Then it's wisdom.

What did Brig do? Maybe I can learn from his example, both positively and negatively. Why not me? Why not now?

Nearly every day I hear stories of folks who have poured their lives into jobs, businesses, or careers that led them only to dead ends and dashed hopes. Others have been part of businesses that robbed the life out of them. Still others have bought into misguided philosophies and now are reaping the consequences of that bad information. Thousands of folks have been the innocent victims of mismanaged companies and have been let go because of downsizing, or "the economy." Simply put: millions of people today have found themselves in the wrong place at the wrong time as the global economy spirals downward, forcing a large number of people to consider alternative ways of making a living. Difficult circumstances beyond our control have dictated that many of us must look beyond the norm to find ways to recover and prosper again.

Life is too short to spend your time doing things you don't fully enjoy doing.

Each week I hear of heartbroken people praying, "God, if you don't intervene in my situation, if you don't change something soon, I don't know what I am going to do. My finances are at an end, and my relationship with my spouse has deteriorated because we are so worried about how we are going to make it." People everywhere want more, and you and I may be the answer to their prayers.

Many people with whom I work have discovered that my simple, systematic way of approaching life works. They are not smarter than you or more talented. They simply desired to change their circumstances and decided to follow the plan of action that I discovered the hard way. Now that I've figured it out, I'm offering it to you. If I can do it, so can you! So as you read my story, I pray that you will see the possibilities of achieving anything that your heart desires, that you will attain all that I've been able to do—and more! My success can be replicated by anyone willing to work at it. Everyone wants more, but not everyone is willing to learn, work, and sacrifice to achieve more. I have come to realize that no one can make anyone else successful; you have to decide that for yourself. You have that option in life: to overcome and become.

Everyone I meet is born equal and has the right to become unequal. What makes the difference? "You just gotta wanna," is how I put it. By picking up this book and reading this far, you have already separated yourself from the pack. You've shown yourself that you wanna. Now, keep going. Don't stop until you reach your goals. If I can do it, why not you? Why not now?

BRIGISM

Life should be a daring adventure. Go for it!

CHAPTER **2**

Miracles Happen

BORN IN DELAND, FLORIDA, as the second in a family of four siblings, with an older brother and two younger sisters, I spent most of my early years in Salisbury, Maryland. I was raised in a typical middle-class family with a strong work ethic. My dad, Robert L. "Bob" Hart, was a wise man, but unfortunately I didn't appreciate it until I had my own "great awakening." He passed on a number of brilliant aphorisms that I still use in our business today. A few of Dad's sayings you might hear me repeating include: "Friends do what friends do," and "If you are going to walk through a mine field, follow someone...at a distance!" He often quipped, "Love makes the world go around, but it's money that greases the wheel." Dad also loved to remind our family of his version of the Golden Rule: "He who has the gold makes the rules."

Dad could be a vicious competitor when it came to business, a fact attested to by another of his favorite lines: "When a good man is down, kick him. When he gets up, run, and encourage him as he pursues." Dad was always quick to help underdogs as long as they were willing to help themselves. He evidently taught me to do the same. I love to help folks overcome and beat the odds.

Perhaps the principle I heard most often from my dad had to do with his work ethic: "Do it. Do it well, and do it right. Take pride in all you do. Always do what is right, but always do the right thing." To that, he added, "Never tell me you can't do something. You can do anything you set your mind to doing." And people say that *I'm* driven!

Despite his energetic approach to life, by 1997, Dad had developed a severe case of inoperable prostate cancer and was fading fast. His doctor said, "There's not a lot we can do," so he loaded up Dad with all sorts of medicine simply to reduce the pain and keep him comfortable.

One day I was home and received a phone call from Dr. Edwin Louis Cole, a man whose spiritual wisdom and discernment I respected greatly. As one of the world's most successful network marketers, I was planning a major function at the Fontainebleau Hotel in Miami Beach. I had scheduled Dr. Cole to speak, so I wasn't surprised to hear from him, but I was surprised when he let me know the reason for his call.

"Hello, Brig, I just wanted to talk to you before the event."

"Hey, Ed. I'm looking forward to seeing you."

"Listen, I've been praying for you, and the Lord showed me that there's something going on with your dad."

"Well, yeah. He's fighting cancer."

"Let me tell you what we're going to do. I want you to get your dad down to Miami."

"Well, Dr. Cole, he can't even get out of bed, much less travel."

"Whatever you have to do, get him there. I want to tell you what's going to happen: God is going to heal your dad."

My dad, Robert L. Hart

Dr. Cole's words nearly knocked me over.

"I've been praying," Dr. Cole continued, "so you just bring him along and trust God. Do you believe that God can do this?"

"I do," I heard myself saying against all logic.

I arranged to have Dad transferred by ambulance from my parents' home in Neptune Beach, Florida, to the Fontainebleau in

Miami Beach, where I was booked into the Frank Sinatra Suite. Dad couldn't move. His face was ashen, his eyes dim, his gaunt skin a pale, yellowish gray. It was obvious that my father was dying.

We went through the entire weekend, and I kept expecting Ed Cole to pray for my dad or do something spectacular, but Dr. Cole was a man not given to the outlandish. "Just relax," he said to me whenever he saw the anxiousness in my face. "Relax."

Dad didn't get out of bed during the event. We brought in special meals for him, but he could barely eat or drink.

On Sunday morning, we held a nondenominational, voluntary worship service, as we usually do at my events, for those who attended the weekend business conference and who wished to participate. At the close of the event, a large number of people responded to an invitation to put their trust in Jesus Christ. We were thrilled at the results of the weekend, but I still wondered about my dad.

Finally, after all of the scheduled events were concluded, Ed said, "Gather your leaders and people who have faith and meet us up in your suite."

Within a few minutes, we had assembled about three dozen of my leaders and friends in the suite.

"Now, go get your dad," Ed instructed.

A few of my friends and I went to Dad's room and carefully assisted him downstairs to meet with Dr. Cole in the living area of the suite. The people standing around the room could barely conceal their concern at seeing Dad's condition, and Ed seemed to pick up on it.

"Y'all just pray," he instructed.

Dr. Cole reached his arms around my dad and supported him with a bear-hug-type hold, steadying him on his feet as he held him. He then looked into Dad's eyes and asked, "Bob, do you want to live?"

"Yes," my dad answered feebly.

"Bob, do you want to be healed?"

"Yes," Dad answered with what little strength he had left.

"Bob, I'm going to pray for you," Dr. Cole said, "and God is going to heal you."

Dr. Cole fully embraced my dad, his face cheek-to-cheek with Dad's, as he whispered into his ear a simple prayer, commanding Dad to be healed. Thirty or more people in the room watched in awe as my dad's countenance dramatically changed before our eyes. His skin went from the pale, sickly color back to a healthy-looking hue and texture. Over the next hour

Dad with my brother David and me in
Salisbury, Maryland, in 1953

or so, Dad's countenance changed, his eyes brightened and sparkled. His frame straightened and strengthened. His entire body went through a complete restoration.

But Dr. Cole wasn't done. "Bob, I prayed for you to be healed in the name of Jesus," he said matter-of-factly. "Now, are you ready to acknowledge the One who healed you?"

I felt as though I were witnessing a New Testament miracle as my dad tearfully and joyfully prayed and expressed his faith in Jesus Christ. It was one of the happiest days of my life! When Dad left Miami and went home, the prostate cancer was gone.

God gave him an extra five years of life as a result, and those were some of the best years in my dad's and my relationship. We became a true loving father and son, but beyond that, we became the best of friends, enjoying the type of father-son relationship for which both of us had longed. Dad's and my relationship over the years had been strained, to say the least, but now I wanted to be around him as much as possible to draw from him his unique insights about life. We had some wonderful and memorable times together.

Dad had grown up on a working farm with some acreage in and around Washington, North Carolina. In his senior years, he missed having space to roam and explore outdoors. As my wife, Lita, and I prospered financially, in 1996 we acquired a 350-acre working thoroughbred horse farm in Ocala, Florida, while Dad was still alive. It was one of my Dad's dreams to be able to wake up in the morning and wander around that beautiful acreage. He

Every boy wants his dad's approval.

had his coffee and cigarettes in hand as he made his way to the track on the property to watch the horses' workouts. As often as we could, Dad and I traveled from Jacksonville Beach to Ocala to spend time at the farm. It was worth everything for me to be able to see my dad's joy, and it was tremendously satisfying to see him so proud of our accomplishment. I loved helping Dad see one of his dreams come true.

Every boy wants his dad's approval. I had always wanted to please my father, but I never felt that I could measure up.

Now, Dad was so loving and kind to me and to his grandchildren. My dad adored his grandbabies! He regarded grandparenting as a second chance at raising his kids, and he did it with style. My kids—Brittany, Daniel, and Paul—

A proud moment with Dad prior to my going to Parris Island in 1971

so loved their grandfather, or Papa, as they called him. I'm grateful that they had such a wonderful time bonding with my dad. They will remember him as the kind and loving and lighthearted man I got to know in those latter years of his life. Many of my early experiences and memories of my dad weren't quite as cheerful, however.

CHAPTER **3**

Our Lovable, Huggable, Dysfunctional Family

I GUESS ALL FAMILIES are dysfunctional to some degree, and ours was no exception. I love my family and wish things could have been much different from what they were, but it was what it was, and we all survived those years. My dad had a love for real estate and enjoyed a rewarding career in the business on the Eastern Shore of Maryland for more than twenty years. When I returned home from the service, I relocated in Florida, where my older brother was living. Mom and Dad decided to do the same. Most of Mom's extended family resided in and around Jacksonville Beach, and she had always hoped to return and settle there. After a two-year stint in the Winter Park–Orlando area, she and dad moved to Neptune Beach in 1974 to help my brother David and me run our newly opened surf shop.

Dad renewed his real estate license in Jacksonville Beach and continued in the profession he loved. His passion for real estate was so contagious that, for a while, I decided to give it a try, although mostly to support Dad's habit. Dad also discovered the stock market and dabbled in penny stocks and later the full market. He did rather well. I supported him in his efforts and played right along with him. For the first time in our lives, we enjoyed working and being together.

Dad was a voracious reader. He especially enjoyed studying business books and books about the two world wars. He had served four years in the U.S. Navy in the Philippines during the Second World War as part of the Seabees. He had a vast knowledge of every general in the two wars and could speak intelligently about a wide variety of subjects. He often quipped, "I'm just packed full of trivial and useless information!" But I learned something new from him every time we were together. People say that the apple doesn't fall far from the tree, and in a real way, to understand me, you need to know a bit about my dad.

Robert Linberg Hart was known as Bob by his friends and kin. He hailed from Irish and Native American roots. His family operated a working farm near Raleigh, North Carolina. Dad didn't take too well to raising hogs and cattle or harvesting tobacco, so he decided to pursue his education. After high school, Dad ventured south to attend Stetson University in DeLand, Florida, where he studied business and marketing and learned to fly an airplane, all with the help of the GI Bill. While in college there, he met and married Cornelia Hargraves, my mom.

Mom came from a military family, so she had moved a number of times before she finished high school. Moving to a new part of the country was no big deal to her. During Dad's second year at Stetson, Mom became pregnant. So before Dad could finish his degree, life kicked in, and providing for his family became his most important priority. With his BS degree in business, Dad was offered a sales position with Lorillard Tobacco Company in Baltimore, Maryland. Jobs were scarce, so Dad jumped at the opportunity. My brother David was born in 1951, and I came along a year later in October 1952.

I was the first baby born at the Fish Hospital in DeLand, Florida— well, actually in the ambulance on the way to the hospital. The way Mom tells the story, she loved the beach and was there when she went into labor with me. I guess my later love of surfing and water sports came naturally. Why was I born in DeLand rather than in Maryland? Mom says that since Dad was working all the time, and she wanted to be around her family when she gave birth.

After arriving on the Eastern Shore of Maryland, Dad worked for two years with Lorillard, until he was offered a job in real estate by a dear gentleman, Bill Ahtesmy, in Salisbury. During those two years, my sisters Cam and Robin were born one year apart, Cam in 1954 and Robin in 1955. We moved into a thirteen-hundred-square-foot home that sold at the time for around seventy-five hundred dollars and was financed by a

VA loan. With four children under six years of age, Mom and Dad set up housekeeping in Salisbury, Maryland, where Dad worked diligently to develop a thriving real estate business and made a living by building and selling small homes.

Dad loved interacting with people, so falling in love with the real estate business was a natural for him. Nothing thrilled him more than to see someone get into a new home. Most of the folks in Salisbury knew and loved my father, and in truth, he gave more to other people in the community than he did to his own family. He was a good provider, but he had little involvement in and with our family.

Nevertheless, Dad was a mentor to me in many ways. He was wonderfully wise, a hard worker, and had great street smarts. He had an awareness of the God of the Bible and lived by many of Christianity's principles, but he exerted no real positive spiritual influence on our family. Mom insisted we attend church, however; so we loaded up the car each Sunday and attended a church where most of the services were conducted in Latin. In my early years, my brother and I were ordained as acolytes. The robes and garb we wore were pretty cool, and the ceremonies were interesting, but we gained little spiritual content. It was mostly outward religious experience with no real meaning to us.

It was always a chore for Mom to get us four kids up and ready to go to church, so one day I asked my mother, "Why do we even go to this place?"

"What do you mean?" Mom answered, somewhat taken aback by my question. "It's church."

"Yeah, but the priest is anything but the perfect role model for us. He smokes and drinks more than most people in the church. So why do we bother going?"

Mom didn't have a good answer, or at least she didn't provide one, so rather than switching to another congregation, we eventually quit going to church altogether.

Early in my life, Dad started drinking, and the alcohol changed his personality, exposing a volcano of anger that seethed just below the surface of every conversation. The slightest provocation or unexpected pressure caused an often violent eruption. Thus the atmosphere in our home was not peaceful by any means. We lived in constant fear and tension, as the alcohol spoke more frequently. Dad was a good guy for the most part, but when he started drinking, it took over his life. Alcohol was the drug of choice for many families in those days. On more than a few days, I came home from school to find Dad passed out drunk on the couch.

Even when Dad wasn't drinking, he didn't mince words. If I did something wrong or disagreed with him, he let me have it verbally.

Dad was disciplined about everything he did, and he hated waste of any kind. He could improvise well, finding a way to get a job done with whatever resources he had while always seeking out new ways to do things better.

In his own way, Dad was a visionary and an innovator. Against the advice of the well-established local builders and developers, he bought an old gas station, converted it into a sales office, and opened Bay Shore Realty for business on the banks of the Wicomico River. Dad and his partner were hard-working men. They put in an enormous number of hours every week, and the business soon became Dad's top priority at that time in his life. He worked tirelessly listing and selling residential homes. He also built and developed small parcels of properties, and he took great pleasure in helping folks understand the value of homeownership. Dad had an uncanny ability to see a property and determine its highest and best use. Dad could see potential where others did not. He constantly sought ways to improve homebuilding. He appreciated the value of building structures that would last. He always used the best materials, not necessarily the most expensive, so he could give his clients the best value for their hard-earned dollars. He took time to explain the various features and differences between the homes he offered, and he took every home sale personally, making friends with every transaction.

As a businessman, Dad wasn't afraid of change, nor was he afraid to take a risk. When precut homes came out, Dad was one of the first builders in the Salisbury area to promote them. In the same way, when slab homes came out, Dad was quick to offer his customers the less expensive, no-basement homes built on a cement slab.

Interestingly, my dad built entire homes—and many of them—on nothing more than a handshake. He knew his business, his word was golden, and people knew they could trust him. To this day, I tell people that a paper contract is only as good as the people who signed it. I saw that in my dad.

Friendly almost to a fault, with a perpetual smile on his face, Dad was always upbeat about business. He enjoyed inviting people home with him, and the next thing we knew, Dad was building a home for them. To the day he died, he encouraged people, "You need to be in a home and have some roots. You need to have an investment that will pay you later. Real estate is not going away. They aren't making any more land."

Dad had a different approach to selling real estate than most of his contemporaries. He did most of his business on the front porch. Rather than transporting clients from property to property, he'd interview his customers on the front porch while drinking coffee, smoking a pipe, and talking with them about their lives, their family, their needs and desires, their hopes and dreams. After a while, Dad would get a grin on his face. He'd look the folks in the eye, reach over and touch them on the arm, and say, "Guess where we're going? I'm going to show you your new home."

He listened to his prospects' needs rather than try to sell them on his. Once he quoted a price to them, he refused to alter it, even if circumstances increased his costs and reduced his profit margin. Dad sometimes even lost money on a deal rather than to go back on his word. He always made things right, even if it meant doing so at his own expense. To Dad, his word was his bond. If he said it, you could rely on it.

I recall Dad and Mom having more than a few heated discussions over some of his business deals.

"What are you doing, Bob?" Mom would fret.

"I shook the man's hand," Dad said. "I gave him my word, Cornelia, and I'm not going back on it now, just because the cost of materials went up."

Dad took great pride in every home he built. He was an astute and dedicated builder. Moreover, he had a natural gift for seeing how a building should be erected. He could look at a house from the street and discern that a window was off kilter by 2 percent. He could tell whether the concrete was curing too rapidly in a foundation. When I worked with

---

SUCCESS PRINCIPLE FOR LIFE

Listen to the needs of others, find out what their dreams are, and then help them achieve them. The key to building your business is to help others to succeed!

Dad, he rarely allowed for putty or caulking to cover up any mistakes. "Cut it right," Dad demanded. If something wasn't correct, "Do it again," Dad would say. Things had to fit near perfectly.

He instilled that passion for excellence within me, although I must admit that I didn't appreciate it back then. To me, his constant correction was simply more proof that I could never please the man, that I could never win his approval, or do anything that would be good enough for him. That lack of approval from my dad left an indelible impression on my life, one that followed me into adulthood and affected me for many years.

FOR MANY summers during my childhood, I attended summer Sunday school, similar to Vacation Bible School. I had a knack for drawing, and I loved sketching the Bible stories that the teachers told us. I drew everything from the Creation account and Adam and Eve to the stories of Moses and Jesus. I especially liked the stories of David and Goliath and Samson. No doubt, that idea of the little guy facing the giant and defeating him appealed to me as a young boy. How Samson, another seemingly ordinary guy, did such extraordinary things. These true-to-life stories still appeal to me to this day.

NOWADAYS PSYCHOLOGISTS might refer to a family like ours as being dysfunctional. We would never have used such a term. All we knew was that we seemed to be experiencing some sort of emotional pain.

"Why is Dad so mean to you and to us?" I frequently asked my mom. She never had a good answer. Later I learned about the deep emotional pain inflicted by an addiction to alcohol, how it hurts the person addicted as well as the loved ones affected by the addicted person's attitudes and actions. But at the time, I didn't fully understand it.

I respected my dad for providing a good living for our family, but his role in our family was also a major point of contention between Mom and him. Mom practically had to beg Dad for money whenever she needed anything: groceries, school clothes, gas, or when she wanted to do something a little extra or out of the ordinary with us. Dad had the money, but he always put up a fuss about giving it to Mom.

Any time Mom and Dad argued, we could count on hearing Mom shouting, "Once these kids are raised, I'm leaving you!"

Dad countered, "Don't I provide for you?"

My dad, like most dads of that generation, didn't see or understand the need to provide emotional or spiritual support for his family. To Dad, it was more about survival than enjoying life. He felt that the greatest way he could show love for his family was by providing financially for them. That meant working constantly and earning enough money to pay the bills. Dad would not understand that we kids, and Mom too, all spelled *love* T-I-M-E. A lot of dads today still haven't figured that out.

So in the heat of their arguments, Dad was quick to remind Mom that he took care of her financially. "Don't I provide for you?" was his answer for any of her desires.

Of course, as any woman knows, that answer was insufficient and only exacerbated Mom's pain. She wanted Dad to be more than a mere provider; she wanted him to be a loving husband and father.

Family was so important to Mom. She did a stellar job of raising us four kids, and I will be forever grateful for her bold and caring example. She deserves a medal of honor! Mom read widely and avidly until the day she passed away in September 2010. Like Dad, she loved books of all kinds, and getting lost in a novel was far better entertainment for her than going to the movies or watching television. When she wasn't reading, Mom stayed busy as a homemaker, and long before "soccer moms" was a familiar term, she was carting her four children from one sporting event, dance recital, or school activity to another.

Every year that we lived in Salisbury, immediately after the last day of school, Mom packed up our blue Chevrolet Impala convertible and drove us four kids to Jacksonville Beach for the summer. Dad remained in Maryland except for infrequent visits, while the rest of the family spent the summer on the beach with Mom's extended family. We stayed there until the week before schools reopened in Maryland, and then Mom drove us all the way back home—thirteen hundred miles one way. She did the same thing for most Christmas celebrations with the family.

With four kids each a year apart, Mom never worked outside the home, except for a short season when she assisted Dad in his real estate business. Having a stay-at-home mom wasn't considered as much of a luxury in the late 1950s and early 1960s as it is today. It was more of a call to duty. Mom was one of the few in her social group who made it a point to be a stay-at-home mom. She was always there in the morning to send us off to school and there when we came home. I shudder to think how my siblings and I might have turned out had she not been there for us. Thanks, Mom!

GROWING UP, one of my best friends in Salisbury was Rex Willing. His family lived across the street from mine. We started school together at Beaver Run Elementary and remained friends all the way through Wicomico High School. As a boy, nearly every Friday night, I packed my little suitcase and went across the street to Rex's to stay overnight. Sometimes my brother David would come along too. Big Rex, Rex's dad, and Ruth, his mom, were good friends with our parents, and they realized that our dad was drinking too much, so they always welcomed us to stay with them. I was like a second son to them. Later, when Rex and his family moved about five miles away, I rode my bike to Rex's house. Rex's mother always grilled the most delicious, mouthwatering hamburgers on Friday nights. That alone made the five-mile bike ride worthwhile!

Rex and I were like blood brothers who played together almost every day, and we didn't need to be doing anything fancy to be content. We played sandlot baseball all the time, and we could pitch a ball back and forth for hours in his backyard and be perfectly happy. Rex was a good basketball player, so when we weren't playing baseball or table tennis or swimming, we'd be on the basketball court. When we were old enough, we played against each other in Little League, but we remained true friends. Rex was a good pitcher, but he sometimes purposely served up a slow, easy pitch with my name written all over it, just waiting for me to wallop the ball—and I did. Rex always made me look better than I was.

We often went to the movies at the Ulman Theater, which featured more than its share of science fiction movies. Rex and I loved to sit in the balcony, and when the lights were low, we tossed popcorn and candy at the people below, trying to hit one of them. We were pretty good shots and caused quite a few disruptions for folks who were only trying to enjoy a flick. We were even better at not getting caught, at least for a while. It was only a little mischief and some cheap entertainment at other people's expense. Rex and I would talk and laugh about these incidents for hours.

Sometimes we'd go to the Boulevard Theater, where the admission price was thirty-five cents for kids under twelve and fifty cents for those twelve and above. Because I was small in stature, I could talk the girl at the ticket window into selling me a thirty-five-cent ticket. Since Rex was bigger than me, it irritated him no end that I could get away with it. "Good things come in small packages," I'd jaw at Rex. Bigger isn't always better.

Rex was a musician, and a good one too. His dad was a big-band jazz musician, so it was no surprise when Rex became an outstanding drummer in the school band. We loved to go to Watson's Smoke House, a mixed bag of a store that sold pipes and tobacco products to adults and records to kids. In the back of Watson's was a room where kids could listen to albums and 45s before they purchased them. Rex and I spent hours listening to all kinds of music in that backroom. While several of my friends and I enjoyed dabbling in music, Rex took his music seriously and went on to become a professional drummer. After a stint in the air force, Rex returned to Salisbury and opened his own drum shop.

WHEN IT came to school, I wasn't what you would call a good academic student, even though I was fairly intelligent and had some common sense. I simply wasn't book smart; I couldn't apply myself to the curriculum. I was too busy building air castles in the sky and dreaming of much bigger and better things than figuring out the square root of some number or merely memorizing answers for tests. I was good at memorizing, though, so I figured out the system well enough to get by in school. I was a C student. You might say that I just tried to *see* my way through!

I was also good in physical education. I loved PE. With my energetic personality, staying physically active came much easier than studying. In school, I won the Alonzo Stagg award for the President's Council on Physical Fitness several years in a row. Physical fitness and keeping myself in shape have always been important to me. In junior high, Nick Christianson, our gym teacher, noticed that I had a gift for gymnastics and that I had great strength and flexibility in my body. So he took me under his wing and helped me develop my natural talents. He encouraged me to excel on the mats, the pommel horse, the high bar, and

I had some common sense. I simply wasn't book smart.

the rings. His belief in me was a rock of stability during the years of my often tumultuous and stormy home life. I loved the challenging workouts. Mr. Christianson taught me that I could go far beyond my perceived abilities if I would only practice, practice, and practice some more. All that hard work paid off. I lettered in gymnastics each year I participated.

When I wasn't working at my gymnastics, I played community league baseball and football at the Red Shield, an organized sports program for kids, similar to the Boys Club. Since I was small and fast, I proved to be an outstanding fielder. Occasionally, I'd pitch or play third base, but mostly I loved shagging balls in the outfield. My involvement with the Red Shield and community league teams provided a sense of achievement in my life outside of school, and it was tremendously meaningful to me. I shared a sad commonality with most of the other boys on the team, namely, our dads were too busy to be part of our lives, and most of our dads drank too much. Like most of the other dads, my dad never attended my games.

Mom pretty much raised all four of us kids by herself, and she was not bashful about reminding our dad, "As soon as these kids are grown and gone, I'm leaving." We lived with that ominous threat echoing through our minds even in the best of times. Mom was true to her word; she left Dad when we kids had all left home.

Her leaving was enough of a shock for him that he came to grips with his drinking. Dad joined Alcoholics Anonymous and got some help that enabled him to stop drinking. What a glorious day! Mom returned and things worked out for them and us. Mom and Dad stayed together; they never divorced. People of their generation remained in a marriage oftentimes out of sheer commitment, sometimes because of society's much less favorable view of divorce than we have today, and many times out of necessity. For many women in the 1950s and early 1960s, there simply wasn't any place else to go.

Nevertheless, despite their differences, I'm glad Mom and Dad hung in there. I think they'd both say the same thing. Mom and Dad eventually came to terms with life. Dad realized the beauty of having a family, and he

BRIGISM

In every adversity there is the seed of an equal or greater benefit.

The Hart clan in 1996: Dad and Mom, with Robin on the left,
Jim and Cam, center, David, me, and Lita

embraced the concept wholeheartedly, attempting to make up for lost time after we kids had all moved out and moved on with our adult lives. Eventually, he and my precious mom came to faith in Christ, and their lives were forever changed.

Growing up in our family was quite the experience. It was often the school of hard knocks, but as hard as it was at times, I am grateful for my parents and my brother and sisters and what I have learned through them.

CHAPTER **4**

Budding Days

MONEY DOESN'T BUY HAPPINESS an old adage says, but the lack of it certainly affects your level of happiness. I know we're not supposed to love money, but I must admit, I like it a lot. I especially enjoy what I can do with money. If I had to rate the value I place on money, I'd put it one click below air! I've lived with and without it. With it is better. Remember, it's the love of money that is the root of all evil, not money itself. Money is amoral; it isn't good or bad. It's whose hand you put it in that makes the difference. Money merely magnifies or makes you more of what you already are.

I've always had an entrepreneurial spirit—something I've inherited from my dad I suppose—and wanted to work for myself. Looking back now, it's easy to see that throughout my early years, I preferred being self-employed, whether it was mowing lawns, detailing cars, pulling weeds, selling newspapers, or playing music. When I turned sixteen years of age, I worked in retail stores such as a Sherwin-Williams paint store and a Bresler's ice cream shop, but I preferred being my own boss. It wasn't simply that I didn't like somebody else telling me what to do—although I didn't—but I figured that I'd rather work for myself than for someone else.

B R I G I S M

People are going to judge you and talk about you whether
you are good or bad, rich or poor, so be good and rich.
Give 'em something to talk about!

I liked being independent. I rarely asked my parents for money; instead, I'd earn my own money to do the things I wanted to do. I worked and saved my money to buy several used cars before I was old enough to drive one. I loved working to improve the looks and performance of the cars I owned, and I still do today.

Around the age of thirteen, I began having a recurring dream in which I had everything I could possibly want—cars, boats, jets, buildings, even towns named after me—but at the end of the dream, I still saw myself as desperate and searching, looking for meaning and satisfaction. I was empty. In my dream, I seemed to have it all, but I was the only person in the world. I had no one to share it all with. I was distraught at the fact that I had everything but joy, peace, or a sense of satisfaction in my life. I often awakened from that dream in a cold sweat, suddenly realizing how horribly lonely and empty having it all could be. Without friends and people to share it, material wealth has no joy or meaning. Think about it: we all want to please somebody with what we have and do. It is not good for man to be alone, and while that principle applies to marriage, God was showing me even then that merely having money and material things is not enough to satisfy a human soul—my first lesson in "things won't bring happiness."

I saved my money and bought a guitar. I wanted a Fender bass guitar but couldn't afford it, so I bought a lesser quality one to start with.

When you want something bad enough and are willing to go after it, you can get or do anything. True to my nature, I found a way to get the bass I wanted. I worked and saved and eventually bought a Fender bass, an amplifier, and the first-rate gear with it. The guitar was almost as big as I was. Cool!

I took some guitar lessons, and because I had my own gear, I was asked to join a group of guys who were forming a band. Carmen Yates was our lead singer and rhythm player. M. B. Gordy was our drummer. Bob

Nicholson played lead guitar and sang. Ronnie Nelson played keyboards, and more important, his house was available for practice and jam sessions, with no parents around. I was on bass and had a van to haul everyone around. Ronnie and I didn't read or know a note of music, but what did that have to do with playing rock music in the seventies, anyway? We had a blast and became quite popular for the three years we were together. We named the original group "More of Us," and then changed the name to "Love Machine." The name says it all.

We played and sang the most popular tunes of the seventies at gigs and high school dances all around the Eastern Shore of Maryland. We made some extra spending money, but we invested most of our earnings into equipment to further our cause. We basically played for the sheer fun of it, but we developed great friend-ships through the experience, and like a lot of kids at the time, we had a dream of someday making it big in the music indus-try. We also thought being in a band was pretty cool. A couple of the guys actually went on to enjoy great music careers. Drummer M. B. Gordy worked with artists such as Rita Coolidge, Neil Diamond, John Tesh, and the Doobie Brothers. Carmen became a successful songwriter in New York, and Bob played lead guitar and devel-oped a thriving business by teach-ing guitar lessons.

It's okay. I'm with the band.

For me, though, the group was primarily a way to escape my home life and be a part of something that brought me joy. And, of course, to be noticed. Acceptance by our peers was as big a deal then as it is now. Funny thing about peer pres-sure: it never really goes away. The faces change and the ante rises, but the desire to be accepted and af-firmed by the people around us doesn't diminish with age. Some people unfortunately look for love in all the wrong places; others dis-cover it where they least expected.

Yeah, I'm gonna be a rock star someday. I bought my first bass guitar in 1967.

Gosh, I wish we could have made it big with the band. That rock star stuff seemed pretty cool.

I didn't date anyone regularly during high school, as I was more focused on the fun factor in my life at that time. That's not to say I wasn't interested, but dating cost money and time, and I was a bit stingy and selfish with those two commodities. Dating was too much of a distraction to my lively, fun-spirited style at that time. I was too sexy for myself!

I wasn't the most popular guy at school, but I was the life of the party and attracted some of the biggest friends around me. Of course, anyone seemed big compared to my ninety-five pounds and five-foot-two frame. Small in stature but huge in the fun factor—that was me. I was the little guy hanging out with the big guys—sort of Mutt and Jeff—so I'd start the brawls many times, but my big buddies stepped in to finish them. Rarely did anyone mess with us when we were together. Of course, the problem was that we weren't always together, if you know what I mean. That sometimes got a bit messy—especially for me!

MY OLDER brother David and I were competitive from day one. We both loved sports, and usually I could outperform him in most of them. He didn't like to practice; his ability either came naturally or not at all. On the other hand, I worked hard at practicing baseball, swimming, tennis, gym-

nastics, and even football. I really wanted to play high school football, but I was too small. I literally slept with my baseball glove. Immersing myself in sports became a refuge for me, a place where I was not only accepted but wanted and affirmed. The one sport at which my brother always bested me was surfing.

David loved to surf! He hung out a lot in Ocean City, Maryland,

In 1965–66, two short guys (David and me) posed with a long board. It took some teamwork to get that board in the water.

at one of the surf shops, and became friends with some pretty serious surfers. He took to the water like a fish and fell in love with the sport. He still competes to this day, though he's now in his late fifties.

As we were growing up, David seemed to get all the new clothes, so I wore his hand-me-downs. I really didn't mind. I didn't feel an urge to dress in the latest styles to look cool. My dreams were much bigger than that. *Someday, I'm going to get ahead in life,* I'd dream. *I'm going to figure out a way to have what I want and do what I want.* I worked at all sorts of odd jobs—mowing lawns, deliver-

Brother Dave was also known as Crazy Dave

ing newspapers, bagging groceries, washing and waxing cars, almost anything else to make a dollar legally—and I learned to take pride in my work, to do it with excellence. Dad placed a high value on quality work. His attitude was, "If you're going to do it, do it right."

Dad was hard to please, too, and as I mentioned, I grew up under the specter that I could never earn his approval, no matter what I did. But Dad at least tacitly acknowledged when I came close to pleasing him. I lived to hear those words from Dad: "Good job, Brig." Unfortunately, his standards of excellence loomed so high, Dad's praise was a rare treat. He was more comfortable telling me what I could have done better, or how I could have improved the project. And he was usually right. But that subtle implication that I never quite met his expectations colored much of our relationship during my younger years.

BRIGISM

I'd rather be the captain of my own rowboat than the second mate of a battleship.

Maybe that's why from the time I was thirteen years of age until I was sixteen, I rarely lived in my family's home. Unlike kids who threaten to run away from home but never do, because of the constant tension at our home, I ran away often. Usually I stayed at the home of a friend: Ronnie Nelson's or Mike Danmeyer's family. I lived with the Danmeyer family for more than a year, and I lived with Ronnie off and on for at least that long.

Ronnie's mom passed away in 1966, and his dad owned a bar and was working all the time, so Ronnie allowed me to stay whenever I wanted. With Ronnie's dad working at night, Ronnie and I were pretty much on our own.

One time, we left without telling Ronnie's dad and stayed for about two weeks at the home of Ronnie's aunt, who lived about seven miles out of town. When we returned, Ronnie explained to his dad why we'd left. "I didn't feel like you wanted us around."

Ronnie's dad looked surprised. "I didn't realize you had gone anywhere."

At one point during my early high school years, I stayed at Ronnie's house for nearly six straight months. Mom and Dad knew where I was, and they also knew I probably wouldn't stay home even if they forced me to come home.

"You know where I am," I told them. "I'm not trying to hide from you, but I'm not coming home."

Occasionally a truant officer would show up and want to take me back home. "You can take me home, but I'll just run away again," I said. I had gotten to the point where I simply didn't want to deal with all the drama at home.

Although most of my friends understood why I might want to run away from home for good, none of them volunteered to come along. None except for Greg Denson, that is. Greg and I met during junior high, and we became good buddies. He lived down the street from my friend Ronnie, so

---

BRIGISM

Do the best you can with what you have right now, and quit complaining about what you don't have.

we hung out a lot with a couple of other guys. Greg loved to water-ski as much as I loved to surf, so it was not unusual to find us both at the beach.

Greg's father passed away when Greg was only fifteen; his grandfather passed away that same year. Maybe because Greg didn't have a strong male influence in his life, and my dad was gone so much or incapacitated by his drinking so often, Greg and I had a common bond. Of course, as teenage boys, we didn't think that deeply about why we both shared a sort of cosmic loneliness. But that common foundation—or lack of it—was the launching pad from which our boyish energy was propelled as though fired by jet fuel. Greg and I were going constantly, especially once we were able to drive.

We both loved muscle cars and Harley Davidson "chopped" motorcycles and dreamed of having our own bad-to-the-bone rides. We spent a lot of time at Red's Gas Station, the local hangout where everyone took their cars to impress one another. Red's was on a corner lot on the old Ocean City Road, so it was everyone's first stop most every night.

My car was a custom four-speed '62 Chevy Impala convertible. It was red with a white convertible top, a sweet car! And it won the respect of the crowd at Red's. Greg and I also had a couple of vans that we were always working on, trying to convert them into party wagons on wheels. They, too, were sweet in their day.

For more than a year, Greg and I planned to run away from home. We worked out meticulous details for our great escape. I snitched some money from Dad each week and stashed it away, saving it for the day when Greg and I could pack up and leave. We actually hid clothes in a closet in an empty house that Dad had on the market, so we'd be ready to roll at a moment's notice.

At that time, my brother David and I were refurbishing two sports cars: two two-seater 1959 MGA's, a red one and a blue one. The red one wasn't quite roadworthy; it was supposed to be my car eventually. The blue one, David's car, was already licensed and ready to go.

Greg came over to spend the night at our house one Friday night, and we went to the drag races. We had already decided that that night would be the night we would escape, so I pulled out a wad of money and flashed it in front of Ronnie and Greg and several other guys and bought everyone hamburgers and hotdogs. Greg and I got home late, and when Mom fell asleep on the couch, we slipped past her and made our way to the garage.

We furtively raised the garage door and pushed the blue MGA into the street. We didn't dare start the engine, because the sound from the MGA's motor might awaken someone in our house. So we pushed the car down to the house where we had stashed our clothing. We loaded our things on the MGA's luggage rack, revved the engine, and peeled out of town. We were on our way to California—or so we thought.

We drove through the night. By daybreak we were in Suffolk, Virginia, where we stopped for gas and food near a truck scale. We filled the tank and then pulled off close to a grassy area near the gas station, where Greg and I stretched out on the grass to enjoy some snacks.

Soon a Virginia state trooper pulled in to the gas station and noticed two boys lounging in the grass near an MGA sports car. At first the officer passed us by, but no doubt his curiosity was piqued, so he drove back toward us, got out of his car, and stepped over to talk with us. He asked some questions about where we were from and where we were going. Greg let me do the talking, and I tried to sound grown up and cool. I told the trooper that we were on our way to see my aunt who lived in that general area. The trooper wasn't buying it. "You guys look awfully young, out here with this sports car loaded up."

He pointed at me. "You get in the car with me." He nodded toward the patrol car. Then he told Greg, "And you drive the car. I'm on my way to work over at the truck scale. Follow me." There was no point in arguing. Our big plans for running away from home had been foiled in less than half a day.

Several state police officers were inside the truck scale office when we arrived. The officers called Greg's mom and then my mom. Since it was so early in the morning, nobody was even aware that we were missing. Greg's mom had remarried after his father's death, and his stepdad owned a small airplane. While we waited at the police station, my dad and Greg's stepdad flew down to Suffolk.

Meanwhile, Greg and I asked the officers if we could freshen up and change clothes. It wasn't simply that we wanted to look our best when our parents arrived; we wanted to look good before dying. We had packed suits for our anticipated job interviews in California, so Greg put on a three-piece suit with wing-tipped shoes, and I dressed in yellow pants, about three inches off my ankle, and a blue sports coat. The state troopers cracked up when they saw us come out of the bathroom dressed to the nines.

When Dad and Greg's stepdad arrived, the officers released us into their custody. Greg flew back home with his stepdad, and Dad drove the

MGA home with me. On the way back, Dad made me pay all the tolls with my own money. I didn't dare tell him that I had stolen the money from him in the first place. That trip home was one *long* trip!

Our parents didn't kill us, but our friend Ronnie was a bit hurt by our escapade. "What were you guys doing? I can't believe you didn't tell me."

Greg and I stayed close all through school, but during my senior year, Greg went off to a military school in Virginia. When he came home on leave around Christmas, he called me and said to come up and see him. So another friend, Mike Mills, and I skipped school and drove up to Seaford, Delaware, about twenty-one miles north of Salisbury, to see Greg. Mike had a red '57 Chevy, and we wanted to show it to Greg.

After a while, we grew restless for something to do, so someone suggested that we go to Seaford High School, where Greg had gone to school briefly before transferring to military school. Classes were still in session, but we boldly walked into the building like we owned it. We roamed the halls, peeking in classroom windows, looking for any of our friends.

A vice principal collared us and said, "Get out of here. You're not supposed to be on school property."

As we were leaving, walking down the hall toward the parking lot, I spied a fire alarm on the wall. I turned toward Greg and asked, "Hey, do you want to pull the fire alarm?"

"Sure, why not?" Greg said. "We'll go get the car and have it running and ready for you."

I waited till I saw the '57 Chevy outside, and then I gave that fire alarm a yank. The alarm bells sounded instantly, and I ran out the side door, toward the car. Greg had the door open for me, and I dove into the backseat. Mike had the tires screeching down the street before I could even get the door closed. We hauled it out of there, all three of us laughing hysterically.

Before we could get to Greg's house, the police had already called his parents. As a consequence, when Greg returned from military school, he was expelled from school for a year and not allowed to attend Seaford High either. Greg never squealed on me, but he paid a high price for being my buddy.

Later, Greg was one of my first friends to have both a Harley motorcycle and a smokin' hot Corvette. By 1972, he was driving a big chopper, and although our paths didn't intersect for years, to this day we still hold dear those days of our youth. We both were mini-rebel dreamers. And guess what? Today, we both have hot smoking Vettes and sport around on custom Harleys whenever we want to revisit our youth. Greg and I recently

Friends for life, from left to right, Greg Denson, me, and Ronnie Nelson at a 2010 reunion

jumped on our bikes and did a ride from Salisbury down to where, as kids, we had spent some time on the river at his grandparents' place. We walked, talked, and sat for hours, reminiscing about our lives and how dear our friendship remains after more than forty years. Rex, Ronnie, and Greg are true examples that friends are friends forever. (Love you guys!)

✦ ✦ ✦

DURING MY younger years, although my friends and I were mischievous, we never got into any real trouble. But when we had our own cars and some money in our pockets, we moved from miscreant behavior to more serious misdemeanors. Drinking and semimalicious mischief became a way of life for me, since alcohol and drugs were readily available to kids in the mid-1960s. We were doing what felt good and what most others our age were doing. Marijuana, speed, and acid were the most prevalent drugs during that time, and lots of the so-called cool kids were doing them. I really wasn't so interested in doing drugs, but because of my desire to be accepted, to be a part of the in crowd, I succumbed to the temptation and soon became captivated by them. For me, drugs and alcohol became the means of escaping the reality of my life, especially the hurt I was harboring in my heart and mind. I was on a road to nowhere. When the drugs and booze wore off, I was even more empty and confused about life than I'd been before.

✦ ✦ ✦

I GRADUATED from high school by the skin of my teeth in 1970. Mom attended my graduation, but since I had destroyed another car after the prom just a few weeks earlier, my graduation did not exactly engender a party atmosphere around the Hart home.

About that time, Dad planned to take a six-week boat trip, cruising from New York, down the Intracoastal Waterway, to Miami. He had just bought a new Cadillac Sedan DeVille, and he entrusted it to me to wash and wax while he was gone. Dad had barely passed the city limits before I called several friends and announced that I had a new set of wheels. "Let's party!"

The local Elks Club, of which my parents were members in good standing, was hosting a big golf tournament. Dad had originally joined the club because of the bar and used his membership to network and make business contacts, while Mom and we kids spent a great deal of time at the club's swimming pool. Since the club was preparing for the tournament, the golf course was even more impeccably manicured than usual: every flower in place, the greens and fairways cut to perfect heights.

That night, as usual, my friends and I overindulged and got crazy drunk. I was driving up a hill in the park next to the golf course when someone in the backseat shouted, "Police!" and pointed to the patrol car rapidly coming up behind us. With the car loaded with beer and our pockets stuffed with other "natural" substances, we panicked. I had already received several citations from the police for misdemeanors and mischief; I knew if the police caught me driving drunk again, I'd be headed to the slammer for sure. But rather than slow down and drive more sensibly, I floored it.

I was driving much too fast for any conditions, and the road was slightly wet, making things even more precarious. We careened around a turn, and Dad's brand-new Cadillac slid, spinning off the road and plunging over a ten-foot embankment—flying through the air and landing on one of the golf course greens. I didn't need a mechanic to tell me that the impact of hitting that surface had bent the frame on Dad's car, and I didn't even want to think about the damage we had done to the green. But I certainly wasn't going to wait around to find out!

I slammed the car back into gear, hit the gas, and proceeded to spin the tires across the eighth green. The Cadillac was equipped with a special feature, known then as positive traction, which meant that both rear tires were spinning and tearing into that beautiful turf. We launched off the eighth green, diving into and out of a lower sand trap, and then on to the ninth fairway.

One of my buddies jammed the gearshift into Park, and the car jolted to a stop in the middle of the fairway. I paused just long enough for my four buddies to bail out, then I roared down the fairway, through a sand trap near the ninth hole, and weaved across another green, where I blasted through the barricades and back on to the road.

It wasn't like the authorities in our small town wouldn't know who was driving Bob Hart's new Cadillac Sedan DeVille. I knew there was no escaping, but there was no use in taking my friends down with me.

The police were waiting in the living room when I got home. They arrested me and hauled me down to court the next day. As I stood before the judge to answer for my misdeeds, I was given a court date when he would decide what to do with me. The headlines in the local newspaper the next day read: CADDY ON THE GOLF COURSE! Another headline joked: LONGEST DRIVE OF THE DAY. This was not a good moment for me.

By the time Dad returned home from his waterway adventure, I had, with Mom's help, formulated a plan to make things as right as possible, so my dad wouldn't kill me. We called in favors from everywhere, I used every penny I could muster up to repair Dad's car. A family friend helped. But the moment Dad saw the Cadillac, he knew something was very wrong. After all, the frame had been bent, the doors had been jammed so hard that they hardly opened, not to mention the numerous dings, scrapes, and scratches on the paint that had to be refinished. If there was ever a time my dad wanted to kill me, I'm certain this was one of them. And I deserved it.

About that same time, the United States was embroiled in the Vietnam War and had reinstituted a military draft system in which all eligible young men between the ages of eighteen and twenty-six were given lottery numbers. The lower your number, the greater the likelihood of your being drafted for military service.

When I received my notice from the Selective Service, the draft board, my jaw dropped. I was number thirty-five, which meant my future in the U.S. Army was a virtual certainty unless I contracted some mental or physical malady that might keep me out of the service. My low draft lottery number meant my days of free-spirited carousing were numbered as well. I was aware of several young men from our area who had gone to Vietnam as robust soldiers and had returned home in body bags. I admit, I was scared. I had no potential deferments, no legal reasons for not landing in Nam, so for a while I considered running away to Canada. I couldn't remember the words to "O Canada," so I figured that wouldn't work.

When my day in court for my sentencing arrived, I knew immediately that things were not going to go well for me in any way, shape, or form. While I stood before the judge, he shook his head while he read over my record. He knew me well, so his tone was familiar and almost friendly, but no less firm. "Brig, I see you're back again. I've read the report on your shenanigans. You're on probation, right?"

"Yes sir," I answered contritely.

"Drinking and driving again?"

"Yes sir."

"Okay. You destroyed a bunch of property, which you will pay to repair. You've been locked up, in and out of jail several times this year." Exasperated, the judge sighed heavily, shook his head again, and looked down at me from the bench. "Brig, what am I going to do with you?"

I knew better than to answer.

The judge continued, "I have no choice, but I see here that you've been drafted and you are supposed to report to the army in a few weeks. Is that right?"

"Yes sir," I replied quietly.

"Well, I'll tell you what. I'm going to give you one of two choices today. The army is not good enough for you, Brig Hart. I'm going to give you a couple other options. One, you can go to the Green Beach for an extended stay." The judge paused to let his words sink in on me. I knew what Green Beach meant. That was a euphemism for the jail on the Eastern Shore of Maryland.

The judge continued, "Or, number two, you can go become a marine today. They have a voluntary draft. What's your choice?"

I could tell the judge was not messing around, that he had made up his mind that this was going to be a turning point in my life—or else.

"Well?" The judge glowered at me. "I'm waiting."

"Judge," I replied, "I've always wanted to be a marine."

THE POLICE officers walked me down to the Marine Corps recruiting office that very day. I filled out the paperwork, and then I went home to ponder and prepare for my departure a few weeks later.

Looking back, I realize how this crazy episode set me up for some of the best teaching and discipline of my life. God protected me through my many antics, and now He was going to use the U.S. Marine Corps to shock me back to reality.

I was ordered to board a bus and report to boot camp at Parris Island, near Beaufort, South Carolina. The moment the bus pulled into the base, a drill sergeant bounded onto the vehicle to welcome the new recruits. He greeted us formally, almost kindly at first, but then he turned into Attila the Hun. "You have five seconds to get your gear outside and line up on the yellow footprints on the ground," he roared. "You will not say a word! You will not look to the left or to the right! You will stand up straight, eyes forward! Get off my bus! Now move!"

After preliminary instructions, the drill sergeant ordered us to line up outside the marine barber shop, a stark room filled with marine "stylists." When it was my turn, I plopped down in the barber's chair and looked around at several other recruits in chairs lined up in the hall. It didn't look as though there were a lot of choices in hairstyles.

"How do you want it?" the barber working on me quipped.

"Oh, just take a little off the sides," I said, shaking my head slightly so my shoulder-length blond hair swept out of my eyes.

"Sure thing," the marine barber replied. *BZZZZZZZ!* The hair clippers burrowed straight back from my forehead, right through the center of my hair, all the way down to my neck. The marine smirked a bit as he repeated the motion several times, denuding my head in about thirty seconds. "You're done."

I got up, stared downward, and saw every strand of my hair strewn in piles on the floor. I was afraid to look in the mirror. Not to worry, though. There was no time for primping.

"Outside on the line!" came the order. I pushed in closely behind the newly bald soldier in front of me as the drill sergeant instructed and almost immediately felt another man behind me equally as close. We squeezed into that line as we moved through a battery of inoculations. It was hot in South Carolina, and the line was stifling. At one point, after my first group of shots, I actually fainted while standing up, but I didn't fall down because the line was so tight. I was simply dragged to the point where I received another battery of shots. After a while, I came to and found myself being poked, probed, and prodded again.

The Marine Corps boot camp lasted thirteen weeks, and because of the Vietnam War, everything was intensified. Many of the recruits were trained, then sent to field training, and then immediately assigned to overseas duty in Vietnam. We had to learn how to respect authority and to submit our wills to it. We learned to respond to orders without questioning, how to develop camaraderie, how to be a team and work together to help one another, and we had to learn it all quickly, or else somebody was going to get hurt. There was no debate about personal preferences, or any other challenges we might have. Any backtalk or slowness to respond to the drill sergeants brought a strong, instantaneous response. Marines allowed no segregation. We weren't black, white, or yellow. We were all green. The goal for each of us was to become a lean, mean, fighting machine known as a marine.

Of course it took a few weeks to figure that out, and in the meantime, there was a lot of infighting among the new troops, each one clawing for respect. I quickly learned the system in the marines: one of the best ways not to be bothered by the big guys was simply to be so wildly crazy that they'd be afraid of you, regardless of their size. A few weeks into basic, I heard a rumor that the guys were going to pull a prank on me, because I was going along with our drill sergeants too much. (I was only going along with them because I was scared of the consequences if I didn't!) I knew I had to mark my territory, so I picked out the biggest guy in our platoon, grabbed a big trash can, and smashed it over his head. He hit the floor, and the moment he did, I jumped on top of him and bit his ear. Blood gushed in every direction. After that, I had the respect of my entire platoon. It was a survival tactic. I'm really not that bad a guy—really!

Much of basic training involved making a clean break with the outside civilian world and adopting a new lifestyle, that of a marine. The training emphasized physical fitness, which was right up my alley. We ran three miles every morning before breakfast, and fat bodies soon became buff bodies. I enjoyed the physical training and was never in better shape in my life. I received one affirmation after another and even became the platoon leader. For the first time in a long time, I was beginning to feel better about myself.

We trained in everything from close-order drills, Marine Corps history, to martial arts, weapons training, and survival techniques. We crawled on our bellies under barbed wire while sharpshooters fired over our heads. The first few times we did it, the sharpshooters did not fire live ammunition, but by the end of our training, they were using real bullets.

The day I graduated from boot camp was one of the greatest days of my life. Putting on those Marine Corps blues, my formal dress blue uniform,

Graduation day for USMC Platoon 3014 on February 8, 1972

and feeling the pride our class of new recruits shared was a monumental experience for me. I'd made it. Mom and Dad attended the ceremonies at the base, and it was obvious that Dad was never more proud of me.

Following my basic training, the corps sent me from Parris Island to Camp Lejeune, North Carolina, for field training, and eventually I was stationed at Camp Elmore in Roanoke, Virginia, where the marines taught me more about myself in two years than I had learned in my entire life up to that point. Those lessons would prove invaluable in the years ahead.

About the time I got to Camp Elmore, a decision was made at the Pentagon to begin pulling the marines out of Nam. None of the troops at our camp were sent to Vietnam, although we served in various support capacities. During my time in the corps, I was given top secret clearance and worked as an administrative clerk for a colonel. But the best lessons I learned from the marines involved self-discipline and the concept of being on a team. I fell in love with my country and the armed forces that protect it. I also gained a tremendous respect for the men and women who served our country during that time, and still to this day, I honor all who serve and have served. May God bless America and the men and women who fought to secure the freedom we enjoy and cherish today. Thank you to all who have served in any capacity.

CHAPTER **5**

Surfer Dude

To the surprise of many—including me—after the initial shock to my system, I thrived in the Marine Corps. My attitude was that I was going to make the best of a bad situation. I received two meritorious promotions and played on the marines' championship fast-pitch softball team while at Camp Elmore. Upon earning an honorable discharge from the marines in late 1972, a surfer friend and I mustered up a couple hundred bucks, and I financed a new Chevy van, which we loaded up with all the necessities for a West Coast surfing safari. We landed in Southern California and stayed for two months, surfing and partying until our funds ran low. I then returned home to Salisbury for the next year or so.

I teamed up with my old friend Ronnie Nelson, and we took advantage of our time as two young veterans returning from the service. For us, drinking, dancing, and partying was our world, especially in light of some difficult economic times. Ronnie and I created "BrigaRons," festivals in which we rented the local armory, hired some popular bands, and secured a license to offer kegs of beer, all with local police oversight. We promoted and sold tickets to the weekend events, which we billed as the ultimate party: live music, dancing, and all the beer you could drink. The BrigaRons were a huge hit and financially successful. Ironically, the BrigaRons earned me some grudging respect from my dad. He was impressed that I had actually founded a profitable enterprise.

I decided that perhaps college would expand my horizons. I enrolled at Delaware Technical and Community College in Georgetown, and in theory I was there to study business, although I honestly don't remember learning too much about real-world business. Mostly we talked about business theories. Boring!

One of the best things to come out of my college experience was a friendship I forged with Larry Parsons. He was a larger, rowdier version of me, about six foot two inches tall and around 240 pounds. We met in class at Delaware Tech and hit it off instantly. I was the little guy with the big mouth. I'd talk us into trouble and Larry would fight us out of it. He'd glare at me, and say, "When I get done beatin' up this guy who was trying to beat on you, I'm going to beat you too!" Nevertheless, Larry and I were a lot alike. We both had entrepreneurial blood in our veins, we both looked like long-haired hippies, we both liked to surf, and we both liked to smoke dope. And we were both Maryland boys. Larry was from Pocomoke City, and I was living back in Salisbury. We were also both bored in the classroom.

About four months into the first semester, Larry and I decided to go surfing at the Indian River Inlet one afternoon before going to an accounting class. On the way back, we pulled into a convenience store, and I purchased a quart of malt liquor, which I downed on the way back to campus, while Larry smoked a joint. By the time we arrived at class, neither one of us was too interested in accounting principles. We stumbled in and took our seats as the elderly professor was writing on the chalkboard. Larry's seat was in the same row as mine, about two seats from the front and a few seats ahead of mine. The only sound in the room was the professor's chalk scratching against the chalkboard.

Not in the mood for accounting, I tried to get my buddy's attention. "Larry!" I whispered as loudly as I could. I was certain Larry heard me, but he ignored me and pretended as though he hadn't, so I tried again. "Larry!" Same response. The third time I practically called Larry's name out loud. "Larry!"

Larry turned around in his seat, still somewhat bleary-eyed, and said, "What!"

As loudly as I could, I called out, "Hey, man! Let's get out of here."

The professor turned around and stared at me. "Mr. Hart and Mr. Parsons, I think that would be a good idea."

Larry and I left college that day and neither one of us ever went back, but we remained great friends and great surfing buddies. Larry's parents and his sister welcomed me, and we hung out in Pocomoke City for most of the semester.

Larry was a musician, a drummer, and the only white guy in an all-black horn band. One of the guys went on to play with James Brown. Larry and Ronnie and I hung out a lot together, but when Larry's dad developed multiple sclerosis and was confined to a wheelchair, Larry returned home to take care of the family business, the Twin Towers, a small hotel and restaurant. I didn't see much of him for years, and for a while we lost contact, but eventually Larry became a born-again Christian and a youth minister and a Mennonite pastor. Talk about a supernatural transformation!

Years later, when I needed someone I could trust to help me launch a new business, Larry came to work for me without a salary for nearly six months. To this day, Larry is one of the best friends I've ever known.

ONCE I had been home for a while, I realized that most of my friends hadn't grown a lot. They were still doing pretty much the same things they had been doing two years earlier. Many had married their high school sweethearts and were already raising children and establishing some roots or settling into a more conservative routine. I was too young and carefree for that, and I certainly wasn't ready to be a husband and dad. That was just not in the cards for me at that time. I had too much living to catch up on. So I said my good-byes and made for the great escape, not knowing what I was going to do or even where I was going. I loaded all my earthly possessions—including my surfboard and a bit of contraband—and filled the tank on my latest vehicle, a 1969 Chevelle 396 SS, and headed south

BRIGISM

If you don't start something soon, you may never start.

> ## SUCCESS PRINCIPLE FOR LIFE
>
> Dreaming is fun and healthy. Risking is also part of the deal in life
> if you are going to achieve anything worthwhile. Go for it!

on Interstate 95. I landed in Jacksonville Beach, where my brother had moved several years earlier. I had no idea what I was going to do, but I was footloose and fancy-free for the moment, even though I was broke and had nowhere else to go. Isn't youth wonderful?

I resumed my freelance carpentry, picking up odd jobs here and there. My brother David worked for the city at the time, and we shared a common desire to make a living by doing what we enjoyed most: surfing. A simple conversation turned into a plan. We borrowed a few hundred dollars from Mom and Dad, bought a business license for fifteen bucks, and we opened a surf shop in a tiny house, providing surfboards, T-shirts, and beach equipment to the local surfing crowd. We were actually in business within two weeks from the conception of our idea. It was a meager beginning, but to two young entrepreneurs like us, it was tremendously exciting.

Sometimes ignorance really is bliss. My brother and I were honestly excited about what we might be able to accomplish. I'm one of those guys who believes you need to go with the flow. Get an idea, but don't overthink it. Work out the details and adjust as you get moving. Too many wait for everything to be just right before launching out. Those folks never get started in anything. My philosophy: do something and do it now.

David and I lived in the rear of the building, and the shop occupied the front two rooms. We worked our regular jobs, and whenever we could, we opened the shop to service our small but growing clientele. We did whatever we had to do to make the business happen. Because of our zeal and passionate interest in the surfing business, we soon attracted a modest following. The surfers

It was a meager beginning but tremendously exciting.

knew that we were the real deal, that we not only spoke the language, but we knew the surfing culture. We provided an honest service to people who were interested in the sport, and we loved every minute of it.

David was a fanatical surfer, and he excelled at it. Surfing was his sport. I loved surfing as well, but the business side of it became my real interest. David had surfed in Ocean City, Maryland, along with Dewey Webber, a legend in the surfing world, who now designed, built, and sold his own brand of surfboards in Southern California. We called Dewey and asked if he would be interested in our carrying his line of surfboards on the East Coast. We had enough money to buy only three Webber boards but no skegs (the fin on the bottom of the board that improves directional stability). We couldn't afford those. Dewey not only agreed to let us sell his surfboards, but he allowed us to incorporate his name with our first shop. I promptly went to work and painted our first sign, bearing the name Hart's Webber House Surf Shop, and hoisted it above our front door. With three surfboards and a sign, some high hopes, and a lot of zeal, we opened our first real enterprise. We were open for business. Look out world, here we come!

A half dozen other surf shops dotted the beach within a short distance from us, and our competitors scoffed at our

The first Harts Surf Shop (and my home) opened at 1973 First Street South in Jacksonville Beach, Florida.

opening another one. "You guys will never make it." (Has anyone ever told you that? That kind of remark steams me up and fuels my belly!) But we ran our business differently than most ordinary shops. We didn't have regular business hours. We'd open at any hour of the day or night, whenever someone wanted or needed something we carried, regardless of the hour.

Before long, Hart's Surf Shop became known as the locals' place to go if you wanted any kind of great surf- or skateware or just to hang with the locals for some good beach conversation. It was cool to hang with the kids in the know about anything having to do with the surfing culture in and around our area. We had what you call status, which meant we didn't have any money. We reinvested every penny in building an inventory and developing a legitimate competitive edge. But our profits didn't allow us to take much of a salary, so we did what we had to do in that start-up phase, like work three jobs and learn to sleep fast. Sleeping and eating weren't high priorities in our lives at that time.

P.S. You will survive, it's part of the learning process. It's called paying a price.

One thing Dad had instilled in us was a strong work ethic, so both David and I held down other jobs for the first year as we tried to get the surf shop off the ground. I was good at carpentry, so I built all the display cases, board racks, and even the furniture. We did what we had to do, and we enjoyed and took pride in our work. I also did some custom work on vans and cars. I worked at all sorts of menial jobs, including cleaning rest rooms at gas stations along the interstate. I scrubbed toilets: five dollars for a single-holer and eight dollars for a two-holer.

A friend, Matt Mason, and I wanted to open a cleaning business for office buildings, and we had to start somewhere. For a two-man operation, we were amazing. We'd blow into that rest room, and in ten minutes it would be spotless, and we'd be on our way to the next location. When we solicited

> **In every adversity there's the seed of an equal or greater benefit.**

office-cleaning jobs, however, we discovered that potential employers wanted us to be licensed, bonded, and insured. So we got creative and printed up some business cards that included the words *licensed, bonded,* and *insured,* none of which were actually true. We were fortunate that our clients bought our sales pitch. Our work spoke for itself.

I've always said that in every adversity there's the seed of an equal or greater benefit. Scrubbing toilets was filthy work, but the benefit was that scrubbing those filthy toilets cured me of my ferocious fingernail biting habit!

SUCCESS PRINCIPLE FOR LIFE

Sometimes you have to do some things now that you don't really want to do so you will be able to do the things you really want to do in the future. The lessons learned during these times will be invaluable to you.

SUCCESS PRINCIPLE FOR LIFE

Change your business model. Don't expect people to come to you. Go to where the customers are!

The surf shop remained my primary interest, however. Any idea we could implement—from promoting new or unique surfing or skating products to hosting special events—we were on it big-time. Although David was the front man, working in the store was not important to him. I'd wake up many mornings to find the shop still locked down and David out doing his thing—surfing. I'd groggily look out the window and think, *We need to open the doors for business.* By that time, David had already been surfing for several hours. Our priorities were a bit different. Since I wasn't the sort of person to sit idly all day in the shop, waiting for someone to come in and buy something, I went out after customers. And where were most of the people who might be interested in our wares or services? On the beach, of course. So that's where I applied most of my efforts, fair-skinned as I was, walking up and down the beach, talking to people about our services and handing out flyers.

Our simple but effective marketing plan—singleness of purpose and sheer tenacity—paid off, and despite intense competition, our surf shops survived. After a while, we started carrying our own brand of surfboards. I've always been big on branding, promoting and making a name for ourselves on the products we carried. So after a few years, when Dewey became very ill, we developed our own line of boards. We continued to carry a few other brands as well, and we renamed the shop: Hart's Surf Shop.

I've always been big on branding—show and tell what you have.

About that time, a group of Jacksonville Beach businessmen were looking to cash in on a popular national trend: skateboarding. They decided to turn a vacant piece of prime property into a skateboard park. They knew little about the particulars of skateboarding, but they recognized that it was popular and in demand. They named the park Landallee Skateboard Park in Jacksonville Beach, one of the first skateboard parks on the East Coast. They sought out David's and my services and expertise to attract customers and to run the park. Since we were always looking for ways to better our position and leverage the opportunities that came our way, David and I saw this as a chance to market our wares in their facility. So we commandeered a small area and opened a skate shop in the park. We were becoming good at figuring out how to get things done with limited resources. We knew the surfing crowd already, and many of the kids on the beach knew of our shops, so I felt certain we were going to make a fortune. We might have pulled it off had it not been for the unforeseen obstacles we faced because of insurance hassles.

Every day kids lined up to get into the park. There were so many skaters we had to break up the day and evening into one-hour skating sessions. That way, we limited the number of boarders in the park at any one time. The kids wore helmets and pads, and most of them did fairly well. We suffered few serious accidents among the young skaters. But outside the park, the parents weren't so agile or balanced. Merely trying to stand on a skateboard resulted in innumerable injuries among the adults. In short, it wasn't the kids' injuries that caused us the grief; it was the adults trying to be kids. As a result, regardless of how safe our parks were, enormous insurance premiums caused us to shut down. Sad to say, the skateboard park closed, not due to lack of business, but because no insurance company would provide coverage at a reasonable rate. I packed up my skateboards and went back to the surf shops.

The surf shops did well for a while, and we expanded to three stores in Neptune Beach and Jacksonville Beach. We also opened a shop in Orange Park, which we referred to as "Town." But rather than paying attention to the business, both of us embraced the party lifestyle throughout the day and far into the night. It wasn't long

> **Our outgo was greater than our income, so our upkeep became our downfall.**

before things spiraled downward. David and I weren't the most astute businessmen, so we didn't know how to read business trends and cycles. In 1977, the nation went into a recession that hit us hard. Gas prices soared to nearly fifty cents a gallon. Since we had no idea how that might affect our business, David and I expanded. But we failed to consider our market. Kids weren't usually the ones who bought the $150 surfboards and the $100 skateboards; the kids' parents purchased them. When gas prices went through the roof (by 1970s standards and compared to 1970s

One of the seven Harts Surf Shops we opened over a
thirty-year career, from 1973 to 2003

incomes), David and I didn't realize that all our products were petroleum-based. Our suppliers passed on the increase in costs, and our products doubled in price almost overnight. The shock caused a dramatic downturn in our business for an extended period of time. Our outgo was greater than our income, so our upkeep became our downfall. Translation: we were broke!

By 1978, we were going broke fast. I knew we were in trouble when I didn't have enough money to pay an eighteen dollar electric bill at the shop. No bank would give us a loan, and we didn't have any rich benefactors from whom we might borrow some money.

I was extremely frustrated because we couldn't turn the business around. This is where I learned a lesson about hard work. If working hard and working long alone makes you successful, I should have already been a multimillionaire. I became increasingly discouraged and turned to drugs and alcohol to mask the pain and depression I felt. But that didn't help, but rather served to make the situation worse. I was on an emotional roller coaster as David and I watched the business we had built with five years of blood, sweat, and tears dwindle away. My self-worth was tied to my accomplishments in the business, and as it tanked, so did I—to the point where drugs and alcohol caused me to think that suicide might be a viable answer.

Isn't it amazing how easily we can be deceived if we don't know what has real value in life? To me, there seemed nowhere to turn, no reason to go on. I was mad at myself, broke, busted, and disgusted.

This chapter in our lives was quickly coming to an end. But there were more changes ahead.

CHAPTER **6**

A Fresh Start

SOMETIMES WHAT LOOKS LIKE the bottom point in your life is actually just a great place to start again. Sailors who have lived around the sea all their lives say the night is usually darkest just before the dawning of a new day. I was twenty-five years old, looking up from the bottom of the barrel, trying to find my way out of the dark. That's where I was languishing when opportunity found me.

I had been asking around, trying to find a bank or an individual who would loan David and me enough money to make it through another month, when someone told me about a group known as the Jaycees, "young businessmen in action." The Jaycees monthly meeting, an informal gathering of local businessmen held at a clubhouse in a mobile home park on Beach Boulevard was coming up. Technically, I was an owner of a failing business, but a business nonetheless, so I decided to attend.

Sometimes you don't get what you want, but you get what you need. I actually went to the Jaycees meeting in hopes of finding someone from whom I could borrow eighteen dollars to pay the surf shop light bill. There I met Doug Grissom, a man I guessed to be in his mid- to late thirties or early forties. I was impressed with him, though, because Doug wore

---

SUCCESS PRINCIPLE FOR LIFE

Are you at the bottom of your own barrel? Does it seem like
the doors have suddenly shut in your face or that you've
been knocking on locked doors? Maybe you have the
opportunity of a lifetime staring you in the face, but you'll
have to see with a new view to recognize it.
When God shuts a door, He opens a window.

---

a suit and drove a nice Monte Carlo. He didn't offer me any money, but the next day he called me to tell me about a business opportunity and to invite me to a business meeting.

A business opportunity? You want me to take a look at a business opportunity? I'm trying to bum eighteen bucks just to get by, and you're offering me a *business opportunity?*

This was just too strange for me to turn down.

> **Sometimes you don't get what you want, but you get what you need.**

"Are you interested?"

"Well, yeah. I guess."

"Good, come to the meeting tomorrow night, and wear business attire. You're welcome to bring somebody with you if you'd like."

"Okay." I hung up the phone.

I thought about Doug's call for a few seconds and quickly dismissed it. I had no intention of attending a business meeting. First of all, my car was not licensed or insured at the time. Nor did I have any money for gas, and I certainly didn't have any business attire. Moreover, I wasn't about to ask someone else to go with me to something that I didn't know anything about. I blew off the meeting.

The next day Doug called. "Hey, what happened? I thought you were coming to our business meeting."

"I just couldn't make it. I didn't have a way to get there." Then I launched into my litany of excuses. "And you said something about wearing business attire. Surfers don't wear *business attire.* I didn't want to embarrass you or myself."

Doug didn't argue with me. He was quiet on the phone for a few moments. "Would you mind if I stopped by the shop after you close tomorrow evening?" Doug asked. "Maybe I can fill you in on the opportunity then."

"Sure, Doug. Whatever floats your boat."

True to his word, Doug came to the shop the following evening after I'd closed. We talked a while, and there on the top of an electrical power line spool that I had turned into a makeshift table, Doug drew out several circles on a piece of paper, outlining a marketing plan. I knew nothing about direct marketing, let alone network marketing—I didn't run in those circles—but I was truly mesmerized by Doug's presentation. Not that he was so good at presenting the program. I was simply ready to hear anything that might help me out of my desperate situation. Doug's presentation sparked hope in me, and I responded to it. It was more of a spiel that he practically recited, but what appealed to me was that I could get into a business with little up-front money and almost no overhead, no equipment, no inventory, and no experience. Just register, get in, and start showing the plan to others.

The way Doug explained things, it wasn't rocket science: buy products at wholesale prices for yourself, merchandise a bit to other customers, and teach other people to do the same thing. Seemed simple enough to me. Doug briefly outlined at least six ways I could make money in this business opportunity. It wasn't real deep; I saw it as something almost anybody could do. My only initial expense was a starter's kit and some support tools (pamphlets, books, and audio materials to help me build my business) that sold for about three hundred dollars. After that, I needed to move about one hundred dollars a month in volume to stay active in the business and to qualify for bonuses from the company.

But what really got me was when Doug began to describe how the business could grow through the process of *duplication*. According to Doug, here's how it worked: I would sponsor a few people and help them get started, then those people would help a few others, who again would help a few more. The business success was not based on my efforts alone,

---

BRIGISM

Believing starts with wanting to believe. Hope is
nothing more than premature faith.

but on the efforts of each of us doing a little bit, which could add up to a lot of business. We all were paid commissions on all of the products moved by everyone in our "down-line organization," the people we had recruited as well as all those whom they would sponsor. In networking, this process is known as the law of exponential growth, although I doubt that Doug called it that as he explained the program to me.

I had no marketing experience on which to draw while I tried to process what Doug was telling me. Nevertheless, I was intrigued. I watched in amazement as Doug showed me how the profits could mount expo-nentially. I'd make a small percent-age from the company as a reward for the sales successes of everyone that I sponsored as well as those

Success is the progressive realization of a worthwhile goal or dream.

whom they sponsored. Wow! I didn't have to be a great salesperson. I could just share what I knew with other people who might be interested in mak-ing some extra money—and everyone I knew was interested in that!

In the process of explaining the plan, Doug uttered a statement that he'd probably memorized and tossed out to potential clients a thousand times, but it scored a direct hit with me. "Success is the progressive realiza-tion of a worthwhile goal or dream." That statement connected with me at such a deep level that I adopted it as my own.

"Do you want to succeed?" Doug asked blandly.

"Yeah, sure I do, Doug."

"Well, what's your dream?"

"My dream? Are you kidding me? I want to pay an eighteen-dollar light bill; that's my dream. I want to have enough money to put gas in my car. I want to eat on a regular basis."

Doug chortled as if I were joking with him. "If you could do all that, then what would you do?"

"Why would I think beyond those things, Doug? I can't even do that right now."

Doug didn't know it, but my dreams had long since been buried under a load of oppression. Like so many other folks, I had allowed my dreams to be snuffed out by the realities of life. I spent most of my time just trying to survive. I was twenty-five years old and had given up hope of doing anything significant with my life.

"But what if time and money were no problem?" Doug probed.

I looked back at Doug, and thought, This guy is a nut case. He's asking me these questions as though I really know the answers. But I'll play along. After all, nobody else has asked me these kinds of questions in a long, long time. Maybe never.

"Okay, Doug," I began almost sarcastically, "I want a beachfront home, and I want to drive around in luxury automobiles."

"What kind of car?" Doug interrupted. "What color?"

"A Cadillac," I responded quickly, thinking of the nicest luxury cars on the market in the midseventies. "Black. I want a black Cadillac Eldorado."

"What else?"

I didn't realize it, but Doug was causing me to think for the first time beyond my self-imposed limits. And his questions were forcing me to be specific about my dreams, not merely describing them in vague, ambiguous, nonachievable terms. I've since learned that such specific goals are absolutely essential for true success, but at the time, I was just humoring myself at Doug's expense. Nevertheless, the more questions Doug asked, the more I had to admit that a change for the better sounded pretty good. I was starting to have some fun with this.

"Well, I wouldn't be living here in the surf shop, that's for sure. And I wouldn't be working all the time, night and day, just to make ends meet. I'd go to work because I wanted to, not because I have to. I'd take some time to travel to other places to surf. I wouldn't ask my date to go dutch with me. In a restaurant, I'd read the menu from left to right, rather than right to left, always checking out the prices before I order. I'd be out of debt and have some discretionary cash for myself."

Specific goals are absolutely essential for true success.

I was just playing along with Doug, but his questions sparked something deep within me and got me dreaming again. Most people suppress their dreams and live in survival mode. If you are weighed down by your past experiences, and you don't know where you are going in the future, the present can be a pernicious place. Why put yourself through the misery of hoping for anything better? If you have no hope for the future, you have no power in the present, and if you have no power in the present, you have no path to take you forward.

Doug was on a roll, so I let him talk, and I dropped my defenses for the moment and became genuinely interested. Doug wrote two words on his yellow pad: *success* and *dream.* "Success," Doug said as he pointed at the word, "is not all about just dollars and cents, as he circled the *u* in *success.* It's all about you. You and your Dream." He looked up to see if I was following him.

"Hmm, okay, I get that," I said. "Success is based on a dream. Okay."

"But it takes four things," Doug said. "A dream, the willingness to work—"

"No problem there," I interrupted. "I've been working all my life."

"Working hard and smart," Doug said.

> **If you have no hope for the future, you have no power in the present.**

"Smart might be a hard one for me," I quipped.

Doug smiled but was undeterred. He continued scribbling and wrote the word *attitude,* then alongside it, he wrote the letters, *PMA.*

I wasn't familiar with the acronym. "What's PMA?"

"Positive mental attitude," Doug replied. "You have to develop an optimistic way of looking at life. Your attitude is your key to success. Ninety-nine point nine percent of all success is attitude. If you think you can, you can. If you think you can't, you can't. You're right either way. The glass isn't half empty; it is half full. So much depends on how you view the same circumstances."

"How can a guy like me do that?" I asked.

"By reading good books and hanging around with successful people."

"Okay," I nodded. I was a pretty happy-go-lucky guy. I could develop a brighter outlook. And most of the friends I was hanging out with were in the same shape I was, so I was up for a change. After all, anything would be better than the rut in which I was stuck. "What else?"

"Number four: it takes a vehicle, a way to get you where you want to go. You can have a great dream, a willingness to work, and the right attitude, but without a vehicle to get you there, you can't be successful. If one of the elements is missing, it isn't going to work."

By vehicle, Doug didn't mean an automobile; he was talking about a business opportunity that could help me get to where I wanted to go. Doug drew two intersecting lines on the paper. "Where opportunity and readiness meet in life is the point that determines success." He looked up from his paper and looked me in the eye. "This is why I'm here. Are you ready to make a decision to start on your journey to success?"

I nodded my head and barely whispered, "Yeah, I am."

"Okay, the opportunity I've been sharing with you is the Amway business. Have you ever heard of that?"

I had never even heard the word *Amway*. At that time, I didn't even know the business existed. "Is that like Amtrak?" I asked.

Doug looked at me as though I had just dropped down from outer space. "Yeah, just like it," he replied shrewdly.

"Oh, good. I like Amtrak," I said. "I'm in."

Doug drew several circles on the page. "This first circle represents me," Doug said. "And this circle represents you. I'll sponsor you." He drew a line from the first circle to the second.

"You'll sponsor me?"

"Yeah, I'll get you into the business and I'll help you. I won't do it for you, but I'll do it with you. I'll help you every way I can. Now, watch this." Doug drew six circles with lines extended to four more circles, then from the four to two others, all connected to mine. He looked up and smiled at me. "It's called the 6-4-2 program," he said. "All those circles represent people who do a small amount of volume, and when added together monthly, they can create a lot of group volume." Doug explained how that volume translated into personal bonuses for me. Now that got my full attention.

Attitude is 99.9 percent of all success. If you think you can, you can. If you think you can't, you can't!

"Really?" The fascination in my voice must have been obvious to Doug. "That's all?" I was thinking about a traditional business and what it would cost to open a new surf shop. I was seeing all the up-front expenses we had to pay for—overhead, equipment, inventory, employees—before we could ever sell anything, not to mention that it was all a huge risk. The business Doug was telling me about posed a relatively small risk with potentially huge returns.

BRIGISM

I would rather earn a little bit of a lot than earn a lot of a little bit.

"The business can actually gain a life of its own in time," Doug explained, "so you can earn ongoing residual income."

"And I am only required to do a small amount of volume each month," I confirmed.

Doug nodded affirmatively. He explained that once I had the 6-4-2 structure in place, I would be running about seventy-five hundred points in monthly volume, which translated into a two thousand dollar monthly bonus for me. That seemed like all the money in the world to me at the time. I was knocking down a cool eight hundred dollars a month and spending a lot more than that struggling to survive.

My mind was racing. "Can I help more than six people? What if I sponsor a hundred people?"

Doug smiled. He wasn't used to someone asking if he or she could do more. Most people wanted to know how few people they had to talk to, or how little time they had to invest and still make money. "Sure, sponsor as many as you want. You get paid for all that volume," he replied.

"Can I work at this every day?"

"As much as you want to," Doug answered. "It's your business."

"And can I go to other towns, like maybe Orlando or Daytona, and get some people in the business there?"

"Well, sure. If you want to."

"Do you mean I could meet a total stranger and invite him to get into the business?

"Yes, you could." Doug was amused. He was accustomed to people asking, "Do I have to do anything?"

Not me. I was taken by the fact that I had no limits or geographical boundaries to confine me. I could talk to whomever wherever and when-

---

SUCCESS PRINCIPLE FOR LIFE

Sometimes we have to reach the bottom before we're ready
to look for a way out and to consider new ways of doing things.
Are you tired of doing the same things, weary of exerting
so much time and energy only to reap the same old
results? Identify the limits of your current situation and
commit to finding a way to begin building a new future!

ever I chose. I couldn't wait to get started. Why? Because I was broke. I saw this business as my way out.

Prior to this conversation with Doug, I had never before seen or heard of network marketing, but it instantly made sense to me. I mean, I *got* it. I could see clearly the idea of exponential growth achieved by compounding the efforts of a few people who were helping a few more people, and that soon grew to many people. It just made sense. In each of our surf shops, we had several vending machines from which we made passive income. I likened the network marketing business to them. Each of the machines created a small profit for us with minimal effort on our part. So as I considered network marketing, I figured there were a whole lot more people out there than there were locations for vending machines! I was excited about the possibilities.

"And what kind of products do you market?"

"We have all kinds of great products," Doug said as he pulled out a brochure, showing pictures of laundry detergent, liquid hand soaps, toothpaste, and all-purpose cleaners. The products were mostly household items that ordinary people would use every day. Compared to selling surfboards, they were rather nondescript, but I had to admit that more people bought laundry detergent than surfboards.

It all sounded so simple to me—maybe because I saw it that way. What could be easier than finding people who wanted to make some extra money simply by changing their buying habits? They'd be buying everyday items at wholesale rather than retail prices, and then having those products delivered to their front door. Then all they had to do was to replicate that process with other people. Simple.

"You just have to talk to people," said Doug, "and tell them about the opportunity, sorta like I've told you."

"I can do that."

Doug smiled. "Yes, you can."

He told me several inspiring stories, attributing the success of numerous people he knew in the business to their faith in God. I wasn't the least bit interested in that aspect of what he had to say. In fact, I recoiled against it. "Look, we'll do real fine if you keep that God stuff out of this," I said. "If there is a God, why am I in this position?"

"Okay, fine." Doug quickly glossed over the subject. "No problem. You don't believe in God?"

Images of the pictures I had drawn as a boy in Vacation Bible School flitted through my mind. "Nah, I don't believe in all that heaven and hell stuff. Do you?" I asked. "Do you mean to tell me that you believe that God parted the Red Sea for Moses and all those stories about David and Goliath, Jonah and the Whale?"

"Why, yeah," Doug said, somewhat aghast that I might not.

"How do you know it's true?" I asked.

"Well, when I get to heaven, I'll ask them," Doug said.

"But what if they ain't there?"

"Then you ask them," Doug deadpanned.

I quickly changed the subject. "So how much does it cost to get started in this business?"

"Not much," Doug replied. "Around three hundred dollars."

"Will you take a check?"

"Sure."

Now think about that. Just a few nights earlier, I was asking Doug if he could loan me $18 to pay my electric bill, and now he's going to take a check for $318 from me! I dutifully wrote out the check, knowing there was not enough in the bank to cover it. Some people might call that faith. Others might call it foolish. The police call that passing bad checks. I love educated folks!

The next day, Doug returned with my sales and marketing kit, along with some support tools that would help me get my business off the ground. I was on my way.

CHAPTER **7**

The Power of What-If

FOR THREE STRAIGHT NIGHTS I could barely sleep. I kept seeing those circles Doug had drawn and thinking, *What if?* There's incredible power in those words: what if? What if those circles began replicating, if I really could get a few people interested in this business, each of whom would get a few more, who would enlist a few more. I was so excited I couldn't wait to get up and get started!

Of course, on the third day, reality poked a hole in my balloon of idealism when Doug came back and said, "Hey, Brig! Your check bounced."

"Well, duh! Of course it bounced. I told you that I didn't have any money."

Doug was not happy. He wanted his money, so I scraped up everything I could and had a yard sale. I sold my most precious possessions—my television, surfboard, wet suit, and little bag of green stuff—and paid Doug. I owned my new business debt-free. Boy, does God have a sense of humor.

ARMED WITH my sample products, I set out to find some other people who might be interested in my new business. Since I was already a partner with my brother David, he was the first person I attempted to enlist. I told him about Doug and some of the other people he had described to me. David scowled through my entire presentation and then said, "You don't think that will really work, do you?"

"Well, it's working for them."

"Nah, I ain't gonna do that. I'll stick with the surf shops."

"But David, we're broke. We gotta do something to make some money."

"You can do it. But don't bring it in here."

I called Mom and Dad and told them about the business.

"Isn't that a pyramid scheme?" Dad asked. "That sounds like that Glenn Turner guy who got in trouble for selling mink oil distributorships?"

"Pyramid? Who's Glenn Turner?" That was the first time I'd heard the term *pyramid* in a negative context. I thought pyramids were in Egypt, and I was totally oblivious to the scheme in which Turner's followers lost more than forty million dollars. Nor was I aware of the scandals that had plagued early legitimate network marketing businesses. Later I discovered that Amway, in fact, was not a pyramid scheme, that it did not have exorbitant entry fees, nor did distributors get paid simply for recruiting other people, and it had a legitimate product line—all key differentiations. But at that moment, I'd never heard of a pyramid scheme, although it certainly wouldn't be the last time that I heard that term.

"Isn't that illegal?" Dad suggested.

"No, I don't think so. These guys are in business. I've seen their products."

Dad and Mom weren't interested. Nor were any of my surfer friends. Nor were any of the other two hundred or more people to whom I talked about the business over the next two weeks. I sponsored only thirteen people in the next few months, and none of them did much in the business.

BRIGISM

Facts can sometimes be the enemy of truth. People closest to you may discount something due to their own opinions. Some folks make excuses; others make money.

Looking back, it's easy to see why I elicited so little enthusiasm. Doug had helped me to make up a list of people I could contact about the business, but I didn't really hone my skills in making my presentations. I was calling on people merely to sponsor them rather than to qualify them, to see if they were really looking, to discover whether they were the type of person who was looking for a business opportunity with plenty of potential. I regarded the business simply as a means of making money. I didn't care all that much about the products, even though the products were good. Consequently, most of the people I contacted said, "No, I'm not interested." In fact, most people wouldn't even allow me to sit down and show them the business plan, so they weren't really saying no to the business. They were saying no to me.

I could get appointments with people, but most of them weren't interested in me—a long-haired, destitute surfer—telling them how they could be successful.

"Why would I listen to you?" somebody asked.

Yeah, why would you listen to me? I asked myself.

I continued cleaning toilets to earn enough money to buy food. But everywhere I went, I met people and handed out my new business cards.

I talked a lot of people into joining me in the business, many of whom quit after a short time. It wasn't their fault. I had pulled them into network marketing for the wrong reasons and with the wrong expectations. I thought the goal was to get a bunch of people to work for me. I'd call my people and ask, "What are you doing in your business?"

"Nuttin'," most of them replied.

"Well, you gotta get out there and buy or sell something or I'm not gonna make any money." I wasn't really concerned about the people I had encouraged to get into the business; I thought it was all about me.

I did better with referrals than I did with my friends. I'd ask people, "Who do you know who might be interested in this kind of business?" A lot of people were willing to give me names of others as long as they were one step removed from me.

Eventually I met Kim Magdalein and Dick Souther, who were both sales representatives in Jacksonville and were my direct up-line in the business. Kim and Dick taught me better ways to approach and build my business.

Paul Stanley was another highly successful person in my up-line of sponsorship. A single guy from North Carolina who rode motorcycles,

Paul was a bit of a rebel when he first got into the business. He was more relatable to me, and I liked him immediately. Paul had experienced some great success within his first three years in the business, so I gravitated toward his teaching. Paul shared his story with me, including how he had to overcome a lot of adversity as he achieved higher levels of success. I was impressed, especially since Paul was driving my dream car (a Cadillac Eldorado) and living in a pretty nice home. Paul had no choice but to mentor me, because I showed up anytime he was in the area. I watched his mannerisms, observed how he engaged people, and I listened to every word that came out of his mouth. Then I did my best to replicate his words, actions, and activities. In the process, I grew personally, my business improved, and Paul and I became good friends.

I learned to talk about the business to people anywhere and everywhere. My dream and desire drove me to overcome my fear and inhibitions. I was locked and loaded and focused on becoming more than what I was. I decided I would not be denied the success others had earned. Anytime I'd get in a conversation, and someone would ask me, "What do you do?" I'd tell them about my new business venture. "I'm looking for a few folks who want more than what they have and are willing to do something about it. Do you know anyone in that position?" I assumed that everybody has a dream that they can't fulfill through what they are currently doing— just as I did. I later learned that although everyone may have a dream, not all folks are motivated to do anything to see their dreams fulfilled. That just didn't compute to me, but I encountered that attitude often enough to recognize its reality.

I'm a KISS kind of guy: Keep It Super Simple. My greatest ability is to take the complicated and make it simple. I don't use a lot of complex business terms or other fancy words. My vernacular was everyday, down-to-earth, and conversational. "I've stumbled into a gold mine," I'd say, "and there is more than enough for me and my family. Want to dig?" This was a simple way of finding out where a person stood on the desire level. "If you're interested in hearing about it, let's get together and talk."

I got good at qualifying people (determining their openness to a new business opportunity) and then presenting the business opportunity in five to fifteen minutes, depending on their responses. Sometimes it wasn't so much what they said, but how they said it and what their body language said, that gave me insight into their interest level. Although I didn't realize it at the time, I was developing a skill in understanding people and a valuable gift of discernment. It got to the point where I could almost determine a person's interest level within moments of our being together. I learned to ask good, direct questions, to get to the heart of where people were in life and what they wanted in their future.

Every week there were meetings somewhere, usually in the home of a distributor, and I attended as many as I could. I no longer had a licensed or tagged car, but I was determined to get there, so I'd ride my bike to the meetings. I'd walk in wearing flip-flops and casual beachwear, slightly sweaty and disheveled from

My greatest ability is to take the complicated and make it simple.

the ride, with my wind-blown long blond hair flowing down to my shoulders. The people in their business attire would look at me askance, but I didn't mind. I was excited about the business, and I wanted to learn how to operate it better. Eventually, I made some personal concessions. For instance, I started shaving prior to meetings, pulling my hair back into a ponytail, and bathing regularly.

I encouraged all my potential distributors to attend the meetings with me. I'd tell them, "Look, I know a little bit about how this works, but there are some people meeting nearby this week who know a lot more than I do. You're welcome to come with me as my guest, so you can check it out for yourselves." I was so excited and convinced of this newfound opportunity that I could almost always get people to attend informational meetings. I developed an ability to pique people's curiosity, causing them to want to check out the business opportunity. My contacts didn't always get involved in the business, or last very long if they did get in, but I became proficient at getting folks in front of the presentation.

People respond more to emotion than they do to logic. I got into the business because I was excited about the possibilities. The business gave me hope. Nothing else in my life had really changed, but networking stoked a fire in me. My enthusiasm about where this business could potentially take me was contagious, so people wanted to hear more about it. Even today, I'm convinced that excitement sponsors folks and enthusiasm breeds enthusiasm. I was taught in the beginning just to play dumb and be excited. The dumb part came honestly; the excitement continued to grow.

Occasionally, I'd attend larger meetings held in a more public venue, a hotel, or an auditorium. At many of the meetings, we began with the

Pledge of Allegiance, and at the end, we often sang "God Bless America." At first, I thought that was a bit strange for a business meeting, but as a marine, I appreciated that. I also enjoyed the teaching about embracing an entrepreneurial spirit and a strong work ethic. The people at these meetings not only taught but demonstrated how to exercise kindness, gentleness, honesty, faithfulness, and diligence in working with business associates. I learned many other basic success principles at these meetings as well. I especially enjoyed hearing the stories of how other folks from all walks of life had entered the business and had overcome various obstacles to become the successes they were today. Each time I would think, *Why not me? I can do what they have done!*

> **People respond more to emotion than they do to logic, and enthusiasm breeds enthusiasm.**

The how-to aspect of the meetings provided practical tips for improving myself and honing my skills in building the business, but the personal success stories provided the emotional side of the business equation, and that's what appealed most to me. People genuinely cheered for one another as they celebrated each person's success. Where do you find that kind of attitude in the world today? That impressed my socks off. This was a new and exciting world for me.

The meetings were beneficial to me in other ways as well. I often picked up nuggets of information that helped me not only in my business but in my everyday life. For instance, the business helped me immensely by encouraging me to read positive books and to listen to uplifting audio materials that sparked creative ideas in me. I wasn't a big reader, but I started reading books and listening to material such as Norman Vincent Peale's *The Power of Positive Thinking,* Napoleon Hill's *Think and Grow Rich,* Dale Carnegie's *How to Win Friends and Influence People,* and of course, oil tycoon J. Paul Getty's classic business book *How to Be Rich,* in which he shares his formula for success: rise early, work hard, strike oil. Getty's book also piqued my interest because he posed the intriguing question: Which is better, to earn 100 percent of what you can do, or to earn 1 percent of what a hundred other people are doing? Making a little bit of money from the sales of a lot of people appealed to me.

Eventually, I became good at replicating what I learned. But I also realized early on that people were only going to follow me to the extent that I could feed them helpful information. That's why I told my new recruits, "I'll help you, but let me tell you about this up-line of people who know a lot more than I do. They're willing to help you too." I understood that if I succeeded, the people above me succeeded and the people down-line could succeed too. I leaned heavily on my friends in the business who gave me some credibility when I didn't have any. I borrowed their success for a season.

I posed for pictures with some of the more successful individuals in our business, and I wasn't bashful about showing those photos to my prospects. "Look, do you see this guy who owns this big, fancy house and that gorgeous car? He's really successful in this thing. He's helping me in this business. And I'm going to help you." That was exactly how Doug Grissom and others had influenced me. "See these guys in our up-line? They are available to help you in your business." That intrigued me; nobody else had ever offered to help me succeed. Now, these guys were willing to help me. They'd take calls from people in my organization and encourage them far better than I could, and I didn't pay them a dime to do it. They weren't even charging me a consulting fee for their expertise.

I know now that what my mentors were doing is a basic principle of success: you must help others succeed if you hope to be successful yourself. In true network marketing, it is impossible to succeed until someone else on your team succeeds. But here's the deal: the more people you help to succeed, the more successful you will become.

Today, I'm still looking for people who get excited. I look for people who have a *why*, a deeply seeded reason for wanting to do more and have more in life. If they have a dream they are willing to fight for, I am their man. I am not the message but the messenger. I want them to have a well-defined why—a why that makes them cry.

My why (why get involved in a network marketing business) was simple. It didn't require a lot of complex analysis on my part. It wasn't so much what I wanted; it was what I *didn't* want. I despised being broke. I just wanted out of my situation. I didn't like where I was in life. I hated the fact that I was in perpetual financial bondage. I wanted to get to a place where money didn't control me, where I was financially free. I dreamed about having some discretionary cash. I wanted to fill up my gas tank or shop at a grocery

> **You must help others succeed if you hope to be successful yourself.**

BRIGISM

Learn to observe what the masses of people do in life
and do the opposite in a positive direction.

store without fear of overspending. I dreamed of going to a restaurant and reading the menu from left to right rather than from right to left.

For all my excitement, however, my first fifteen months or so in the business were a wash. In my best months I made only about three hundred dollars a month, and I was spending most of that trying to recruit more people. The surf shops were barely surviving, and I was constantly scrambling to get some carpentry work to pay my bills. I was struggling personally too, since I had alienated myself from most of my surfer buddies because I wasn't partying with them as much and I was trying to get ahead in life. They looked at me as though to say, "Who does Brig think he is?"

That was tough. But it's important to understand that when you decide to do something with your life, there will be some separation. Some people won't understand, others won't want to be around you any longer, and there will be some folks you don't want to be around any more. But the key is this: if you want something greater in life, you must learn to observe what the masses of people are doing, and then do the opposite in a positive direction. Be different. Weak fish swim with the tide; strong fish swim against the tide. If you want something different, do something different.

At the same time, having gotten one step removed from my beer-guzzling, pot-smoking buddies, I could see how futile and fickle those relationships were. As long as I had money and was buying the beer or pot, I had plenty of friends. When my money ran out, so did my friends. I didn't hold it against them, but more and more, I realized their attitude was "What's in it for me?" Those were conditional relationships.

I was discouraged and lonely. Nothing seemed to be working for me. I felt like a failure. I became depressed. I tried every way I could to keep things going, but I was sinking lower with each passing day. I bottomed out when my credit company tried to repossess my Ford Econoline van. Thinking that my business was going to take off any day now, I had done some carpentry jobs and scraped up enough for a down payment to finance the new van. Now, since times had gotten tight, I didn't have enough money to keep up the payments, and the repo man was on my doorstep again. As I'd done before, I tried to hide the van, but I was pretty easy to track.

The Bible says that, without a vision, the people perish. That is a dangerous place to be (and right where the devil wants you, by the way). Not only did I have no vision, I felt as though I had no value or purpose. With no true friends, no love in my life, and my fledgling business dreams dashed, I despaired of life once again. If I had taken one more step in the wrong direction, I could have easily destroyed my life. Looking back, I must have had really good angels looking out for me.

CHAPTER **8**

A Changed Hart

I T'S OFTEN FUNNY TO look back and recognize the many potentially life-changing encounters we have, to realize how God was working in our lives even if we never gave Him a second thought. I recall attending a large business function and sitting next to a nattily dressed fellow on the front row. "What brings you here?" he asked.

"My friend Paul Stanley invited me," I replied.

"Really?" the sharply dressed man replied. "Paul invited me to come too."

"No kiddin'? What do you do?"

"I'm going to be speaking here today."

A short while later, I sat and listened while Dr. Charles Stanley—the man I'd met on the front row—mounted the stage and presented some powerful business-building and life-changing principles. When Charles returned to his seat, I leaned over and said, "Hey, Charles, that's some pretty good stuff. If you'd leave God out of all that, you know you'd probably get a lot more people."

Dr. Stanley laughed and said, "Oh, *Lord!*"

In sales, it's not always the steak that people are buying. Often it's the sizzle. I liked the sizzle I saw, heard, and felt when I was around my new business associates, many of whom were Christians. I was living for months as I thought a Christian might live, but I was not really a Christian. Oh, sure, I had accepted the principles, the mannerisms, and external lifestyle, but I had no spiritual reality within. Interestingly, I used to curse every other word, but once I began spending more time with people in this business, I noticed very few of them used profanity. It was an environmental change for me, and that environment was influencing me for the better. I quickly realized that such degrading comments were unacceptable in our business, so I refrained from cursing. Nobody sat me down and lectured me; I simply stopped cussing.

I wanted what they had, but I thought the secret was merely outward change. I even bought a suit and tie so I would better fit in with the business crowd. I still kept my long blond hair, but I went to J. C. Penney's and bought a ninety-nine dollar polyester suit with two pairs of pants, a reversible vest, and a jacket. I wore that suit with an olive green shirt and a colorful tie. I didn't yet understand that the real change I needed wouldn't happen simply because I changed my clothes. It could only come as a result of a transformation within me, by establishing a relationship with Jesus Christ. I didn't know anything about that. I even cautioned some of the people I was bringing into the business to avoid the God talk.

Whenever the business leaders conducted weekend conferences, they almost always included a Sunday morning worship service before the crowd dispersed and went back home. I'd tell my organization, "Don't pay any attention to all that Jesus talk, but the rest of it is pretty good stuff." Sometimes I'd even stand outside the hall, saying, "Don't go to the Sunday meeting.

> **I wanted what they had. But more important, I wanted to be what they were.**

They're just going to have a church service and take your money. Don't go in there." To me, I thought, *Why ruin a good function?*

But I didn't know at the time that the Word doesn't return void if it is sent out with love. Those seeds that they had sown in love were taking root in my soul.

I WAS becoming a people magnet, friendly and personable, and a bit of a natural communicator, so I could produce people for my mentors' meetings. No matter when the guys in my up-line scheduled meetings, I gathered a crowd for them. Ironically, most of the people at those meetings were there because I had invited them. My zeal, excitement, and belief came through and piqued their curiosity. I soon learned to use the credibility of people in my up-line to leverage the value and urgency of the opportunity being presented.

"Where are you getting all these people?" the up-line distributors asked in amazement.

"I got up this morning," I'd answer, "and just talked with the folks with whom I came in contact with today." To me, every day was a fresh opportunity. No matter who I met, sooner or later, I'd find some way to guide the conversation naturally toward the business opportunity. "You know, I've been introduced to a business that offers anyone the opportunity to have some fun and make some good money."

"Really?"

"Yeah, would you happen to know anyone who might be looking?"

I had learned to use the third-person approach to relieve people of feeling any pressure. Most folks would respond, "How about me?" Most people I met were not only interested in making extra income, they were fascinated with why I was so excited about this particular business opportunity.

Ironically, in contrast to my own attitudes at the time, I found a group of people in the organization who genuinely cared about me as a person, not simply about what I could do for them in the business. Kim Magdalein and his wife even invited me to their home and treated me as a member of the family. Ironically, they let me in their house when I wouldn't let someone like me in my own place! Even today, I caution my associates to be careful about whom they share the business opportunity with. You want only people whom you love, trust, and believe in. It's the quality of the people, not simply the quantity, that makes for a good network marketing organization. I teach people never to sign up someone for your business

---

BRIGISM

Every day is the first day of the rest of your life.
Each new day is a fresh opportunity.

whom you wouldn't trust in your own home with your own family. But Kim liked me, perhaps because I was so free-spirited, and he took me on as a personal project. He often allowed me to stay overnight at his home. I know now that he was sharing God's love with me, but at the time, I just thought he was being nice.

In August 1979, some of the active members in my up-line invited me to join them for a leadership getaway at Black Beard's Lodge on Ocracoke Island, North Carolina, on the Outer Banks, near Cape Hatteras. The group loved to fish, so they promoted the event as a "fun, food, fellowship, and fishing weekend." I wasn't the least bit interested in fishing, and I was stuck at a low point in my financial life, so I told the up-line I couldn't afford to go and declined the invitation.

This is me in 1978 in my first suit (like the hair?),
looking good with Dex and Birdie Yager,
a couple of Amway big kahunas.

Dick Souther, one of my up-line distributors with whom I had a good relationship, called and encouraged me to attend the conference despite my financial dilemma.

"I'm not going to any leadership meeting," I said. "I haven't got the money and I haven't made the last couple months' payments on my van. They're about to repo it. The business isn't working for me, so I'm backing off." *End of conversation,* I thought. I hung up the phone.

BRIGISM

People can and will find the time and money to
do what they really want to do.

Dick called me right back. "Brig Hart, I care about you, and that's why I'm going to talk to you straight up. I don't give a flip about how broke you are or anything about your van. You're going to get in that vehicle, and you are going to drive that thing to the Outer Banks and be with us this weekend."

Dick was unusually straightforward and hard on me. I didn't understand that God often uses our circumstances and other people to get us right where He can touch us. I now realize that I was in the midst of a spiritual battle. Someone—or some *thing*—didn't want me to be at that gathering. Had Dick not been so emphatic about my participating, I might have missed the greatest divine appointment in my life.

Because I respected Dick so much, I heard myself saying, "Yes sir. I'll be there. Somehow."

I figured if I drove my van to the event, the repo man couldn't find it. I also knew that there was pretty good surfing at Hatteras, so I was able to justify the trip. I talked a friend into going along with me, and he loaned me some money for gas. We also found enough cash for one or two cases of lager refreshment and some "natural herbs." We loaded up and headed north, partying all the way. Isn't it amazing? People can and will find the time and money to do what they really want to do.

The weekend schedule promised some business aspects to it, but most of it was simply intended to build our relationships with one another. I probably wouldn't have gone had it not been for Dick encouraging me and for the possibility of surfing on the Mid-Atlantic coast. Running away from my negative situation for some momentary relief was also in the mix.

Most of the people attending the retreat were married. I was one of the few singles. The married couples impressed me with the way they treated one another. It seemed as though they genuinely loved one another. I watched, listened, and took it all in. Each couple talked about their relationship with each other and how the Lord had changed and blessed their lives. The conviction with which they spoke, and the tears that flowed naturally as they expressed their love for one another, touched me deeply.

Even more powerful to me was that throughout the weekend, almost to a person, each man and woman came up to me and expressed how much they loved *me*. I felt awkward and didn't know how to respond, especially when the men said things like, "I'm glad you're here, Brig. I'm praying for you. I love you, Brig." I had grown up in a family where the men weren't so effusive, not to mention the fact that I'd spent a few years in the Marine Corps. Most marines don't go around gushing about how much they love one another! Still, there was something real about these people, something so powerfully contagious that I wanted to find out what made them tick.

Saturday night, I heard Paul Stanley and Dick Souther tell their stories. At the close of the Saturday night session, someone announced that there would be a worship service in the morning, featuring the testimony of T. Aldred, a successful real estate businessman in the Charlotte, North Carolina, area, as well as a distributor in his network marketing business.

Great, I thought. I can sleep in a little longer.

Sunday morning, I pulled the covers up over my head and tried to sleep, but almost every person in the group came by and knocked on my door. "Come on, Brig. Let's go to the service."

"No, thanks," I'd call through the door. "You go on ahead. I'm not coming. I'll catch up with you a little later." I rolled over and squeezed my eyes shut.

I had no sooner closed my eyes when someone else knocked on the door. "Hey, Brig! Come with us. You'll love hearing T. Aldred."

"Nah, I'm sure he's great, and I'll look forward to hearing him some other time, but I'm just gonna hang out here for a while."

"Oh, please, come with us, Brig." One by one, they kept knocking at my door until I thought it must be a conspiracy of people trying to yank me to a church service.

SUCCESS PRINCIPLE FOR LIFE

A very valuable lesson I have learned is that if you build relationships
with people, people in our industry will build the business.
Friends will do what their friends do.

Finally, I acquiesced, threw on my clothes, and reluctantly stumbled to the gathering. Everyone greeted me enthusiastically. I found a seat and tried to be inconspicuous, though of course, that was impossible.

Despite my reluctance to attend the gathering, I was nonetheless interested in hearing what T. Aldred had to say. I respected T. and knew he was a multimillionaire who had been wildly successful in the real estate business—my dad's line of work—and in his network marketing business. I once had asked him, "T., why are you doing this?"

"So I can help people," T. replied.

His response didn't make sense to me at the time.

That morning at the lodge, T. Aldred didn't preach or tell sad or funny stories; he stood up by the fireplace and simply read a familiar passage from the Bible, 1 Corinthians 13, known as the love chapter be-

True love never fails.

cause of its emphasis on *agape,* unconditional love. "True love believes all things, bears all things, endures all things...but true love never fails."

That's all T. did, but the words pierced my heart and mind. I had never before heard that Scripture. "Does that kind of love really exist?" I asked when he was done.

I could feel tears welling in my eyes, and I fought to maintain my composure.

T. held out the Scripture passage for me to read. "You see it," he said, nodding toward the individuals seated around the room.

I could barely contain myself as it seemed something like emotion, but much stronger, overwhelmed me. I tried to divert what I was feeling by raising an intellectual defense. "Who wrote that?" I asked.

"Would you like to know who wrote that?" T. wisely replied.

"Yeah, I would."

"Would you like me to introduce you to Him?" T. asked.

"Yes, I would."

"Okay, bow your head and close your eyes."

"Why? What is he? A ghost?"

T. smiled and said, "Yeah, kinda." T. led me in a prayer, acknowledging that I was a sinner and asking God to forgive me and inviting Jesus Christ to come into my life. It wasn't a fancy or liturgical prayer, like those I'd heard in church. But it was real.

Suddenly, it seemed as though the weight of the world lifted off my shoulders. I didn't understand it, but I felt clean and free for the first time in years.

Afterward, T. showed me some scriptures in the Bible as he explained further, "Brig, you are born again. You acknowledged you were a sinner, you asked for forgiveness, and you welcomed Christ into your heart. So you are now born again. God has given you a new chance." He kept things real simple.

Everyone in the room surrounded me and hugged me, welcoming me into the family of God. Many of them were crying tears of joy. Most offered words of encouragement and of- **I felt clean and free for** fered to help me learn more about **the first time in years.** Jesus. Before we left the lodge, T. took me aside and offered a final word of encouragement. "Not everyone is going to get excited about what you have done here," he cautioned. "It's not easy to be a Christian, but it's worth it. Don't think that life is always going to be blissful, but here's the good news: you never have to walk alone anymore. We can't always be with you, but God will be with you. Keep your eyes on Jesus."

On the way home, I dumped out my beer and tossed my marijuana out the car window. Nobody told me to do that, but I felt so good, almost like a natural high, and I didn't want to mess it up. So I pitched out the artificial stuff. I didn't go through any rehabilitation programs; I was simply ready—ready to trust the Lord with my life and ready to change. Change is hard to live with, but it's impossible to live without. It's the only constant thing in life.

For some reason I didn't understand at the time, the first thing I wanted to do was to go to my parents and tell them what I had done. So I drove to their home in Jacksonville Beach. "Mom, Dad, I've been born again, and God is giving me a second chance in life," I tried to explain. "I just want you to know that I've been forgiven for all the rotten things I've ever done, and I feel so free and clean. God's forgiven me, and I'm asking you to forgive me also. Please forgive me for being such a lousy son. I want to start over, and I want to show you that I've changed." I babbled and gushed about the change I had experienced so far, and all the while, Mom and Dad just sat there and stared. Mom teared up a bit, perhaps recalling our

BRIGISM

Change is hard to live with, but it's impossible to live without.

early upbringing in church, but Dad appeared unimpressed. He sat puffing on his pipe without saying a word. Finally he spoke.

"You're kidding," Dad said. "So you're in this Amway thing...some sort of cult...and God forgave you for all the things you've done improperly. Is that right?"

"Yeah, that's it!" I figured there was no use explaining that Amway wasn't a cult, especially since Dad had basically nailed the forgiveness part.

"God may have forgiven you, but we ain't," Dad said bluntly.

Amazingly, Dad's reticence to forgive me didn't affect me greatly. Whether the person I offended accepted my apology or even understood my request for forgiveness wasn't the most important issue to me. It was still worth it to express my remorse. I needed to say those words: "I'm sorry. Would you please forgive me?" So with my heart filled with genuine joy and exuberance, I merely brushed off Dad's comment.

"Well, I can understand that," I replied. "I'm just telling you that I'm going to change."

"We'll see," Dad responded.

For the next three months I devoured the Bible. Kim Magdalein had given me a Bible after the weekend at the Outer Banks, but he really didn't tell me where to start reading it for the most benefit. Nowadays, when I introduce someone to Jesus, I usually encourage the new believer to start in the gospel of John, reading and asking the questions, "Who is this person, Jesus Christ, and what can He do in my life?" But Kim just gave me the Bible with no instructions. Fortunately, I found some helpful study notes by Porter Barrington, and those notes helped me better understand the New Testament. I appreciated the gift, and I couldn't wait to dig in and find out what this new life was all about.

Ironically, I started my reading in the book of Ecclesiastes. I was attracted to the story of King Solomon because he was one of the wisest and wealthiest men on the planet and had accomplished marvelous things during his lifetime. He lived in a grand palace where he was catered to by seven hundred wives and three hundred concubines, yet he declared all of the usual quests in life to be meaningless. Vanity, vanity, all is vanity, he lamented. Having a lot of money? Meaningless. Fame and fortune? Power and position? Meaningless. Solomon's words surprised me, so I embarked on a mission to better understand his conclusions.

If a person doesn't read the book to its powerful ending, Ecclesiastes could really discourage you! But I found what I was looking for as I read and reread the Scriptures. Fortunately, the king finally gets to his main point: that nothing on this earth can satisfy a person except for a deep trust in the living God. "Obey God and keep His commands," Solomon summed up a life well lived. All the other stuff comes—or goes—as a by-product of our obedience to God.

I knew a little about Solomon from my time in Sunday school and Vacation Bible School. I was intrigued at how God was so pleased with Solomon in his younger years that He had allowed Solomon to ask for anything in the world. Rather than asking for gold, power, or fame, Solomon asked God for wisdom, especially wisdom to rule God's people correctly. God was so impressed with Solomon's request that He not only gave him wisdom, but He also lavished on the young king wealth far beyond his comprehension. God gave him fame and enormous power as well. I was also fascinated by Solomon because he was a builder and a motivator. He built the ornate Jewish temple in Jerusalem, and under his rule, the nation of Israel prospered immensely.

Unfortunately, Solomon didn't always use God's gifts for God's glory but instead began to bask in his own success. In the book *Why the Mighty Fall,* Jim Collins lists five reasons why great companies slip into decline. The first step down is hubris brought on by success. If that could happen to Solomon, it could happen to you and me too. We need to be constantly on guard and stay dependent on God.

I didn't know all that about Solomon when I first began reading the Bible. I was simply enamored by Solomon's great wisdom, the marvelous gift he had received from God. "Where's that story about Solomon?" I asked somebody. Rather than pointing me to Solomon's life story in 1 Kings and 1 Chronicles, he misdirected me to Ecclesiastes. Nevertheless, I read it faithfully, wondering, *What's this all about?*

My recurring dream from years earlier came back to mind, and I realized that, like Solomon, I could gain all the things the world had to offer, but without a relationship with God, life would be meaningless and unsatisfying.

I was hungry to know more of God. I began attending church services at a small Baptist church, where I was baptized as a new believer. I bought the Bible on tape and studied or listened to the Scriptures constantly. I couldn't let a day go by without getting the Bible into my heart and mind. The book was life to me. In the Old Testament, I discovered another book associated with Solomon, the book of Proverbs, in which many of Solomon's wise insights are recorded. I dug into that part of the Scriptures as well. Every time an invitation was given at our church, an opportunity to publicly proclaim my faith and trust in Jesus Christ, I went forward and was born again—again!

> **Without a relationship with God, life would be meaningless and unsatisfying.**

I didn't know that what was happening was part of the deal, that God was refining me. His Spirit was teaching me, showing me new things, as well as convicting me about some areas that I'd never previously thought about. My heart was sensitive to God, so every time I'd think of something else that I'd said or done that might be wrong, I went down front at the church to repent. There was nothing wrong with that—in fact, there was a lot of good going on in my life as a result of my obedience to God—but I later found out that I could keep short accounts with God by repenting on the spot when I said, did, or thought something contrary to His Word. I didn't necessarily have to run to the front of the church every time the Lord shined His searchlight on my heart.

People in business invited me to attend church services with them, and I visited a number of congregations. I felt most at home at the First Baptist Church in Jacksonville, where Pastor Homer Lindsey clearly taught the Bible in a way that I could understand it and apply it to my life. I became involved in classes and groups in the church and was growing spiritually by leaps and bounds.

Amazingly, about that same time, my business took off. Although I would not claim a direct connection between my newfound faith in Christ and my success in business, when you stop to analyze it, the growth made sense. It wasn't because I had acquired more knowledge or business acumen. No, something had changed within me. My attitude had changed. I was seeing myself through a different set of eyes. No longer was I attempting to talk people into doing business with me for my benefit. Now, I honestly hoped that they could benefit by taking advantage of the business opportunity I offered them. It sounds simple, but believe me, the change was revolutionary! Before committing my life to Christ, I tried to recruit just about everyone I met into my business. Now, I genuinely desired only people for whom the business might be a benefit.

I soon catapulted ahead in my business, achieving the pearl level in 1980. That same year, I earned more than $102,000, working my business part time, in the evenings after my day jobs. Prior to gathering momentum in my network marketing business, I had been working full time at two other jobs and had netted only $18,000 that year. Ironically, that was the highest income I'd ever earned in my life! I realized that my full-time work was not producing near what my leveraged network business was earning, so I made a corporate decision. I quit my full-time work to go part time. It was a new beginning for me.

> **Motive matters!... No longer was I attempting to talk people into doing business with me for my benefit.**

What made the difference? Simply this: the way I saw people and approached them had changed almost overnight. Prior to coming to faith in Christ, I saw people as objects to be used in achieving my goals, stepping-stones to help me get to wherever I wanted to go. Now, I saw them the way God saw them and realized that I was supposed to be serving them, rather than them serving me. It was a major transformation not only in my business but in all of my personal relationships. Now, I was *serving* them rather than selling them: selling them on my dreams, selling them something they may or may not have wanted to help fulfill their dreams. People can smell selfishness a mile away. And I reeked of it! Of course, if you'd have asked me if I was a selfish person, I would have vehemently denied it, but it was obvious to a lot of my potential clients that my emphasis was, "When you sell this much, I get this. When you do even more, I get even more. When you hit that level, I'll hit the higher level." Guess what? My selfish goals did not inspire other people to reach for their stars.

After my spiritual rebirth, I simply shared my business and hoped people could see it. If they did and were willing to jump in, I told them, "I'll help you. I'll help you do meetings. I'll help you present the business plan. I'll help you get where you want to go." What a difference!

I, me, and *mine* were virtually erased from my conversation, but even more importantly, from my motivation. That change was partly due to

Dale Carnegie's books, but a lot of the credit goes to the Word of God. How absolutely satisfying it was to be giving rather than looking to receive. How wonderful it felt to end my day thinking about the good I was trying to do for others. I became addicted—this was a good addiction—to helping others find hope and joy.

Ironically, I got to a point where I could sponsor just about anybody. I now know that he who serves best normally wins. My success was nothing more or less than God's favor on me. I didn't try to coerce or convince; I simply shared what I knew with people who were interested. It wasn't just the business; they wanted to hear my story and to hear how my life had changed. People seemed to like me. I call it the *likability factor.* People will get into business with people they like, and they did. I told others how being around the right sort of people had changed my life physically, financially, emotionally, and most important, spiritually.

> **People can smell selfishness a mile away.... Now, I was *serving* them rather than selling them.**

Most refreshing, I was finally telling the truth! My friends who knew me well saw that something real had happened in my life. Interestingly, some of the changes surprised even me. I remember the first time I had to pay taxes. "Why?" I asked. "This is my money." I had never made more money than could be reported on a 1040 EZ form nowadays. Now, suddenly, I was contributing to the federal government's coffers far more than I'd ever made in my life!

One thing I did not do. I didn't go out and spend excessively. Oh, sure, I bought some trinkets. I bought some nice clothes, some cool jewelry, and even paid cash for my first Cadillac. But I also saved and invested. I had never before had this kind of money, and I sure wasn't going to take it for granted. Besides, I wasn't sure how long all this newfound prosperity would last, so I wanted to make sure that I handled it carefully.

I really got it. I fell in love with the people and decided I was not in the product business, but rather I was in the *people* business. I enjoyed setting people up to succeed. Amazingly, as I did so, I created more and more volume, which earned much more money than many of my mentors. I read again J. Paul Getty's *How to Be Rich,* in which he said he'd rather earn 1 percent of a hundred people's efforts than 100 percent of his own efforts. That was my tact too. Rather than having personally sponsored just one leg of business, I developed many legs! It was rather rare for a young single man to be so successful in the business at that time, so I received a lot of attention as well as invitations to speak all across the country at various business functions. I became one of the most sought after speakers in the business, simply by telling my story and encouraging other people. Maybe after seeing and hearing me speak, people figured, "If he can do this, I can certainly do this." And they were right!

But there was trouble on the horizon. During the early 1980s, the network marketing industry as a whole was going through trials and tribulations, and our business in particular was under fire. Although I was **Trouble on the horizon.** making money, to admit to being in network marketing during those days often evoked the same sort of response you might get by admitting you were a used car salesman. People were automatically suspicious.

About that same time, a lot of negative information dominated press reports about pyramid companies, mischaracterizing many legitimate network marketing businesses as being of that same ilk. I was still making money, but I wasn't having as much fun.

Then one weekend in late summer 1981, I attended a meeting in Orlando, where I met the woman of my dreams. I didn't know it, but my life was about to change again—big-time! Another divine appointment.

CHAPTER **9**

Lita

THE MOMENT I SAW the pretty brunette with the bright eyes and contagious smile, I knew that she was the woman for me. I was ready when I met her. In good businesslike fashion, I had actually written down a list of characteristics that I wanted in a woman: physically, emotionally, financially, and spiritually. I hoped to find a physically attractive woman who was a hard worker, someone who managed money well, somebody who wasn't into drugs or alcohol, someone with personal integrity and values consistent with mine. I established a list of character traits that I felt were important in a potential marriage relationship. Most of all, I wanted a woman who was a genuine Christian, someone who would not only be a great wife but a good mother, with whom I could raise a family. I didn't date a lot, but I occasionally prayed, "God, if you have someone for me, please reveal her to me."

LITA GREW up as the youngest of four siblings in a home almost as dysfunctional as mine. Lita's mom was Jewish and her dad was Catholic, though neither practiced either religion regularly. Instead, their real religion was hard work. The family owned and operated an air-conditioning and heating business. Lita's father, Celestino (Chester), was a first-generation American who had immigrated from Spain, along with his family. Lita's mom, Faye, grew up in Michigan, and that's where she and Chester met and married. Shortly after Lita was born, they moved to the warmer climes of Melbourne, Florida, and set up housekeeping.

Lita's family was not affluent, but because they owned the company and worked night and day, they lived a comfortable middle-class lifestyle. Her mom worked in civil service jobs during the downturns in the heating and air-conditioning business, which occurred all too often.

Lita's eldest sister was nine years older and had married a young man whose father owned a jewelry store. As a teenager, Lita worked as a sales clerk at the family-owned jewelry store rather than a typical first-time job for most sixteen- and seventeen-year-olds. The environment was better and healthier at the jewelry store, and she learned a great deal about running a business.

Because her parents didn't have a lot of extra money for luxuries, Lita worked from the time she was old enough to legally hold a job. She bought her own clothes, car, and even her own dirt bike. Her dad drank a lot, and the alcohol took a heavy toll on the family. Raising four teenagers during the 1970s hippie generation would have been challenging anyhow, but with marijuana and other drugs readily available on the streets of America, Lita's family was not immune from the effects. Their home life was not a comfortable, cozy en-

Lita often joked, "I'm never going to own my own business!"

vironment due to the tension revolving around a sister who was three years older than Lita and frequently getting into trouble. Lita's dad would fly into a furious rage over the kids' malfeasance, causing the entire family to walk on eggshells. Her mom tried to manage the stress, and her dad dealt with the strained relationships by taking another drink. For this generation, even though it was a simpler time, many did not have role models for healthy marriages, but God can transform hearts and lives when we allow Him.

Work at the jewelry store soon became a refuge for Lita. She gravitated to work even when she didn't need to be there, just to avoid going home. She was busy with school too, participating as a cheerleader in junior high, and later noted as the friendliest in her freshman class. As graduation day approached, Lita began grappling with what she wanted to do next. College seemed a likely choice, and Lita looked forward to completing her education and then working for someone else for a while. Because she grew up with her parents owning their own business, Lita often joked, "I'm never going to own my own business!" (Don't let your past dictate your future!)

After high school, she attended a business school, but then she transferred to a community college. She was still working at the jewelry store when a co-worker invited her to a get-together where Lita was in-

In September 1981, I proposed to Lo-Lita, the girl of my dreams.

troduced to network marketing. She attended some home meetings and was impressed with the positive attitudes of the people and what seemed to be a healthy, upbeat environment. She got into the business and even recruited a few friends, and slowly she began to build. She attended a few more home meetings and some regional meetings, where she heard about a fun-loving, single surfer guy who was becoming successful in the business.

Within a few months after that, Lita attended a meeting in Orlando, which I was attending as well. I was not the main speaker, but I presented a testimonial about the benefits of the business, attempting to fire up the troops. After the event that evening, a lot of people stayed around, mingling and talking. When I saw the attractive brunette still in the room, I made my way toward her. I introduced myself, asked her about her involvement with the business, and we exchanged business cards. I knew immediately that she was something special.

When she said she was from Melbourne, I replied spontaneously, "Oh, I have some people in Cocoa Beach. I get down that way pretty often. In fact, I'm coming through that area in a few weeks."

If I didn't have a meeting in Cocoa Beach planned, I did now! (I actually did have a meeting in that area on my schedule.)

A few weeks later, I was in Cocoa Beach for a company function, so I called Lita and asked her if she would like to go along with me. We went to dinner before the meeting, and I enjoyed talking with her so much, I almost forgot about the business meeting.

Lita was everything I was looking for, but she was not a Christian. I had read the Bible by now and knew how important it was to be "equally yoked," on the same page spiritually with your partner. I recognized that it wasn't enough simply to have a physical attraction or even a lot of mutual interests. The best relationships are those in which a man and a woman are in agreement spiritually, with similar worldviews, attitudes, and ambitions. The Bible cautions against a relationship in which, like an ox and a wild bull, one pulls in one direction and the other tugs in the opposite direction. No wonder life together for so many married couples is so tough. They are unequally yoked. They need to get in agreement with each other, and that includes the physical, emotional, financial, and spiritual aspects of their relationship. I was committed to having that kind of relationship with a woman or none at all. I wanted the whole package, and that included the spiritual dimension.

Lita and I dated frequently over the next few months. I say dated lightly, though, because most of our dates involved events having to do with our businesses. I pursued her, but I knew we couldn't allow our relationship to get too serious since Lita was not a believer. She was attracted to the positive values and principles of Christianity,

> **The best relationships are those in which a man and a woman are in agreement spiritually.**

and had even attended church with her friends, but she had never truly put her faith and trust in Jesus Christ and entered into a genuine relationship with Him. Obviously, she knew about religion, with her mom being Jewish and her dad being Catholic. But Lita quickly realized that there was an enormous difference between having a religion and having a relationship with Jesus Christ. She had never really read the Bible, but she was looking for a new outlook on life.

She came to a function in Miami, and on Sunday morning, at the close of the weekend meetings, when an invitation to meet Christ was extended, Lita responded and walked forward. I joined her at the front of the room, and we prayed together as she invited Jesus Christ to take over her life.

"I felt as if a huge weight had lifted off me," Lita later described her experience. She was so excited about her new relationship with Christ that she immediately wanted to tell her mom. Although not an orthodox Jew,

Lita's mom was not overjoyed about Lita's newfound Christian faith. Her dad was more conciliatory. He recognized the lightness in Lita's spirit, and

"How are you going to take care of my baby girl?"

he was happy that she was attending church more often. "It can only help," he said.

The fact that Lita and I were now in agreement spiritually sealed the deal for me. Within a few days, I asked her to marry me.

She responded positively but with one caveat. "You'll have to ask my father for my hand in marriage," she said with a mischievous smile, "and he may have some tough questions for you."

I visited Lita's family in Melbourne. Her mom was real sweet to me, but I was nervous about her dad. We sat around the kitchen table, and when I asked Lita's father for her hand in marriage, he did nothing to hide his skepticism about my involvement in network marketing. "How are you going to take care of my baby girl?" he asked bluntly.

Lita blushed in embarrassment.

"Well, I don't have a job," I said. "I'm generating income in a business that is going to keep going whether I do anything or not."

Lita's dad didn't understand, and he didn't want to understand.

"I've worked at this a couple of years," I continued, "and it has taken care of me. I don't know that I'll ever have to do anything else to take care of your daughter. We can do whatever we want to do."

"That sounds good," Chester softened.

"I love your daughter, and I want to marry her."

Chester's eyes moistened, and he gave us his blessing.

I later joked with Lita that I had really been looking for a blonde.

"That's okay," Lita fired right back. "Most blondes were brunettes at one time or another."

We decided to be married at the First Baptist Church in Jacksonville rather than in Melbourne, since Lita didn't really have any spiritual ties to a church in her hometown. On November 21, 1981, Rod Walker, another mentor of mine and a distributor in our business, conducted the wedding ceremony. Lita and I were husband and wife, and we felt like two ecstatic kids going out to conquer the world together. We were married within four and a half months of our meeting.

After the ceremony, Lita and I packed into my '78 fire-mist green Cadillac Eldorado, about the size of a small boat. We headed north to Banner

Elk, in the Blue Ridge Mountains near Boone, North Carolina. In our excitement, we hadn't bothered to check the weather forecast—we had other, more important things on our minds—so the farther north we drove and the more we traveled over the mountainous terrain, the more snow and ice we encountered. We had to stop and have chains put on the tires to climb the mountain road and make it up to our cabin. We didn't even attempt to come back down the slippery road for about a week.

After our honeymoon, we headed back to Jacksonville Beach, where we established our home in the first of many houses we would eventually own.

Lita and I worked in the business together and were simply enjoying life. We conducted meetings in people's homes as well as events in hotel conference rooms and ballrooms. Lita was impressed at my ability to speak in public and to talk to almost anyone about our business. "I think you came out of the womb talking!" she teased. "You could talk to a rock!"

We bought a new home and were making good money, but we decided to pull back from our networking business. Along with our good friends Lu and Don Crews, who were twenty years our senior and were like surrogate parents to Lita and me, we got involved in some other business ventures. We invested in some real estate deals and also bought into drilling shallow oil wells in Kentucky—a huge mistake! We invested our personal time and money into a few other small businesses, selling storage sheds, doing window tinting, and even developed a sports photography franchise throughout Florida and Georgia. At the same time, my dad and I were speculating and building single-family homes on lots we were buying at the beach. I was by no means bored at this point in my life.

For a while, Lita and I basically let the network marketing business run on autopilot. We didn't sponsor any new distributors for nearly three years. One of the beauties of network marketing is the passive income that continues to flow even if you are not working at it. Unlike a doctor or a dentist or an auto mechanic who stops practicing and suddenly has no further income, in network marketing, the passive income—or residual income as it is known in our business—keeps flowing as long as others in your business keep producing volume for the company.

The years we had invested in putting people in business for themselves were now paying us for that time and those efforts. We had been fortunate enough to find some good folks who took ownership of their own destinies and saw the network marketing business as a means to their financial security. It was their business, and we received the residual benefits from them, because we were the ones who had helped to establish them. That was huge, and we didn't exactly learn to appreciate that until a bit later in life. But for now, life was good!

WE WERE growing spiritually during this time. I was hungry for more, because it is my nature to keep searching for the next level. That carried over to my spiritual life as well. I studied the Bible daily and started wondering, *How could those early disciples be so afraid after the Crucifixion of Jesus, but then fifty days later, when they came out of the Upper Room in Jerusalem, they were boldly talking about Jesus and were willing to face death rather than deny their Lord?* I concluded I wanted that same difference in my life.

Something within me longed for more. I was on a quest, and I wanted more from God. I bought a study Bible and read it day and night. I read Oswald Chambers's classic devotional material, *My Utmost for His Highest,* and my thirst for more in my Christian life intensified. I discovered that many great men and women of God from diverse backgrounds had experienced a deeper relationship with God some time after their initial salvation experience. That let me know that what I was seeking was not confined to one particular group or time, but it was available for all who believed.

I had read about people being anointed with oil in the New Testament, so I grabbed a bottle of Wesson cooking oil and took it with me to meet with an elder from my church. I pointed out passages in the Bible to him and said, "I'm not dreaming this up. If you will pray for me and anoint me with this oil, I think I can have an encounter with God."

"Come with me," he said.

I followed him outside, where he had a small motor home parked. We climbed into the motor home, and without telling me where we were going, he drove us out of town and out some country road.

"Wait, stop," I said. "Where are we going?"

"Oh, we're just going to go out of town a little ways," he replied kindly. We drove until there were no more vehicles on the road. Finally, he pulled over to the side of the road, shut down the motor home, and said, "Okay, now we can talk."

I felt like we were two spies sneaking around to discuss some covert operation, but I didn't care. I believed there was more to the Christian life than I had experienced, and I wanted him to pray with me about receiving more. I thrust the bottle of Wesson oil in his direction.

He applied a few drops of the oil to my forehead and he prayed for me. There were no external signs at the time, but a deep and lasting spiritual transaction took place that day in his motor home. My life has never been the same since! I was free. I no longer needed to respond to every invitation to meet Christ. I had been healed, delivered, and set free from any yokes and burdens I had been carrying. Looking back, I now realize the issue was not Brig's getting more of God; it was God getting all of Brig.

I went home and told Lita, "I've experienced God on a whole new level. You can too!" We simply believed the Bible with a childlike faith, expecting God to do for us what He had done for others. Sure enough, a few days later, Lita also had a similar and wonderful encounter with God. In and through this encounter, God was setting us up for a relationship that would take us to a whole new level.

BRIGISM

You have to exit a place before you can enter a new place.

✦ ✦ ✦

IN MY newfound desire to surround myself with positive influences, I had been listening to a Christian radio station during the day, when I heard Pastor Paul Zink expounding on practical applications of the Word. I was fascinated by the way Pastor Zink clarified the meaning of the Scriptures. He was more of a teacher than a typical preacher. So I had Lita listen to him, and she also was impressed. One day, at the close of the program, the announcer said that Pastor Zink would be speaking at the Ramada Inn in Jacksonville Beach.

"The Ramada Inn is literally two blocks from our house," I said to Lita. "We have to go."

That Sunday we attended Pastor Zink's church service. There were only about a dozen people gathered in a small conference room at the hotel, but we met Paul Zink and were tremendously encouraged by his teaching. Afterward, he said to us, "You're welcome here. We're a nondenominational fellowship. Here's our mission statement, and here's our doctrinal statement. We're looking to make a huge difference in this town."

We attended church services at the hotel, and soon the small group began to grow in numbers. We moved from one place to another over the next three years as the congregation grew from twelve people to five hundred. We purchased a former Jewish synagogue and conducted services there, until we outgrew that facility too. Eventually, we purchased some property and built a whole new facility, including a sanctuary that seats more than two thousand people, as well as a preschool and school that now has over thirteen hundred students. It's amazing what can happen when people have a vision and the willingness to go after it. Our community and our city have been so blessed by this work. We remain in awe of what God can do through obedient people.

Paul Zink introduced me to many of the people who would become my spiritual mentors and encouragers: Oral Roberts, Harry and Cheryl Salem, Kenneth Copeland, Mylon LeFevre, John Mason, Edwin Louis Cole, Eastman Curtis, and so many others. Paul himself was a tremendous gift to me, and I valued his wisdom and advice, and even more important, his friendship.

✦ ✦ ✦

TOWARD THE end of 1984, Lita and I began grappling with what we wanted to do business-wise. I was frustrated, and my lack of direction spilled onto

My pastor and friend Paul Zink (left) shares the marketplace ministry with me.

everyone around me. At one point, Lita became so irritated with my moodiness, she picked up an ice chest and hurled it across the room at me. "Quit your whining," she chided me.

We talked with Paul to help us sort through our various options. We explained to him that we wanted to pour our lives into a business in which we could have a spiritual impact. We looked carefully at the businesses Lita and I had started since we'd backed off from our network marketing business a few years earlier. None of them seemed to hold the opportunity for a profound spiritual impact. "What do you think we should do, Paul?"

Paul stroked his beard thoughtfully and said, "Well, all of these other businesses are making money for you, but it seems to me that the one that holds the best potential for you to have the spiritual impact, or to have eternal value, is the network marketing business." Paul took his marking pen and crossed out each business until the only one left was the networking business. "Networking is more people oriented, and you are a people person, Brig." The pastor drew a large elliptical line around the name of our network marketing company. "If you want to invest in eternal rewards, that is the one I'd spend my time on. The eternal fruit you are looking for—people whom you influence and inspire for Christ's sake here on earth—seems to be in the networking business."

That was not the message Lita and I had expected to hear. We had grown disillusioned with the industry and the way it was usually done, with its focus on using people and loving money, rather than loving people and using money to help others. But we considered Paul's advice carefully and pondered the implications of his words in our hearts for nearly a year.

CHAPTER **10**

All In

LITA AND I HAD been married five years when God blessed us with our first baby, a gorgeous little girl we named Brittany Nicole. The day Brittany was born, as I held that beautiful, precious little baby and looked down into the face of that miracle—every new baby is a miracle to me—I made a decision. I looked at Lita and said, "Okay, today I'm starting. I'm going Diamond in our network marketing business." Something about the incredible responsibility of raising another human being stirred me to do more than I ever had before. Brittany's birth was my wakeup call. I wanted to get on with the life I knew I was destined to live. I hadn't sponsored anyone in more than three years, but on that day I went out and sponsored two people in the business. I was a motivated dad!

I had been reflecting quite a bit and considering Pastor Paul's counsel, and I had decided that he was right. I knew I needed to act on his advice, but I was waiting for something in my life to kick me out of neutral. The birth of our first child showed me the trust God had in me.

Prior to that, Lita and I had been dormant in our business for several years, from 1983 to 1986, and all the while, I had been stewing on how we could do the business differently. I coined a new term, relational marketing, which meant our focus would be on relationships with people, not simply regarding them as cogs in the network machine. We refused to foster the idol worship that many network marketing businesses enjoyed foisting upon their people. Sure, any successful business loves to extol the virtues of its top performers, but some of the attitudes and actions that we had witnessed were far more than setting a good example for distributors. The only guideline seemed to be the more ostentatious, the better. Good leadership filters down from the top—and so does poor leadership. Consequently, the admiration of successful people in the business hinged on a warped adoration, and this was rarely discouraged by the leadership.

I was young when I became involved in the networking industry, so I emulated much of what I saw, whether it was the healthiest environment or not. In the ideas of what it meant to be successful there was a tendency to be ostentatious and to flaunt material success. I enjoyed the accoutrements that accompanied success, and I still do, but I've learned that material possessions are not always a sign of true wealth. Nowadays a person can acquire many of the material things associated with success and not be able to sleep at night because he or she is in debt up to their eyeballs. To me, that is not freedom. That is bondage.

Worse yet, from a business standpoint, some of the old ideas and methods used by those leaders to build a team and reach new people weren't bringing results. The old guard in our business was not adjusting well to change, and they didn't want to adapt. It seemed silly to me to simply perpetuate the past when the times and culture had changed. If something wasn't working, why do more of it? When I asked why we continued to do things that weren't working, I received little or no response. The attitude of the people above me was, How dare you ask why? This is how we have always done it.

SUCCESS PRINCIPLE FOR LIFE

When considering counsel for your life, be careful who you ask for advice. Don't reject counsel simply because you initially disagree with it. Consider that counsel of this nature may mean you are getting closer to the answer you need. Don't be afraid to seek another spiritually mature opinion. Scripture teaches that there is safety and wisdom in a multitude of counselors.

Moreover, unlike some networking businesses, Lita and I were committed to being absolutely honest with people rather than merely pumping them up with lofty expectations that had little chance of being fulfilled. We told people, "Yes, you can make money at this business. Yes, it allows you to choose your own hours and how much you want to work. But it does require work! Lots of it. It's called work for a reason." I'd add, "Success doesn't happen by accident." We taught people to live life on purpose. Dream it, believe it, and you can achieve it, but don't forget the work part of it. The wisdom of the world reminds us that there are no free lunches in life. Or as one ancient Chinese saying expressed it: "The man who stands on the side of mountain with his mouth open waits a long time for a roast duck to fly in."

I was convinced there was a better way to help people build their businesses. So I developed a systematic plan that I could teach people, with some simple steps they could repeat, steps that would almost inevitably lead them to success. Ideally, the patterns and principles I came up with would work when applied on a regular basis, regardless of what product or services they were marketing. I like to break things down to their simplest common denominators, so I summed up my approach to the business in three words: use, merchandise, teach.

- ✦ USE the product yourself.
- ✦ MERCHANDISE a small amount.
- ✦ TEACH others to do the same.

With everyone doing a little bit of business, the benefits add up to a lot over time through the duplication of efforts.

I wrote constantly during this downtime in our business. I noticed in the Bible that sometimes God took His men out to the wilderness so He could teach them some things that were going to help multitudes of people. Although I can't claim any divine inspiration for my writings out there in the desert period of my life, I believe God got my attention in a fresh way. During that time, I produced the essence of a simple, step-by-step action plan I believed would help people to get oriented and started properly in their own businesses. Today, that document has evolved into one of my most popular pieces, the *Maximum Action Plan,* commonly known to our distributors as the MAP book. I have since written numerous support tools that can assist anyone from the newest network marketers to the most

The MAP book and calendar are key to my ten-step pattern to success in networking.

seasoned to become effective and productive in their business efforts.

I wanted a pure network, a group of people who had a united plan that could produce harmony and synergy by using common steps to build the business and then to maintain and replicate the business model. I kept my plan as simple as possible, including activities that we could actually measure to see if a person was making progress once they engaged in building the business. I came up with a ten-step pattern describing the activities that would help people to produce positive results. These ten steps are expanded in the *Maximum Action Plan* (see the list of resources at the back of this book). Here's the incredibly simple, yet profound, ten-step pattern that has helped hundreds of people to become millionaires and will continue to do so for years to come. I still use this pattern to this day.

1. *You must determine and define your **dream**.* Dream a big dream and describe it in detail. Find something that you want so badly that you can't wait to get up each day to make it happen. Dreams are big and small, tangible and intangible. Dreams are the fuel for your soul, your *why* that drives you. It all begins and ends here. Without a vision or a dream, we are not going to live; we will only survive. Dare to dream!

2. *Set some **goals**, so you know where you are going, when you are going to get there, and what you must do to accomplish each goal.* A goal is basically a dream with a deadline. It's a promise to yourself about what you plan to accomplish and when you plan to accomplish it. Trying to succeed in business without a specific goal is like trying to play basketball without a hoop. Without a goal, you're

Without a goal, you're a wandering generality, dribbling your life away.

a wandering generality, dribbling your life away. Goals help you to measure your progress, or lack of it, so you can quantify your actions. What you can't measure, you can't manage.

What's the difference between a dream and a goal? A dream is the reward you get for accomplishing that goal. For many in my networking business, a goal is a particular level in the business that they want to accomplish. That level carries a certain income. So the level they achieve allows them to purchase a certain item or service they desire, which oftentimes helps to fulfill their dreams.

Many people have lofty dreams, and that's good. Too often, though, those dreams remain fuzzy and nebulous in their minds, more like images of a fanciful fairy tale or, worse yet, a picture of never-never land. They neglect to make specific plans about how they will achieve their goals. Consequently, those goals remain in the dream or fantasy category and never get fulfilled. If you want to see your dreams come true, you must do three things: (1) determine what you want, (2) determine the price of what you want, and (3) pay the price. Each day, everything we say and do is moving us either in the direction of the goal we plan to achieve or away from it.

A goal is a dream with a deadline.

3. *Make some **commitments** in time, effort, and substance.* You're going to have to invest yourself in something before you can expect a return. Why not choose something that can bring a return far beyond your own efforts? Investing your time, energy, and hard-earned substance into something that can gain a life of its own just makes good sense. Remember, if you sow sparingly, you will reap sparingly, but if you sow abundantly, you will reap abundantly. Give of yourself—your time, energy, and wisdom—to others, and then enjoy seeing a multiplied return on your investment.

4. *Make a list of **prospects**.* Regardless of what industry or business you are in, without people participating in your service or product, you have nothing. So, in essence, we are all in the people business, attracting people to what our interests are. Jesus chose twelve men, discipled them for three and a half years, and turned the world upside down. We want to attract

---

SUCCESS PRINCIPLE FOR LIFE

Sometimes people become so ingrained in the way they've always done things that they fail to adapt to changes around them or to think creatively to meet new challenges. The often-quoted definition of insanity is doing the same thing over and over and expecting a different result. If what you're doing isn't working, stop and ask yourself if it's time to consider a radical change!

people whom we can partner with to take our vision from idea or concept to fruition. Build a list of everyone you know everywhere. Don't prejudge anyone, but prequalify everyone. There is no lack of people on the planet who want more than what they have. You just have to find them. Do you plan on meeting anyone new between now and the rest of your life? Great! Keep a prospect list of everyone you meet anywhere. Divine appointments are in your future when you purpose to make something special out of your life.

5. *Contact and* **invite** *the folks on your list to see and hear what you are excited about.* Names on a list are nice, but lists are useless if you don't actually do anything with them. Once you contact people, you have to qualify them to determine their level of interest. In a day of voice mail, video-conferencing, e-mail, and texting, we have almost disconnected ourselves from personal contact and interaction. Use all mediums of communication, but keep in mind, there is something magical that happens when two people interact face to face, or at least, voice to voice. I've heard it said that the eyes are the window to the soul. You can't see into someone's heart without being there. Hearing you and seeing your demeanor is key to having folks buy into your vision. On this one, Dale Carnegie's *How to Win Friends and Influence People* is still a must-read to become proficient at contacting and inviting folks to hear what you are excited about. Anything you keep practicing on you can improve on, so keep on swinging. You never know if people are looking for anything more unless you do this one thing: ask them! You will be amazed at who is receptive and who is not. Often the folks who respond positively are the ones you least suspect. We are all lookers looking for other lookers.

6. *Have a meeting or* **STP** *where you can present the product and the opportunity.* The best way to do that is one-on-one, but a home meeting where a number of people gather in one place is often preferable so you

---

SUCCESS PRINCIPLE FOR LIFE

Change is the only constant. Nothing ever stays the same.
Change is hard to live with, but impossible to live without. I wanted
to win so badly, I was willing to change. Some people are so
afraid to change, they are willing to lose.

can be more effective and efficient with your time. I call this STP, or show the plan.

In this industry, recruitment is key to growth. There is a direct correlation between exposing new people to the product and the plan and making money. So the more you STP, the more people will come into the business with you. It's not how you show the plan, it's that you show them the plan. Good or bad presentations have nothing to do with the success you will see. If a prospect is looking, it doesn't matter how good or bad you present it. They are looking for something, and they will get involved. On the other hand, if they are not looking, no matter how good you show it, they are not going to get involved. It's about timing, so STP: stop the procrastination! see the people! share the product! show the plan! Then you can stuff their pockets!

7. *Follow up and follow through.* You basically have done 95 percent of the work that needed to be done after STP-ing your prospects. But the fortune is in the follow-up. Why? Because if you don't follow up with them, they will naturally do what most people do after a presentation: nothing. Life gets in their way, and they are back to the rut and routines of life, too busy to make a decision. The follow-up starts with the meeting. You book a meeting to have another meeting. Most folks will see the opportunity two or three times before committing to engaging. Most folks retain 15 to 30 percent from the first presentation, 30 to 60 percent from the second, and by the third presentation, they are over the hump. This is where reliable information allows them to make a good decision. You *lead* people into a decision; you don't force it. So set the appointment with them to review the plan and help move them into a positive decision. We are not professional visitors. We are there to fish. So don't just cut bait and run!

8. *Get started.* Most prospects, I discovered, did not ask me to get started in business. The ones who most often decided to get into the business were the ones to whom I'd casually said, "What do you like best about the opportunity?" Once I basically see the whites of their eyes, we move into the enrollment and sponsoring process. I get them to sign on the dotted line. Get them a position. Sign them up. Get their initial order and autoship their product, and then get them plugged into the system. It's a basic orientation of what they do next, positioning them to succeed. Here is where the wisdom of those who have gone before you comes in. They only know what you teach them. At no other

time is this statement more true, so you must be very aware of what you say at this point. Don't overdo this. As you teach, tell and show them how to get started. They will forever remember this process and how you walked them through it.

Teach them to focus on what is most important. Yes, you want your new distributors to understand their starter's kit, cases of product, and autoship. But getting them to set a goal, make commitments, and build a list of folks are where they need to be putting their thoughts and energy if you want to help them move forward in the business. I've found that booking a couple of home tastings or one-on-one's to be able to teach them by showing them is important too. Helping them to host their first few gatherings also is a key to a fast start in their business. There's nothing like helping your new distributor to sponsor a few folks within the first couple of days in the business. Nothing encourages success like success.

> **Experience is the best teacher, as long as it is someone else's experience. Then it is *wisdom*.**

9. *Counsel* up-line. In other words, look for advice from those who have done successfully what you want to do, and then be humble enough to accept their insights. In this industry, what separates us from traditional businesses is that you have built-in consultants who have actually gone before you and have already done what you desire to do. You don't have to search them out and hire them to help direct your activities. You want to have the success they already have. So you get the benefit of their prior experience that got them there in the first place. With my concept of relational marketing, I wanted my network to consist of people who were willing to help each other be successful. I'd always heard the saying, "Experience is the best teacher." But a lot of experience's lessons can be costly and time consuming. I tweaked that adage a little to say, "Experience is the best teacher, as long as it is someone else's experience. Then it is *wisdom*." You don't have to make every mistake yourselves. Nor do we need to learn how to do everything right all by ourselves. My dad always said, "If you are going to walk through a mine field, follow someone—at a distance!" Counseling up-line is tapping into the wisdom of those who have a vested interest in your becoming successful. When you succeed, they do too. That's a given in my industry. We are all for one and one for all. But we also don't give unsolicited information; you have to desire it. So when in

doubt, ask your active, working, plugged-in up-line leadership and tap into their wisdom.

10. **Duplicate** *the ten-step pattern.* Help someone else to succeed. Replicate these steps and your own activities through the people you help to get started. Soon they will be helping others in the same way you helped them. Ultimately your success will be determined by your ability to duplicate this proven ten-step pattern through those you sponsor in your organization. The good and bad news of our industry and this business is that people will replicate what you do—good or bad. So if you will follow and teach the ten steps that have taken countless numbers of folks to successful levels, it can be done by you. Don't vary and don't add to or take away from them. McDonald's is successful in business, not because they make the best hamburgers on earth, but

Help someone else to succeed.

because they have adopted and teach a system and pattern for doing business that works. You can't refute it. If you want the results we have seen, then just do what we have done. Paint by the numbers and stay on the tracks. Success will be in your future.

I'VE HONED these simple steps and taught them to others who wanted to partner with me. The results were amazing! Our business took off exponentially. In 1987, Lita and I qualified as Diamonds a mere thirteen months after I had made the commitment to get all in, to do whatever it took to succeed. To this day, I continue to live by those principles, and I refuse to compromise them. Of course, we've had to make some adjustments as we've learned how to handle success—balance has been the key to enjoying the success we've earned—but the ten-step pattern remains the same.

I took Paul's Zink's words to heart and plunged back into network marketing in a big way. Also in 1987, I established U-Can-II, a business centered around my system, my way of doing network marketing within the broader business. Not everyone saw the benefits of doing business according to my system, but many who did prospered. For the next twelve years, we made more money than I ever dreamed possible, and everywhere we took our business, we helped people incorporate biblical principles into each area of their lives.

I designed our weekend meetings not simply as motivational seminars for people in our business but also as times of spiritual uplifting, offering hope and encouragement. People came by the thousands, and before long, hotel ballrooms were too small for the crowds we were attracting. We moved to larger venues and eventually to convention centers and then to major sports arenas and stadiums. In every city, people were inspired by the business opportunity, and thousands entered into an eternal relationship with God.

With the arrival of Daniel Wisdom Hart, our second child, Lita stayed home more, doing the business paperwork and taking care of the baby, but I was running constantly. To succeed in any business nowadays takes a lot of work, and that is true of network marketing businesses as well. It's not easy to grow a networking business built on relationships. Sure, anybody can do it, but you have to work diligently, especially if you want the business to provide your primary income or you have lofty financial goals, big dreams, or some other big *why*. Anything worth doing usually requires a lot of effort. You can't sit around and wait for things to just magically happen; you have to go out and make it happen. I like to say, "Off your rump and on your feet, out of the shade and into the heat!" If I have learned anything about achieving success, it is this: if it is to be, it is up to thee. If you're looking for a hand up, the best place to look for it is at the end of your own arm.

Lita's goals were similar to mine, and she followed my lead for the most part. We wanted to build the business for our children, and we understood that as we prospered, we'd become more financially successful, have more stability, and earn not merely a place of status but a place of significance. Of course, along with our success came the accoutrements. Lita never wanted big houses, boats, or fast, fancy cars. She wanted a comfortable living with financial security and a big savings account. I must admit that I enjoy the toys far more than Lita does. She prefers the cash in hand or in savings, and there is great wisdom in that. But the fun factor is part of why I do what I do. You have to learn to enjoy the journey and to smell the roses along the way. There are no promises of tomorrow.

> **The fun factor is a huge part of what attracts others.**

Most of all, we felt that God was using our lives to have a positive impact on a lot of people. I should have known that where God is blessing, the Enemy works overtime to kill, steal, and destroy. But I would never have imagined the source of the attacks.

Little did I know that by developing and promoting my own version of a support system and distributing my support tools to my own organization, I'd be creating an uproar in my up-line. Basically, they claimed the rights to my intellectual property and wanted the profits from it. To them, it was all about the money, as I came to learn.

I also began having my own U-Can-II events. I arranged the total packages for each person or the couples in my organization. I rented the hotel ballrooms or larger facilities. I arranged for all the advertising, paid for the sound systems, and underwrote the total production of the events. Lita and I also contracted for all of the entertainment and speakers. We took on all the risks and expenses related to putting on these huge events—meals, hotel rooms, and meetings.

At each of these major functions, distributors were encouraged by great speakers and teachers, not just those in the business, but some of the best motivators in the world. I often arranged to buy the speakers' books or recordings of their talks and offered them to our distributors as helpful resources.

As my business prospered and grew in numbers, we attracted the full attention of my up-line. (Evidently I wasn't supposed to succeed to that level the way I had). They reasoned that because I was in their organization, they deserved a major stake of the profits Lita and I were generating through U-Can-II. They were not shy about calling and demanding that I pay them a significant portion of the proceeds. They had no dog in the hunt, but they wanted the bounty. Their contention was a deterrent to our developing any kind of long-term relationship with them, and later it would be the demise of the wonderful organization we had built. Nevertheless, they were relentless in their pursuit of claiming ownership of something for which they had no skin in the game. Back then, tool systems were not regulated. It was a good ol' boy system, one that was destined to be exposed for what it actually was.

BRIGISM

If it is to be, it is up to thee.

Lita and I and U-Can-II were not part of the good ol' boy system, and we asked nothing of them as we pursued building our business. Looking back, I realize folks don't go after other folks that don't have anything. We were the producers who attracted a bunch of nonproducers that simply wanted what we had. It was apparent to Lita and me that they didn't care about the people; it was all about them and the money. Basically, they wanted me to pay them simply because of who they were.

At first, I acquiesced, and said, "Well, if those are the rules that all others follow, I will do the same. I don't want the money to be the point of contention between us. I'll follow protocol, but I'm going to continue to do things as I feel the Lord is leading me to do." I paid them a percentage for everything that I had created and for what I sold to the distributors whom I had sponsored in my own organization. It was crazy! The feeling of being ripped off planted seeds of discontent that would eventually sprout a vicious harvest. But as long as the up-line left us alone, we could do business in the manner in which we had proven to be proper and upright. We paid them a percentage of all our business activities simply to maintain the peace, but rather than being satisfied, they kept demanding more and more.

Mom and Dad were convinced that my former mentors were taking advantage of me. "They're just a bunch of shysters," Dad said. "I don't trust them."

"No, they're good guys, Dad," I tried to defend them. "They just like their money."

"Yes, but you're the one doing all the work."

"Well, yeah, you're right, but that's the way the business works."

I had finally earned a measure of respect from my dad because of my success in business, so it hurt me deeply to think that his assessment might be correct. Mom had so completely changed her attitude that she had come to work for me as my secretary in the years before Lita and I were married. But the infighting with the members of my up-line took its toll on all of us.

Besides incessantly pressuring me for undeserved commissions, certain people in the business attempted to stir up dissension in our group by telling distributors, "Brig is making all that extra money with his system and he isn't sharing it with you." They weren't trying to support our distributors. It was a blatant attempt to discredit Lita and me so they could sway people away from us and into their organizations through their rumors and innuendo.

Lita began to sense before I did that our time with this business and these leaders was coming to a close. Two things we had developed to enhance our distributors' lives ironically turned out to be major factors in our difficulties with our up-line leadership. First was the development of our own system, and second was the increased attention received by the nonprofit spiritual counseling organization: New Life Network.

CHAPTER **11**

Helping People
Connect Spiritually

To me, at all of the weekend conferences Lita and I conducted, the most important meeting was the voluntary nondenominational worship service held on Sunday mornings. At our events, we took seriously our responsibility as leaders to all these precious folks with whom God had given us favor. We rarely referred to them as our down-line; to us, they were our partners and associates. As believers, we had a duty to expose these folks to honest, upright teaching and training based on the truth. We wanted every word spoken from the platforms and every action taken during these conventions to be aligned with the Word of God. Principles, precepts, statutes, and laws must be rooted and aligned with the Scriptures. We felt we were called to feed the sheep and tend them, and that involved providing exceptional examples of folks implementing these principles and values in their lives. Every speaker we invited loved the Lord and was encouraged to speak from that perspective. The Bible says, "So shall My word be that goes forth from My mouth; it shall not return to Me void, but it shall accomplish what I please, and it shall prosper."[2] So every person who graced the U-Can-II stage was prayed up and prepared to deliver their subject matter in a manner that would be pleasing to the Lord.

We seeded the group Friday through Saturday evening, creating an environment for each person to make life-changing decisions on Sunday morning. During each of those services, we presented the gospel as it was shown in and through the folks who shared from the platform throughout the weekend event. Then on Sunday morning, we simply threw the net, giving folks an opportunity to come to know Christ personally.

They came by the multitudes for healing, deliverance, and salvation. Some folks came to recommit their lives to the Lord, but most of those who came were new believers, converts. We relied heavily on the Lord, not on ourselves. The glory goes to God.

We discovered that many folks had never before heard, seen, or experienced the simple, pure truth of God's Word presented in such a loving, caring, practical manner. The difference was obvious. We weren't talking about religion; we were talking about a relationship—a relationship with Christ. I like to explain it this way: religion is how man tries to get to God, while Christianity is God's way of getting to man.

Herein lies the heart and soul of our purpose: reaching people in this world with the truth and teaching them to live a life in Christ. That is the way to the abundant life for which we are all so desperately searching. Talk about treasure! Jesus said, "For where your treasure is, there your heart will be also."[3] That's the true treasure we seek for in all we do with the support system we promote. I'm convinced that if we edify and uplift people, we will be edified and uplifted in turn. How refreshing and rewarding it is to see people drinking in the good news proclaimed at our events.

Everything that happened at the events was phenomenal. Most people went home feeling as though they had tasted a bit of heaven here on earth. But I realized that we had to do something more to help these precious people who committed their lives to Christ, to help them grow and mature in their newfound relationship with the Lord. Otherwise we were tossing newborn babes out into the streets, smiling, and saying, "Good luck and God bless you! You're on your own." After we had taken the time and effort to identify people, connect with them, bring them in, and educate them about the business and about life, I wanted them to retain what they had received. I felt that my obligation and responsibility was to help them build themselves from the inside out.

We are not merely called to make converts but disciples. Yes, the new birth is essential, but that is just the beginning. We are called to help people grow and mature in their newfound lives, to get established in their rightful positions in the body of Christ, and to make a difference in this life.

I had a burning desire to help people connect spiritually, to help them find a local church where they could get into fellowship with other believers and hear the Word of God taught on a regular basis, where they could learn how to live the Christian life and help others to do the same. I wanted to provide these new converts with a network of Bible-believing churches, counseling centers, and treatment centers where people with ongoing needs could be fully supported. But I was a business guy, not a pastor or a priest. I could teach the distributors how to sponsor and create volume. But I needed someone who could bridge the business and spiritual worlds for us and help our newly converted business associates grow spiritually.

Pastor Paul Zink told me about Ed and Cheryl Henderson, a couple in our church that he thought might be able to help. Ed had been a manager on the staff of the regional postmaster general in Memphis before transferring to Jacksonville, and he had tremendous organizational skills as well as a heart for ministry. He and Cheryl had their own part-time evangelistic ministry in churches and in prisons. Cheryl possessed a gift for counseling and encouraging people who wanted to grow spiritually. The couple also had three boys, so they well understood the various pressures involved in husband-and-wife relationships and parenting, two areas of perpetual problems for people in any business.

When I first approached Ed and Cheryl about helping me to develop a network that would help people plug in spiritually, they were interested. I shared with them my vision of ministering to people, not condemning them, but loving them, helping them get connected to a good church, helping them develop stronger families, and assisting them in becoming spiritually grounded. I could tell that Ed and Cheryl's hearts were resonating with mine when I talked about introducing people to Christ and how I wanted to follow up with them, to make sure their spiritual relationships started right and grew stronger. But when I told them that most of the people were finding the Lord through my networking business, I immediately sensed Ed and Cheryl's walls going up. Like so many others, they had been burned by overly zealous and less-than-forthright network marketing distributors, and they held no interest in becoming part of that kind of organization. I encouraged them to attend just one event, "to stay open and see what the Lord would show them." The couple agreed to consider it.

Ed and Cheryl attended my next weekend event in Knoxville, Tennessee, and at the optional Sunday morning worship service, nearly three thousand people responded to an invitation to come to know Jesus Christ. Watching from backstage, Ed and Cheryl were overwhelmed with emotion as tears of joy streamed down their faces. Seeing all those people come to the Lord blessed the Hendersons so much, and although what I was asking them to do with New Life Network was not even on their radar, they knew they had found something very special, and they wanted to be a part of it. Ed will tell you that he had been involved in traditional churches for years, but he had never seen anything quite like what he experienced in this marketplace ministry. Ed and Cheryl were all in.

I'm often reminded that God doesn't call the equipped; He equips the called. That was certainly the case with Ed and Cheryl. Although they had fascinating life experiences from which to draw, they were not necessarily qualified to run a counseling ministry. But they knew that God wanted them to do it, and so did I. Ed and Cheryl loved God and loved people; they had studied at Faith Bible College for three years and were ordained by the World Ministry Fellowship, so they had a deep understanding of the Word of God, and they had a strong foundation in the gifts of the Spirit. In matters most important, they were powerfully prepared.

> **God doesn't call the equipped; He equips the called.**

On the airplane flight home, Cheryl, Ed, and I reviewed the decision cards that had been collected from the people who had responded to the Lord. One man had written, "Man, I've never been to church before. This is great!"

Cheryl looked at Ed in amazement. "Do you mean to tell me that there is someone in America who has never been to church?" I nodded with them as we simultaneously realized that there was a huge mission field within the business community, filled with people who needed to know God and experience His presence and power. Cheryl signed on with us that week; Ed continued working his secular job until 1992 before coming on full time.

We started New Life Network from scratch, with a small office, a computer, and a telephone. As part of our outreach, we decided to have a New Life Network book table at all of my events. I already sold business books and recordings of the speakers at events, most of which were sales, mar-

For more than twenty-five years, Ed and Cheryl Henderson of New Life Network have led our ministry to the marketplace and networkers.

keting, and motivational materials, but I also wanted to make materials available that would help people with their spiritual needs.

We began with one book, the first volume of Germaine Copeland's *Prayers That Availeth Much*. Cheryl later figured out how to interact with publishing companies, counseling services, and local churches all around the country. At our events today, she carries a plethora of helpful materials: everything from books about the family, finances, motivational materials, leadership, and ethics to Bible studies and devotionals. But we began at that first function with only one book on the table. Distributors attending the conference stopped and talked with Cheryl and Ed; some bought the book, but many others simply needed someone to talk with them or to pray with them.

Even as the ministry grew, the book table was never about selling books so much as it was a point of contact. People came to see what books might be helpful to them, but more often, they came looking for someone who cared. Before long, Ed and Cheryl were dealing with every sort of spiritual problem imaginable, from simple disagreements in marriage to problems of adultery, parenting issues, spousal abuse, drug addiction, pornography, depression, suicide, and a myriad of other situations. In every case, the Hendersons pointed people to the Lord and to His Word to find the solutions to their problems. When long-term counseling seemed necessary, Ed and Cheryl were quick to connect people with competent professionals. New Life Network's approach was to pray, to believe God, to love and comfort people, and to find resources to help them.

Ed had a strong corporate background, so he set up our organizational systems and did all the groundwork to help New Life Network become a nonprofit, tax-exempt corporation with me as president, Ed as vice president, and Cheryl as secretary-treasurer. We hold those same offices today. Ed and Cheryl meet with me regularly to help identify some of the spiritual needs of the people who attend our events. Sometimes after an event, they'll tell me, "We met a number of people this week who were having marital problems." Another week, they'd say, "The group this week seemed to have a lot of financial problems." We never discussed personal situations or named individuals, because New Life Network's ministry is confidential, but sometimes the insights I gleaned from Ed and Cheryl regarding the needs of the people helped me as I brought in speakers who would love our people and minister to them.

We established four basic principles that we felt new believers needed in order to get established and to help them to grow in their relationship with Christ:

1. *Read* your Bible every day.
2. *Pray* always and about everything. Talk to God throughout each day.
3. *Testify.* Share with others how you came to know Christ.
4. *Get involved with a local church* where the Bible is taught and people are growing spiritually.

Many of the people who responded on Sunday mornings had never really heard the gospel before, even though they may have attended various churches throughout their lives. But we weren't talking about church; we were talking about knowing Jesus Christ, having a relationship with Him, and allowing Him to be the controlling partner in our lives. Once again, it's about a personal relationship with Christ rather than a religious act that leaves one distant from the Father God.

Our goal is to assist new believers to get equipped for life. We know that we are not merely called to make converts but to help people become disciples, true followers of Christ. We quickly realized that although they may be enormously successful in other fields, or even in our business, when it came to living as a Christian, many of the people responding to the invitations didn't have a clue about how to get started, much less own a Bible. So we provided New Testaments with the same notes that I had used as a new believer, helping people to implement the Word of God into their everyday lives, to invade every aspect of their beings. Eventually we added other literature that we believed would be helpful in getting new believers grounded in their relationship with the Lord, and we always planted the seed that let them know there was much more available from God. This new commitment was similar to a wedding day, a marvelous place to begin the new relationship, but that was not the end. There was a fantastic life to be lived together! It was a new life and a new beginning for each of them.

We attempted to identify local churches around the country where new believers could find help, health, and hope as they began to grow. Major ministries began calling New Life Network and requesting help in connecting new converts to strong local churches. Today, New Life Network continues to connect people from our organizations as well as numerous other ministries.

I am often asked, "I understand you are a person of faith, but why do you include so much about God in your business?"

I'm not bashful about answering, "Because if you want to build a great business, you need to have a strong foundation. And if you ignore the spiritual aspect, your foundation will be unstable and everything you build can be easily toppled. The Bible says: "I am the vine; you are the branches. If you remain in me and I in you, you will bear much fruit; apart from me you can do nothing."[4] I need no interpretation of this: without Him we can do nothing, so why leave Him out? I've tried living and trying to succeed without Him and with Him. With Him is better.

> **When you get the heart right, usually the prospering of your business will soon follow.**

"On the other hand, if the Lord builds the business through you, your investments will pay dividends forever. The Scripture teaches that unless a man builds on the foundation of the Lord, he labors in vain. So much of relational marketing is based on serving from the heart. When you get the heart right, usually the prospering of your business will soon follow."

✦ ✦ ✦

SADLY, ONE of the reasons for the tension between my up-line and me was our focus on ministering to the people who came to our events, not merely trying to help them make money. How ironic that the very organization we set up to help the people in our distribution network would become another point of contention with our up-line. Naturally, people have problems, regardless of their business associations, and New Life Network didn't turn anyone away, whether they were part of our organization or not. When someone came to Ed or Cheryl needing help for their marriage or with their children or any other spiritual matter, we gladly shared our resources with them. As a result, some people in leadership positions within the company grew insecure, and once again, accusations railed against us. The up-line apparently believed that we were trying to woo distributors away from their business groups to ours. They never mentioned that some of their people were hurting and were desperately seeking spiritual help, so they came to us to find what they weren't getting elsewhere.

Ironically, Ed and Cheryl were not even involved in building the network marketing organization, and I never encouraged them to do so. "I have lots of distributors," I often reminded them. "I need you to be fully focused on the needs of these people." Their business and calling was in the ministry.

In the midst of stress and turmoil, it is often easy to get our eyes off the prize. I was about to be reminded what really matters.

WHEN PAUL Brigham, our youngest child, was just a baby, I attended auto racing's version of the Super Bowl: the Daytona 500. Lita was home with the children. Seven-year-old Daniel and one of his friends were in the swimming pool, but they had neglected to close the security gate between the house and the pool. Without anyone's noticing, fifteen-month-old Paul slipped through the gate toward where all the fun was—in the pool. For a while Paul played contentedly at the pool steps, but then something happened.

> "Isn't that your baby brother floating in the pool?"

Daniel and his friend were at the opposite end of the pool when Daniel's friend pointed and said, "Hey, isn't that your baby brother floating

Here's Paul (center) after his close call in the pool, with brother Daniel (left) and sister Brit (right). We can't keep them out of water.

in the pool?" Daniel looked toward the steps and, to his horror, saw Paul floating facedown in the water. Daniel raced to his brother, pulled him out of the water, and rolled him onto the patio. At about the same time, Brittany walked out to the pool area, saw Paul in the pool and screamed. This got Lita's attention. She was in the kitchen, and she ran out and scooped up Paul and ran with him back inside the house, where she began administering mouth-to-mouth resuscitation while the kids' nanny called 911.

> **Life and our relationships were gifts we were determined to treasure.**

With the paramedics on the way, the 911 operator stayed on the line, guiding Lita in her CPR efforts. By the time the paramedics arrived, Paul was beginning to cough up water. The paramedics took over and life-flighted him to a downtown hospital where they stabilized him. Paul was soon breathing normally, although he had some water on his lungs that required some time to dissipate and an overnight stay. By the next day, he was doing much better and ready to break out of the hospital bed. This was truly a life-changing miracle.

Thankfully, Paul suffered no residual problems, despite nearly drowning. His accident put life in better perspective for the rest of our family members too. Thinking about how close we came to losing Paul made our family more aware that life can be short. It also caused us to be grateful to the Lord and thankful for each new day. We were more determined not to take each other for granted. Money could come and go, and material possessions pass just as easily, but life and our relationships were gifts we were determined to treasure. We knew that as long as we had each other, that's all that really mattered.

Little did we know that we were going to need that reminder in ways we never dreamed of in the days ahead.

CHAPTER 12

The End of the Line

TWENTY-ONE YEARS FROM THE time Lita and I first embarked on our networking journey, we sensed that things were about to change again. We knew we were approaching the end of this season in our lives. I decided to go on a fast and seek the Lord's direction regarding what was going on and what He might have in store for us next.

I was ten days into my fast when early one morning, long before dawn, I awakened from a deep sleep and sensed that God wanted me to read a specific chapter in the Bible: Genesis 26. He impressed on me that He was about to show me my past, present, and future through this passage. I knew it was God, because I knew nothing of this particular scripture, describing how Isaac, the son of the Jewish patriarch Abraham, encountered opposition from the people living around him. Isaac's neighbors, the Philistines, were jealous of the young man's wealth and prosperity, so they plugged all of Isaac's wells by filling them with dirt. In the Middle East, water is a precious commodity, particularly in the area of Gerar where Isaac lived, near the desert. To interfere with someone's well was a serious offense, and Isaac had every right to retaliate.

But he didn't. Instead, he chose to keep the peace and simply went to work reopening the wells. When Isaac's workers struck a fresh pool of water, the neighbors disputed with him again, claiming that the water was theirs.

Isaac quietly went about his business and simply dug another well. Once again, however, the opposition raised its selfish head, quarreling with Isaac's workers about that well also. So Isaac moved on and dug yet another well. It was hard work to dig those wells in that arid land, but God honored Isaac's tenacity and diligence. This time, the neighbors didn't squawk, so Isaac named that place Rehoboth. "The Lord has given us room and we will flourish in the land," Isaac said.

Interestingly, that night, the Lord appeared to Isaac and made some incredible promises to him. God said, "I am the God of your father Abraham. Do not be afraid, for I am with you; I will bless you and will increase the number of your descendants for the sake of my servant Abraham." So Isaac pitched his tent there, his workers dug another well and amazingly found water again. Four times, Isaac dug new wells, ironically, all four in land that had been promised to his father, Abraham.

I did a bit of research and discovered that each of Isaac's wells had a name: *Esek,* the well of contention; *Sitnah,* the well of accusation; *Rehoboth,* the well with room enough for all of us; and *Shibah,* the well of God's promise that He is true to His word. The first two wells seemed painfully familiar, and in the third and fourth wells I saw my future.

As I thought about this unusual story of Isaac, a man who chose to move on rather than argue, I could easily see some parallels in Lita's and my experience. At least four times we had to pull up stakes, and rather than creating further division and hurt, we decided to pack up, move on, and dig another well. I'm convinced that is one of the reasons why God has blessed us so bountifully today.

I noticed two other truths from Isaac's story that proved important to Lita and me. First, Isaac stayed in the land of his enemies as God directed. Isaac obeyed God. In this, I believe, God does not make mistakes. He allowed me to see networking like I had never before seen it, perhaps like no one else ever has. God never does things to you but for you. I

B R I G I S M

God doesn't do things to you but for you.

would learn more about why God allowed me to be a part of such a unique industry. I would find that I was to stay in that industry to actually find my destiny.

Second, Isaac's obedience, diligence, and faithfulness brought blessing not only to him but to all his followers for whom he was given leadership responsibilities. Staying true to the calling is so key in all of our lives.

But believe me, it was not an easy journey. I had no idea that the enterprise into which Lita and I had poured so much of our time and energy—as well as our hearts—would take a drastic turn to become one of the most painful experiences we'd ever walk through as a family.

In the mid-1990s, our business was still going gangbusters. At a time when most people couldn't pay others to get into the network marketing business, I could hardly keep them out! I'd walk by and people were almost begging me to get them into our business. I wasn't doing anything different from what I had been doing previously. It was simply the favor of God on our lives.

About that time, two letters from individuals who disapproved of my spiritual stands came to the company's attention. There were only two letters—more than thirty-five thousand people had heard me speak at the Hoosier Dome in Indianapolis and thirty thousand people had attended an event in Charlotte—but two people said, "Brig is a religious fanatic, he's offending me with his 'in your face' Christianity, so I'm going to quit the business."

My actions at the Hoosier Dome must have really grated on somebody. Ronald Reagan was one of the guest speakers at that event, and the sponsors from Michigan made it clear ahead of time that while God and country themes were acceptable, they wanted no other overtly Christian statements made from their platform during the business sessions.

I was on the docket for Friday night at the weekend event, and at the time, I was one of the top distributors in the world. Everywhere I went, people wanted to know how I had become so successful in our business. So on Friday night, during my time on stage, I decided to answer the question once and for all.

"Do you want to know how we've become so successful?" I asked the enthusiastic crowd? "Here's how." I dropped to my knees right on stage

One of my heroes—Ronald Reagan—spoke at our function
at the Hoosier Dome in Indianapolis.

and prayed, acknowledging my absolute dependence on God. When I finished praying, the Hoosier Dome crowd went wild, cheering as though I'd just sunk the winning basket during a basketball tournament. While the folks in the arena were thrilled with my honest expression, the big guns backstage were not amused.

Following the Indy and Charlotte events, some of the top corporate executives called me to meet with them at the home office in Michigan. I assumed they appreciated my outspoken approach and could understand how it might engender some opposition. I acknowledged their concerns and tried to allay them. "Well, there are always going to be people who don't understand or don't appreciate that I speak as a believer." The men nodded their heads. "But I always shoot straight with our people, and I start out by letting them know that if I were a truck driver, I'd speak from the perspective of a truck driver. But I'm just a long-haired hippie-type surfer who got born again, so I'm going to speak from that perspective. So I don't mean to offend anybody, but I did turn my life over to Christ, and since then, I've been a fanatic for Him."

People in the audience often applauded wildly at my straightforward testimony, and inevitably numerous people at our meetings wanted to

> **I assumed they appreciated my outspoken approach.**

know more about Jesus as a result. That was the reason I had started the nonprofit organization known as New Life Network in the first place, to help those new believers get established in their faith.

But I later learned that the concern at company headquarters was not merely over doctrinal issues. Somebody accused me of starting New Life Network as a means of infiltrating their groups and drawing people away from their business organizations to mine. That was silly. I had always honored our leadership and was appalled that anyone would think that I was trying to usurp someone's position or undermine anyone's business in any way.

I looked back at the gentlemen in the boardroom and asked, "Do you have one single example of me doing what you just described, using this 501(c)(3) organization, New Life Network, to take over anything?"

"Oh, it's a nonprofit organization?"

"It's a ministry," I said.

"We didn't know that. So it's not a business?"

"No, didn't you read my mission statement about what New Life does? They pass out Bibles and Christian literature at our voluntary nondenominational Sunday morning worship services and help people to get involved in local churches."

"If this doesn't stop," he continued, "you will be out of this business."

"We heard that you are using that organization as a cover for your own benefit."

"Okay, fine. All I am asking is that you show me one example of my doing something like that."

"This is a problem still," one of the men said, referring, I assumed, to New Life Network. "It doesn't matter what it is or isn't, it's a problem." They even began to criticize some of materials we give to new believers. Ironically, we had previously sent all of these materials, including a New Testament, to the company's headquarters for approval. And the person responsible had approved it.

"I don't understand," I said. "You all are believers. Aren't we supposed to minister to people? I don't have an overt worship service on Friday or Saturday and even on Sunday. We emphasize that it is an optional nondenominational gathering."

"If this doesn't stop," he continued, "you will be out of this business."

I quickly glanced around the room. I realized that everyone else was just sitting there silently. "I don't know what you all are after," I said quietly, again looking around the table, searching each man's eyes. "What do you want me to do?"

"You will not speak on our stage again or speak in the name of Jesus."

"Well, it's your company," I answered. "But tell me something. When did I ever speak on your stage in the name of Jesus? It was at our functions—we paid for the venue out of our own pockets—where I shared my faith."

That meeting was the beginning of the end of my business relationship with that company. I went home distraught and discouraged. I told Lita about the Michigan meeting and said, "You aren't going to believe what I just went through. They're telling me that I can't speak about Jesus from their platforms. The Bible says that if I'm ashamed of Jesus in front of people, He's going to be ashamed of me before His heavenly Father, and I sure don't want that. We're not going to deny Christ. I won't ever speak on their stage again, but there's something much bigger going on here. They're not welcoming us."

It was time for Lita and me to dig another well.

We believe that you should go where you are celebrated, not where you are tolerated. I was beginning to understand that it was time for Lita and me to dig another well.

In retrospect, it's easy to see that it had been becoming increasingly clear to Lita and to me that the season of our being in that particular business was coming to a close. We have learned that no man can close the doors God opens, and no man can open the doors God closes. Discovering His will, then, becomes a matter of listening with your inner spirit, learning to hear His voice, and then obeying His instructions. It was time to fold up our tents and move on. I'm a proponent of following peace.

At one of our last events, hardly anyone responded to the invitation to meet Christ on Sunday morning. Standing on the platform at the close of the service, I looked at Ed and Cheryl and saw the tears of sadness in their eyes. I turned away from the microphone and said to them, "This is it. We're done here." It was as if God was showing us that it was over and it was time for us to move on. As we pulled back, we found that some of our friends and business associates didn't understand. Within weeks, it seemed we were discredited and discarded. Worse still, all sorts of rumors and innuendoes surrounded our departure from center stage. The worst part was the way our children were ostracized and had to endure insults from their former friends because of what their friends' parents were saying about us. "Why don't our friends want to come over to our house anymore?" they asked. It crushed us when our own kids came to us with malicious stories of what their friends' parents had said about us. We said, "We gotta get out of here."

I told Pastor Zink, "I'm done. Evidently God is shutting the door on this. I think the anointing on our lives for this business has lifted." I could still draw a crowd and we could host a fantastic event, but there was little to no peace or joy in doing it. A person must be true to himself or herself—and we were.

Lita said, "I just can't do this anymore." I agreed, but I was still hoping for the best.

A short time after that, Lita and I met with our inner circle of friends and associates. We bared our hearts and shared that we would be going inactive in the business. We had been involved for more than twenty-one years, and we declared that if we couldn't take some time off and enjoy the fruits of our labors, then this thing was a farce. We had generated more than $5.5 billion in sales and had helped untold thousands of folks to earn their financial freedom. Commissions earned by people in our organization over that period were in the hundreds of millions of dollars, and of course, we did well ourselves. But it was time for us to move on and pass the baton. We encouraged the folks and spoke a blessing over them and their businesses.

Initially, our organization was stunned, and some people were downright shocked, but slowly they became more appreciative as I explained our decision. We said nothing derogatory about our up-line leaders, nor did we disparage the company in any way. We thanked our friends for their confidence and trust in us over the years, but we were also emphatic in stating, "We're pretty much done in our active roles. Please honor us and don't call us regarding business matters from this point on."

In the meantime, however, the company decided to censor us, which

---

BRIGISM

Go where you are celebrated, not where you are tolerated.

froze our income. We went from receiving large monthly commissions and bonuses to next to nothing. Worse yet, we soon became aware that information was being leaked to our distribution network, disparaging our reputation and impugning our character. I knew I could always make more money, but a person's reputation is priceless.

At first, our phone rang off the hook. "What's going on, Brig?" people in our business wanted to know. "We're hearing terrible things about you." I tried to explain as best I could, without casting any aspersions on the company or individuals in it. After all, this was still our life's work. Why would I want to kick against the goads, as the Scripture says, or bite the hand that wrote our checks? Before long, however, I found my efforts at explanation were a futile waste of time. The word was out: Brig and Lita Hart are persona non grata, no longer welcome. Almost overnight, it was as though we had ceased to exist as far as that company was concerned.

> **I could always make more money, but a person's reputation is priceless.**

Only a handful of people remained loyal and true to us as friends, and the hurt we experienced was unimaginable. We have since accepted the fact that true friends are those who are walking in when everyone else is walking out. It is a sad fact that many people's loyalty is tied to their finances. The Scripture says that you can serve one of two masters—God or mammon—but not both. Mammon represents power, position, and money. For many folks, their security is in the wrong place.

Talk about a test. This was going to be a hard one for our family to pass. We had to search our hearts for years to come to get through the emotional and spiritual pain. To be honest, it was a day-to-day process. Since then, I have learned that people are most always going to do what is best for them and their interests. Most tend to think and ask themselves, what's in it for me? Fear and necessity are often the common denominators in those kinds of situations. It's the reality of life for most folks. No problem. We will love 'em anyway.

I recognized, however, that our struggle was not against former business associates and friends. Our fight is not against flesh and blood, but against principalities and powers in high places. There will always be battles in your life, but you must learn that the battle is the Lord's. Our job is to stand and then continue to stand; He will see us through. Just watch and see what He does in and through these situations.

I knew that I was on the precipice of something big, and the Enemy was trying to thwart our efforts. Deep down, I believed that God had more for me to do, but apparently the time was not yet right.

WE WALKED away from a business we had spent more than twenty years building, leaving behind millions of dollars. I had learned much during my years in that company, and I had met untold numbers of friends there. Most important, I had come to know the Lord through some dear business associates. Certainly there was sadness in leaving, and as a man, I felt devastated. I dealt with many of the same issues of rejection and failure that anyone confronts when a business goes bust. But Lita and I walked out with our integrity intact and our heads held high.

CHAPTER **13**

Strike Two

POUTED AND LICKED my wounds for a short season, all the while pondering what was next for our family. I knew I had to get up and get going again. I'm not the kind of person to sit around and mope; I am not the best case study on waiting. I am one who needs to be doing something productive. I needed something to do, but not just anything. I wanted to do what God wanted for me. I have always said, "You can be influenced or you can be the influence." Adversity causes some to break and others to break records.

Lita said it best: "When you are drowning, if you want to live, you must become a participant in your own rescue." I understood that change is the only constant thing in life. Good times and bad times have this in common: neither will last forever. You have the choice of either ripening or rotting, getting better or getting bitter. I also acknowledged that choice, not change, would shape my destiny, so it was time to make some new choices.

I had learned earlier in life that God is the God of second chances, that there is always hope for the future, and if necessary, He not only has a Plan B but a Plan C, D, and E. But when those plans change, it's important to learn what God is trying to teach us. I was about to learn that it is not what you achieve in life that matters, it is what you overcome that counts. Jesus said that "in this world you will have trouble,"[5] and sure enough, life kept handing us fresh challenges that tested our faith.

Even before the demise of our network marketing business, I had considered getting into the insurance business as an investment. So as soon as we closed U-Can-II in 2000, which basically took us out of network marketing at that time, Lita and I focused our attention on an insurance business we had started in Lakeland, Florida, with a prior employee and associate. Once again, I jumped into a business that I really didn't understand, but I wanted to do something that could offer my friends and co-workers an opportunity they understood. Gullible me, I always seem to look on the bright side of things without doing my due diligence in searching out the facts of the matter. This was one of those instances.

Lita and I invested a large sum of money in the insurance company and trusted our longtime associate—who served as general manager—and his partners to run the operation. I didn't know squat about insurance. I didn't even have an insurance license. But I knew how to foster an attitude of success, how to make presentations, and how to get people interested in a good product or service. So I helped structure the direct mail invitations and the seminars for the company.

> **It is not what you achieve in life that matters, it is what you overcome that counts.**

The company skyrocketed, creating incredible profits that, for the most part, we poured back into the business. We grew from a few employees and associates who were working in a small, modest office and warehouse space to occupying three floors in a prime bank building on Main Street in Lakeland's downtown area. We furnished the executive offices and conference rooms with the finest furniture, office equipment, and décor. Business was booming and we were on track to hit our two-to-three-year goals. Our three-to-five year goal was to build the business to a

---

SUCCESS PRINCIPLE FOR LIFE

Stick to what you know. Don't expect what you don't inspect on a consistent basis. Trust but verify. It's called good stewardship.

point of great success and then market it to a larger company. Within three years of our inception, several major insurance companies were already looking at us as a potential acquisition.

I had monthly discussions with my management team and associates as to how this could happen and how we needed to position ourselves for a premium sale. The team provided data that showed me how weekly, monthly, and annual sales were all on target and progressing. Of course, I had to keep investing in growth to keep building the base so we could place a higher value on the business as we evaluated its worth each quarter. My advisors assured me that a bigger base at this point could mean greater market value in the near future. So I kept on investing more money in the business.

The plan worked well, except for one slight defect. Several of my key executives and associates inside the company had been embezzling money for more than two years! Other key management folks got in on the deal and were cooking the books. We now had more than one hundred employees, and as I later discovered, many of them were involved in the cover-up, so tracking down the money was no easy task. I always paid our employees well, but apparently greed has no limits. The president of the company, my so-called friend who helped start the company, was being paid a very generous six-figure salary, as were a few of the other top executives. This was all reported to me and I was fully aware of the advances in salaries as we grew, and I was amenable to that. After all, a laborer is worthy of his hire. But one fine day, negotiations with the major insurance companies interested in acquiring our company came to an abrupt halt. When I inquired why, the hard truth came out regarding our company's actual financial position. I learned through some rather heated encounters with my key executives that all was not so rosy in our garden. There were actually two sets of books being kept, and the house of cards was about to come down. The greedy embezzlers had been siphoning off the profits for quite some time. When the cat is the away, the mice will play—and play they did. Some of these guys were secretly taking six- and seven-figure bonuses each year! To my surprise, I found numerous other folks involved in this scheme who were receiving similar unwarranted compensation packages.

Exacerbating matters further, I was soon to find out that the only thing I still owned in my company was its debt. Prior to the embezzlement, Lita and I had owned 90 percent of the company. We were the only investors in the company. When our board meetings were conducted, I usually attended by phone. I later learned that the minutes to our meetings were modified and manipulated to show me transferring shares to my partners. They forged my signature on the business minutes as though I was in agreement with the proceedings.

Can you imagine how violated Lita and I felt when we became aware of this insurrection? We had been negotiating a contract that was worth more than $300 million to the company and to us, only to find out that because the company's financial status was misrepresented to the interested purchasing companies, they all walked away. I was left with nothing but a feeling of being totally violated. Not to mention how angry I was with them and myself. Talk about adding insult to injury. I wanted to die, and I wanted to take some select people with me! My second well had been covered up.

This was another time in my career when I had been taken advantage of by so-called friends and believers. Lita and I were devastated. I pulled out a gun and was ready to use it, either on my former business partners or myself; I wasn't sure who deserved it more. Instead, I called Pastor Paul Zink, and he calmed me down.

Lita and I headed to the company's corporate offices in Lakeland to gather up our belongings from our now-defunct business. We were appalled when we arrived there. It was like a ghost town. Only a few folks were there, scrounging around the complex. Lita and I, along with a few hired hands, loaded two tractor trailers with the remaining furniture and office supplies.

When Lita and I reported the embezzlement to the Florida insurance authorities, they were convinced we had an ironclad case against our former partners. But for a variety of reasons, Lita and I decided that rather than go through the same sort of turmoil we had experienced with our previous business associates, we would choose to let it go. We chose not to prosecute the case. We walked away, believing that God could make up the losses to us. We decided to move on and find another well.

It wasn't easy, and it never will be. It cost us millions of dollars and years of frustration. For nearly half a decade, every time another bill showed up from the insurance business—a bill that should have been paid by the company—Lita and I took several deep breaths, paid the bill, and kept our focus on moving forward with our lives. We refused to allow our hearts and minds to get sucked into the quagmire of hurt and disappointment, anger and resentment. We learned to deal with it and move on.

SUCCESS PRINCIPLE FOR LIFE

It's important to recognize the seasons in our lives and to realize that everything has a time and place—a time to build, a time to uproot. The most important thing is to hold on to your integrity and your peace, knowing that you have done everything in your power to live rightly before man and God.

I suppose this would be a great place to blame someone for this great injustice. But as we processed this, we realized that there was no one to blame but ourselves. We had not been good stewards of the things over which we were given responsibility. God had given us indicators along the way as to what was going on, but we chose not to pay close enough attention to them.

I admit that this was a strong test of our character. It was a trial by fire, and we were facing it big-time. Because this wasn't the first time we had been taken advantage of, and it certainly wouldn't be the last, we knew the direct way to restoration and healing: forgive and move on. I've been told that when you're going through hell, don't stop. In other words, don't camp out there but keep moving.

We wanted to do what was right before God and leave the consequences in His hands. The fire we faced became a refining fire to us, and as you read on, you will find that we came out on the other side better and stronger. We actually found a new level of freedom that we had never experienced before. We knew we simply had to trust God, and we did. Was it easy? No! Was it necessary? Oh, yes.

We tried not to expose our children to the insurance business disappointments. The fallout from our networking experience nearly destroyed our kids' faith in God, in Lita and me as their parents, and especially their confidence in other Christian friends and associates. Our kids had grown up with those families, gone to school with them, gone on mission trips with them, and vacationed with them. Now they were unwanted, ostracized, and considered pariahs by their former friends. Our kids were hovering precariously on the precipice of spiritual disillusionment, so we didn't want to expose them to yet another instance of so-called godly people willing to sell their souls for the almighty dollar.

Although I didn't recognize it at the time, looking back now, it is easy for me to see that for us the insurance business was similar to Isaac's second well, known as the place of accusation and enmity. Although Lita and I had entered into the business with high hopes and lofty ideals, the experience became one of the lowest points in our lives. Making matters worse, during most of the insurance business debacle, our family was dislocated to the mountains of North Carolina. How we got there is a story in itself.

CHAPTER **14**

The Cave Years

AT CHURCH ONE DAY in 2000, Pastor Paul Zink (or P.D. as we had affectionately taken to calling him) introduced Ed and Cheryl Henderson and Lita and me to a group of ministers who expressed hope that they might benefit from my experience and expertise. That in itself was not unusual. Paul was always introducing me to great spiritual leaders, and it was an honor for Lita and me to help them when we felt we should. This particular group included some powerful teachers and speakers who traveled the world and exercised the biblical gift of prophecy—not simply foretelling the future but speaking truth into current situations.

While they may have been spiritual dynamos, their business acumen was next to horrible. They had a lot of products and experience, but their marketing lacked finesse. Their pitch to us was, "We know what we are called to do as ministers. But we are not good at business, and we feel that you have that part down pat. You know how to organize and administrate a business." They wondered if we would consider taking over that aspect of their work so they would be free to do what they do best. We promised to prayerfully consider their offer.

A few weeks later, Ed and Cheryl were at our home when the ministry's leader called me. He expressed absolute confidence that God wanted us to take on this new venture and that we would be moving to North Carolina. "I believe the Lord is saying you guys are the ones to do this. I want you to come on up here, and let's get started." The same week, the ministry leader flew down to Florida in his private plane to take us back with him for a whirlwind trip to North Carolina to have a closer look at the ministry. We met some wonderfully talented and precious people and came away quite impressed with the potential to do something great.

Lita and I are believers in the fact that when you are looking or seeking for something, it's normally wise for you to go with what shows up. Don't miss the boat. Don't let opportunity pass you by. It doesn't come around that often. Don't live life with regrets.

Ed Henderson later went back to Charlotte to examine the ministry's books and to see if we really could be of help to them. Ed felt strongly that we could benefit the ministry by cutting their expenses in half and doing a better job of marketing their materials. Lita and I traveled to North Carolina and found a superb office and warehouse where we could set up shop to market and service the ministers' products.

As we discussed and prayed about our decision, the willingness of our hearts and the circumstances of life seemed to intersect. For instance, the Hendersons had been trying to sell their house for nearly three years with barely a nibble, but now that they were seriously considering the move to North Carolina, the house sold.

For Lita and me, selling our house was equally significant. With the success we had seen in our networking venture, we had built a 12,500-square-foot home, with another 9,000-square-foot multipurpose building and garage housing all of our vehicles and toys. We had a beautiful, three-acre piece of property with 300 feet of frontage on the Intracoastal Waterway in Ponte Vedra Beach, Florida. Over a ten-year period, I had drawn up and designed and then built our dream home. Various appraisals estimated the value of the house between six and eight million dollars.

Selling that kind of unique, specialty property was at best rare. At that time in 2000, it was the most expensive home in the north Florida area. The average length of time for these types of homes to sell required two to three years to attract qualified buyers.

Rather than working through a Realtor, I felt strongly about moving on and going to work with the ministry, so Lita and I put our house and all its furnishing up for auction. If God wanted us to go, we'd be ready.

We really did put our faith in God to bring in the right buyer. This was

My Amway Double Diamond estate was on the Intracoastal Waterway
in Ponte Vedra Beach, Florida. I dreamed it, I built it,
and I sold it after I retired in 2000.

not easy by any means, but it was an exciting time for us, to say the least. As we started the process of listing and preparing for the auction, there were months of solid work and preparation to do. During that time, I had much to consider and think about. I had my doubts concerning the success of such a high-valued property selling in that market. What do you do when uncertainty arises in your mind and spirit? You pray.

Lita and I prayed, and the Lord reminded us of a person we knew locally who was a distant business associate and was the one person we knew who could absolutely afford the house. I picked up the phone and called him. Obedience is a wonderful thing when you are inspired! I suggested to him that he look at the most premiere property in the north Florida area and that he should consider it in his collection of other prize properties he owned. He stated that he already owned a beautiful home less than two miles from me.

My confidence kicked in, and I boldly suggested that there was not another property that compared to this, and he needed to at least look at it. I assured him of the beauty and real value that it offered at the time. He came, he saw, and he bought it that very next day!

We sold the house lock, stock, and barrel in one day (minus some pieces of furniture I wanted to keep—we were like the Beverly Hillbillies, moving from one place to another every year for three years) for the price that we had been praying for and asking God to provide. It was miraculous to say the least. Just consider these details—a former business associate who was living only part time in the area, viewing the property, and buying it on the spot, and writing a check for the full amount—and you can better understand why this was a sign to us that we were in the perfect will of God. How wonderful those situations can become when you listen and obey, but it all starts with trusting God and doing what He directs you to do. It sure seemed as though everything was lining up for us to make the move and head to our next venture in North Carolina. Yeehaw!

To further ease the burden on the ministers, we agreed that I would put up the money to get the products and other business aspects of the ministry organized. As we built the business, the ministers were to give us a commensurately increasing portion of the profits so we could recoup our costs and continue to expand. The goal was for us to eventually take over 100 percent of their products business. First, however, the office building and warehouse we had identified on our discovery trip had to be purchased and retrofitted per our needs. We had to fully remodel the offices, put in computer and phone systems, hire and train about thirty people, and basically do everything else involved in a start-up business.

Despite the unusual details of the arrangement, I felt that moving to North Carolina was the next step for us. Lita, however, had reservations about our deal right from the start. But the more we talked, the more convinced I became that Lita and I had to change our family's environment. With our kids still in school, Lita wasn't quite so sure.

Here's an important truth: when you want to do something, and your spouse isn't in agreement, slow down and pay attention. If you listen carefully, you may just hear the voice of God speaking through your marriage partner. I know how easy it is to get excited about a new venture and to leap before you look. I'm the sort of guy who likes to jump all in. I see an opportunity or a need, and I plunge in wholeheartedly.

> **If you listen carefully, you may just hear the voice of God speaking through your marriage partner.**

Since I believed so strongly in the direction we were going, I got a bit ahead of myself and followed the ready-fire-aim process rather than doing things in the correct order. Sometimes impatience can be an imposter of proper thinking. Since then, I have learned that not being in a hurry for anything is key to achieving peace in your life, but in this instance, I was moving full speed ahead.

Lita, on the other hand, prefers to move more slowly, putting proper steps in place to gradually do something rather than jumping all in. I am more trusting; Lita is the guard dog—a beautiful guard dog for sure, but one with a strong bite nonetheless. I sometimes trust before people prove themselves, whereas Lita says, "Prove yourself and then I'll trust you." Lita has much better intuition than I do about people and projects. Her heart and mind were not in agreement with mine when it came to moving north, but she knew I needed a new challenge, so out of her love for me, she acquiesced.

We sold our home, cars, boats, and almost everything else except a beach house near my mom in Jacksonville Beach. We found some common ground and made the move to Wilkesboro, North Carolina, where we created a fulfillment center for the various ministers and their products.

I supervised the distribution of the ministers' sermon tapes, books, and other materials, as well as coordinating their major events, similar to convention planning, a job I knew well. We arranged to have their materials produced, published, printed, and organized to be sold online and through catalogs. Anything the ministers needed to provide better resources fell under my domain. I felt good that I was using my gifts and organizational skills, even though we were more of a support ministry. I enjoyed it, but I could tell that Lita was uncomfortable.

Part of her discomfort stemmed from the attitudes and conduct of some of the people with whom we were aligned, as well as a continual misunderstanding about what our contributions of time, money, and energy were compared to the group with whom we were working. We paid for the building, the employees, and the manufacturing costs, while the ministers provided the talent and the intellectual properties. Worse yet, we were putting in all the tangible resources but not taking anything out.

FOR NEARLY a year and a half we worked at building the ministry, and we succeeded at boosting product sales and cutting their expenses in half, but our efforts were constantly thrown off track because of the propensity of the ministers to shift gears due to "prophetic revelations." It seemed that every time we turned around, one of the ministers was having a vision or a dream or getting some new idea about how things should be done. These ideas were couched in spiritual terms, so they were difficult to contradict. "God says that we should go this way now."

It is easy to give a spiritual answer to a practical question, and the ministers with whom we were working were pros at that approach to problem solving. But we were learning that prophecy can sometimes be manipulated—that the prophet can receive a word that sounds strikingly similar to what he wants to do—and that sort of answer does not necessarily come from God. Moreover, God does not have ADD. He doesn't say one thing to one person and something totally different to others in the family.

> **It is easy to give a spiritual answer to a practical question.**

Despite the fact that we had turned around the business aspects of the ministry, there never seemed to be enough money for them to increase our revenue and help us recoup our investment and make a profit. That seemed odd to us, because we knew the numbers. We could plainly see that we were making money, yet the leaders always found a reason not to pay us. Lita and I continued to pay expenses and our payroll out of our own pockets. We were spewing out money like water gushing from an open fire hydrant. Finally, Lita said, "We're not going to do this anymore." We put a plug in the money machine.

Two other attitudes we encountered should have been red flags to us. For one thing, our relationship with the ministers and their staffs always seemed to have an element of "us and them." They were the ministry, and we were the business. They had their people, and we had ours. The leaders seemed to have an attitude that the employees were there to serve them rather than the leaders serving and helping the employees to grow. It was not a healthy collaboration in which we felt like partners working together for the greater good of all.

Second, I was bothered by the way the ministers and their staffs treated the women in their organizations, almost as though they were subservient or second-class citizens. Consequently, the women seemed downcast in spirit even when they smiled. It was a strange conundrum—the women claimed to be serving God through their work at the ministry, but they rarely exhibited the joy of the Lord outside of the highly emotional church services conducted by the ministers. In their daily routines, many of the women appeared downtrodden and depressed. Only in church did they perk up.

I also noticed that there were no women in leadership positions within the ministry. In my previous businesses and in our business today, there are no glass ceilings. If a woman wants to work hard and succeed, nothing about our business will impede her. She can rise as high as she wants and make as much money as any man.

In our business today, there are no glass ceilings.

Lita now whimsically refers to our time in North Carolina as "the cave years." Nothing against the state, nor was her discomfort due to her being more of a beach person than a mountain dweller. She recognized, however, that things were out of whack. Consequently, she strongly disliked our time in the mountains.

Before long, the business stress spilled over and created serious tensions in our marriage. We argued incessantly, often over things that would ordinarily not have bothered us, but these were not normal conditions. The trickle-down effect took a toll on our relationships with our children as well. It got so bad at one point that Lita said to me, "Brig, you can stay here if you want, but I'm going back to Florida."

I knew that she was right. She could see that we were throwing money to the wind and not seeing any progress physically, financially, emotionally, or spiritually. In fact, the entire time we had been there, we did not see a single person come to know Jesus.

Socially, the move had been a disaster for our family. The kids didn't enjoy living in the small mountain community. Brittany developed one good friendship while there. Daniel joined the school soccer team, but apart from the few friends he found there, he grew more introspective and sullen. At the same time, he seemed to be slipping away more and more from the rest of the family. Our entire family could easily have fallen apart had it not been for the strong support of the people who surrounded us with prayer. Our longtime friends Frank and Cindy Soucinek were especially helpful to us.

We first met Frank and Cindy during our networking experience. We were all young and naive and didn't know enough to guard our relationships while we were pouring ourselves into the business. Not surprisingly, Frank and Cindy had trouble in their marriage, but they worked hard and pulled it back together. Frank did a 180-degree turnaround in his life, coming back to build trust in their family. Today, Frank is a participant in their family, not simply a provider.

Many men are disconnected from their family; they aren't as emotionally involved as they ought to be because they are always working or always gone for one reason or another. We guys tend to think that if we are providing income, we're doing our jobs. But if the family is to function properly, dad has to be physically and emotionally present. Looking back, I understand now that I was often guilty of being an absentee father and husband. Nevertheless, Frank and Cindy had weathered major storms in their marriage and had come through them even stronger and more in love. They promised us that we could too.

> **If the family is to function properly, dad has to be physically and emotionally present.**

God may have been trying to warn us that something was out of whack with our circumstances. One night, Lita had a dream that overnight our entire warehouse would be emptied of the ministry's materials. When she went in to work the next day and told Cheryl Henderson about the dream, our friend was aghast. "No way," Cheryl protested. "I hope that isn't going to happen."

But sure enough, a few days later, the ministry leader called everyone together, and in a long, rambling discourse declared our "marriage" dissolved. "We got married before we dated," he said in reference to our business relationship. We let more than twenty people go that day, and they were devastated, not simply because they had lost their jobs, but because they had poured themselves into something they thought was God's direction for their lives. Some of them had moved to that part of the country and bought homes there. Now, with the wave of a hand, it was over. That weekend, the workers cleared out all their stock. Overnight, it was done. In one day, all the ministry's inventory in our warehouse was removed.

I felt as though someone had punched me in the gut, but I guess it took that sort of impact to help me recognize that our time with this particular ministry was over.

Following the demise of our work in North Carolina, Ed and Cheryl moved to Albany, Georgia, while other good friends and associates who had signed on with us remained behind to manage the properties and divest us of our responsibilities there.

Lita and I took stock of where we were and decided to relaunch a vision I had for helping people to achieve success through providing a personal support system. The company was called Ultimate Success. The personal development system provided individuals with "fresh manna," as we called it, for helping them to achieve their goals and dreams. It was all biblically based teachings that we marketed in books, tapes, CDs, videos, and conferences. I tapped into all the key relationships I had with some of the most successful folks I knew who had influenced my life. We organized a distribution center for all of their teachings and marketed it through networking. We developed the Word of the Week program, comprised of selected audio teachings from these giants in the faith, and we distributed them through the USA network (Ultimate Success Association). We gave incentives to every independent distributor to promote and distribute these teachings, and we paid royalties to the authors of the messages. We considered this a modern-day university for success. I had all sorts of grandiose ideas for Ultimate Success, but sadly, none of them really came to fruition. I ran Ultimate Success for about a year, from 2004 to 2005, before I felt comfortable in closing it down. It was another well from which I had to walk away. Our time in North Carolina was quickly coming to an end.

I felt as though someone had punched me in the gut.

At first, our lack of success with Ultimate Success was rather depressing. I was accustomed to seeing things work and work well for us. I know I tend to get ahead of myself, and I have always put pressure on myself to perform. I don't like to let others down.

I needed something to happen, and I needed it to happen quickly to provide for the people who were counting on me. But I also knew that things don't always happen according to our time frame. Rarely do they. I am one of the least patient folks you will ever know; waiting is not one of my great virtues. I now know that patience isn't just the ability to wait, it's the ability to keep a good attitude while you're doing it. Happy is the man who doesn't give in when he is tempted.

We sold our home in the mountains and moved back to Jacksonville Beach in 2004. Prior to our move north, we had lived in our dream home, a massive custom estate we had designed and built. When we returned to Florida, our family of five moved into our small beach house that was once owned by my grandmother. The two-story residence was built in the 1930s as an officers quarters for the military based in Jacksonville Beach. It was small and modest to say the least, with no modern conveniences. The house had a tiny kitchen with no dishwasher or other modern conveniences, a living room, and four small bedrooms with three-foot-by-three-foot closets in each of them.

Years ago I had bought my grandparents' home, and we used it as a
beach home. In 2003, when the family returned to Florida from
North Carolina, we settled here and started over.

Lita tried to encourage me, "We don't need all the stuff anyway, Brig.
You gotta live within the means of your closet."

We lived in that little beach house for eighteen months. During that
entire time, I was planning and designing in my mind the next Hart
abode. You just can't keep a good man down.

Nevertheless, the kids and Lita were excited to be home again, and I
was excited to see what God was going to do with us next. Looking back, I
can now see that God was causing me to grow through these experiences,
preparing me for the great things He had in mind for our future, although
it was hard to see that at the time. I do know now that "in all things God
works for the good of those who love him, who have been called according to his purpose."[6]

As LITA and I prayed about what we needed to learn from these experiences, certain principles seemed to surface. First, *be mindful of our own
business.* I had been too trusting of individuals, putting too much stock in
their abilities, and I had not provided proper accountability for their decisions. In my "dig another well" experiences in North Carolina and in

Florida, I had not gotten the specific information about the business in writing, so there was always a nebulous aspect regarding who was going to do what, how the business was to function, and how the profits were to be distributed. I resolved never to allow that to happen again.

Second, *hands on.* We need to be good stewards of the resources entrusted to us. Nobody will take care of our business the way we do. I had gotten distracted by the ministry in North Carolina and hadn't been overseeing the business in Florida, keeping up with matters in the insurance business as I should have been. We took in a lot of money through the insurance business, but we didn't keep a good handle on where the money was being spent.

We realized too late that we always should have had third-party accountants doing our audits and recommending cautionary checks and balances. We later discovered that our partners had spent a lot of money without our knowledge. We also found out later that they were chronic liars. If someone will lie about something trivial, they will lie about something major.

Third, *we're smart enough.* I had always been told that we weren't smart enough to make wise business decisions on our own. "You go do what you do, and we'll do what we do best." That sounded right. After all, I was always the producer rather than the investor, so I had allowed other people to handle our money and investments. Lita and I now realized that we not only had the ability to handle our own financial decisions, we had the responsibility to do so.

On a spiritual level, we learned that we needed to better heed the promptings of the Holy Spirit. Once, while we were still in North Carolina and trying to figure out what was going on with our insurance business in Florida, Lita had a revelation from God that something about the insurance company wasn't right, that we needed to investigate what was going on. But we didn't follow up on it as we should have. That could have been the Spirit of God alerting us, giving us a sign that a person within our ranks was not trustworthy. But we missed it. While we were listening to supposedly deeply spiritual leaders around us, we missed the still, small voice of God's Spirit within us. God is no respecter of persons, the Bible teaches. If you stay open to His leading, He will guide

I had been too trusting of individuals. I had not provided proper accountability.

you by His Spirit, giving you insight and helping you to make good choices just as easily as He does with those high-profile spiritual leaders.

We also learned a great deal about forgiveness. I knew it served no good purpose to harbor resentment toward the people who had ripped us off or those who had disappointed us or used us. Those folks will have to account to God for their actions and attitudes. My job was to keep my own heart right with God. To do so, I could not allow unforgiveness to fester. Bitter-

Better to forgive, forget it, and move on.

ness and unforgiveness will eat a person alive. I've heard unforgiveness called the bait of Satan, and I can tell you, it is. It'll eat you up. Total forgiveness is painful, especially when you believe that the people who offended or hurt you are getting away with something and no one else will ever find out. It hurts to kiss revenge good-bye, but you will find a new level of freedom when you decide to simply obey and do it God's way. Better to forgive, forget it, and move on.

Please understand: forgetting is nearly impossible, but choosing not to remember an offense or to dwell on it is possible with God's help. I don't have time to live in those past hurts, and neither do you. Don't let people who have hurt you live rent free in your mind. Life is way too short and precious for you to focus on those situations. Life is like a camera: what you focus on will develop. So focus on the positive.

I made a conscious effort to forgive every person who deceived us, hurt us, or stole from us. It wasn't easy, and I didn't always feel like forgiving, but I had read the scripture where Jesus said, if you, Brig, won't forgive those who have sinned against you, your heavenly Father will not forgive you. I still have to forgive some of those people every time I think of them. Anytime I feel any sort of bitterness or resentment creeping into my thoughts or attitudes, I do two things: (1) I quickly forgive them all over again, and (2) I choose to bless the people who hurt us. Often I will say those words aloud: "I forgive Joe. I bless Mary." I know how much I have been forgiven, so I try to be quick to forgive others. And I have to

---

BRIGISM

Life is like a camera: what you focus on will develop.

love them, because Jesus said if we just love those who love us, what good is that? We are to love even our enemies and those who have despitefully used us. Ouch! Now, that is tough love.

I have to love and forgive the people who offended us, but that does not mean that I must condone their actions. Nor do I have to do business with them. It is best that we keep our distance from some people. I am commanded to love everyone, and I do, but I am not commanded to like 'em all, and I don't. There is still a lot of room for improvement in my life!

Probably the best thing that Lita and I learned through our "dig another well" experiences was that we will no longer do anything major without being in agreement. We don't spend large amounts of money, we don't invest in businesses, we don't even sow into various ministries unless the two of us are in unity. As Pastor Zink likes to say, "The place of agreement is the place of power." When a husband and wife are in agreement, they have more power than at any other time. If you are in agreement in marriage and in business, even if you make a wrong decision, it will not be as destructive as it might be if one person operated unilaterally in the relationship or made an arbitrary decision without consulting the other person. Jesus says, "Again, I tell you that if two of you on earth agree about anything you ask for, it will be done for you by my Father in heaven. For where two or three come together in my name, there am I with them."[7] Yeah!

We will no longer do anything major without being in agreement.

How you deal with money can be a major source of conflict for a lot of couples. Spending large sums of money without agreeing is a big deal for us. Lita is the conservative and careful one in our relationship. She ponders and deliberates on whether she really needs a new pair of shoes or a new purse, while I can blow thousands of dollars on a new car or motorcycle without blinking. I've learned, however, that we are stronger when we make those decisions together. As I said earlier, Lita doesn't need all the fancy toys; I enjoy them. But I enjoy our unity even more.

In the case of our involvement with the ministry in North Carolina, I knew that Lita had reservations about making that move, and I appreciated her willingness to trust me. Had I paid more attention to the warning sirens going off in our home, we might have avoided a lot of stress, frustration, and financial loss.

At the same time, the North Carolina experience was a sort of sabbatical for me. Few people, myself included, fully understood the dangers I felt for our family after Lita and I left our initial network marketing business in 2000. I had poured my life into that business; I had forged friendships that I had intended and believed to be lifelong. But it all disappeared overnight. I needed a place to heal, to sort everything out in my heart and mind, and a safe place to recoup spiritu-

> **We decided that we were going to do one thing well.**

ally. Although others close to me didn't see it that way, our experience with the ministry in the mountains served me well in that capacity, and I came out of it stronger and ready for the next thing God had for me.

As a result of our Isaac experiences, Lita and I also established our own mission statement. We decided that we were going to do one thing well. Focus and singleness of purpose would be our mandate. So very slowly and very carefully we began considering and looking at various business options. "What will we do with our time, money, and resources?" we asked ourselves. We believed that we could succeed again, that God would continue to bless us because we were givers. Even when people were stealing from us, we continued to give a good portion of our income to ministries that we believed were effectively spreading the gospel. We were—and still are—convinced that the secret to living is through *giving*.

We invested in some real estate because we had never really lost anything on our real estate purchases. I owe much of that to the wisdom I received from my dad.

When we moved back to Florida in 2004—about the same time the insurance mess came to a head—we considered making a career change, staying far removed from any sort of direct sales type of business. I explored the possibilities of everything from real estate to opening a seafood restaurant to a string of automated car washes. Despite getting burned a few times, nothing appealed to me quite as much as network marketing. I actually got involved for about six to eight months in another networking business called Fuel Zone, and it did well for a while and we made some good money, but it was short-lived. Nothing I found seemed to pique my interest or crank my enthusiasm.

Then about a year after we had returned to Florida, I discovered a new business that was going to transform my life, but not before I received the scare of my life.

CHAPTER **15**

When Your Health Goes, Nothing Else Matters

IT'S ONE OF LIFE'S axioms: if you have your health, nothing else matters. Throughout the mid-1990s, while our children were still young, Lita experienced severe health problems that our physicians could neither diagnose nor remedy. She was perpetually weak and fatigued and barely ate. When she managed to get some food down, it didn't stay down for long. We hadn't a clue as to why she was experiencing this dramatic downturn in her health.

In her early years, Lita had several bouts with protracted illnesses. When she was vaccinated as a child, she had a severe reaction that made her so sick that her dad had to pick her up from school. Later, in junior high, she battled a nasty case of mononucleosis that decimated her energy levels for weeks. Shortly after we married, Lita contracted pneumonia and was weak for months. When we first had children, Lita seemed even more tired, but we assumed her lack of energy was due to the pregnancies. For months after each delivery, she remained fatigued and lethargic, as though someone had unplugged her batteries, even though she slept more than eight hours most nights. It seemed that every few years Lita was embroiled in another battle for a normal lifestyle.

Certainly, the stresses of what we went through with some of our businesses weighed heavily on Lita. Then, when we sold or gave away nearly everything we owned and moved to North Carolina to be involved with the ministry there, what I had hoped would be a time of restoration for Lita and me spawned more tension and sickness rather than liberty and healing.

As her health deteriorated again during the mid-1990s, Lita sought help from a variety of specialists. We began to liken her to the woman in the Bible with an issue of blood who spent a fortune with her doctors but never improved. Our search for a remedy seemed equally futile. Fortunately, Lita had more resources than

Without even saying hello, I blurted, "Don, Lita's dying!"

that dear woman in the Bible, but Lita's doctors seemed nonetheless resigned to treating the symptoms rather than the source of the problem. Her encounter with one doctor who was associated with a famous medical institution was typical of many. When Lita confided to the physician how she was feeling, he listened kindly and then said, "It sounds to me like you're depressed."

"Yes, I'm depressed," Lita responded, "because none of you doctors can tell me what's going on."

She went to another doctor who did an exhaustive series of tests, including upper and lower GI tests. All of the tests came back negative, yet Lita's physical condition continued to deteriorate.

Initially, Lita simply believed that she wasn't feeling well due to our hectic, frenetic schedule. We were going, going, going all the time. She assumed that she would get better after some rest. But her condition only worsened. She continued on a downward spiral physically and mentally. Her body was shriveling up, and she was dying before my eyes.

One night when Lita was so sick, Cheryl Henderson was visiting. Lita looked at her with tears in her eyes. "Am I going to die, Cheryl?" she asked plaintively.

Cheryl recoiled at the thought. "In the name of Jesus, you will live and not die!" Cheryl said, quoting the Scriptures.

While I was on the road, Candy Bateman, a woman who had worked with us in New Life Network, stayed at our home with Lita. She cared for Lita, read the Scriptures with her, prayed with her, and encouraged her to eat and rest. Despite our faith, Lita's frail body could hardly function as her health continued to fail.

One night, in desperation, I called Don and Lu Crews in Cocoa Beach. Don and Lu had been our closest friends since the early days of our marriage. In many ways, they had been like surrogate parents for us, and Lu had often encouraged Lita and me to eat more nutritionally. More important, I knew that Lu and Don loved Lita like a daughter and would pray for her.

Don answered the phone when I called, and without even saying hello, I blurted, "Don, Lita's dying!"

He quickly got Lu on the phone, and I described Lita's condition to them.

Lu immediately called a brilliant, licensed naturopathic-homeopathic practitioner in Orlando who specializes in natural and alternative approaches to health. Lu drove up to our home, and along with Cheryl Henderson, we carefully helped Lita into our motor home and into a bed so she could rest as we headed for Orlando. The doctor took one look at Lita and realized the seriousness of her condition. Ironically, rather than immediately loading her up with drugs, he looked into her eyes and asked, "Lita, do you want to live?"

"Yes," Lita weakly replied.

"Okay, if you want to live, I want you to do everything I say."

Lita was in no condition to disagree.

The doctor ran an assortment of noninvasive tests on Lita. Lita was thirty-five years old at the time, but the testing showed that her organs were similar to those of a seventy-five-year-old woman! Three of her organs—her kidneys, liver, and heart—were in serious danger of shutting down. The doctor diagnosed Lita as having the Epstein-Barr virus, similar to an acute mononucleosis in which the immune system has broken down. The doctor suggested some natural health solutions, using nutrition and supplements to change the way her body felt.

Homeopathic remedies are designed to work as "like cures like"; thus in homeopathy, similar to the way when someone is bitten by a rattlesnake, the serum used as an antidote is made from rattlesnake venom. It creates a response within the immune system of the victim.

The doctor prescribed a protocol of natural remedies designed specifically for Lita. When she walked out of office, she carried a bag filled with remedies, but more important, she had something far more powerful. Lita looked at Cheryl and said, "I finally have hope."

Lita followed the doctor's instructions, and the natural approach worked for her. As a result of changing our eating habits, our kids and I received some benefits as well. More than the nutritional change, however, we benefited by spiritually bonding together as a family. This was the biggest crisis we had ever faced together, and Brittany, Daniel, and Paul came together in a marvelous way to support Lita and pray for her.

It took more than a year for Lita to regain her health, and during that time, she studied everything she could find about various natural medicines and how the body works constantly to heal itself if given the proper nutrition. God turned Lita's illness into a strength that she has been able to use to help many people. I sometimes only half-jokingly call her "Medicine Woman" because of her intense study and education about health and the human body. In Lita's adversity was hidden a desire and a talent that she had now discovered.

By 2004, Lita and I had been out of the past businesses for more than five years. She was feeling much better, but for the first time in my life, I was about to experience some serious health issues myself. I've always been healthy, but in the spring of that year, I developed debilitating and extremely painful back problems that eight months of physical therapy and chiropractic treatments did little to alleviate. Here's how it happened.

Since I was now semiretired, when we left North Carolina and moved back to Florida, we bought some land, and I wanted to build a new home using some of the construction skills my dad had taught me when I was a boy. I loved getting my hands dirty and especially enjoyed playing in the dirt and digging holes. I bought a tractor and backhoe for some therapy in the dirt. I felt empowered simply by sitting at the controls. I could dig trenches, move mounds of dirt, and knock down small trees. My dream toy at that time was not a yacht or a plane, but a Caterpillar D9 bulldozer!

Lita understood my obsession with the backhoe. "Where are you going?" she'd ask when she'd see me dressed in work clothes.

"I'm going out to play in the dirt and dig a few holes."

She would laugh, shake her head, and roll her eyes.

We began building our new home in the spring of 2004. I loved everything about the building process and did much of the work on the house by myself throughout the summer. At one point, I worked for three solid days, laying a stone floor with a centerpiece portion of granite. On the third day, I had worked for more than nine hours, lifting those heavy stones by hand, positioning them, mixing my own mortar, and laying each piece while on my knees. I was finally ready to put the last piece, the beautiful granite centerpiece, in place. I reached over and picked up the heavy piece of granite, and as I was about to put it down, I heard a sudden snap and felt a searing pain shoot through my back. I fell face first right on top of the granite, barely able to move. The pain was unimaginable, unlike anything I had ever before experienced.

I heard a sudden snap and felt a searing pain shoot through my back.

Fortunately, I had my cell phone, so I called Lita, and she immediately raced to the construction site. She found me still sprawled on the floor. Lita slowly and carefully helped me into the car, and she drove straight to the emergency room at our local hospital. The doctors there did all sorts of x-rays and found that my L5 vertebra was destroyed; there was no cartilage around it, and it was now a bone rubbing against another bone. My sciatic nerve was fully pinched. All the years of skateboarding, surfing, and mistreating my body had set me up for failure. Moving all that granite was simply the last straw.

The doctors told me that I could either have surgery to fuse my vertebrae, or I could try a new German experimental program using technology designed to stretch my back, or I could just live with the pain. In any case, there were no guarantees of improvement, much less success.

I didn't want anyone cutting on my body, so I decided to give a chiropractor friend a shot at me. For the next eight months, I went to him for treatments almost every day—and the treatments weren't cheap. I was frustrated and disappointed and a bit angry with God for allowing me to go through this torture. Prior to this time, I had never been sick a day in my life, but now I was practically living in doctors' offices.

About that time, I discovered I had another health problem. Growing up in Jacksonville Beach and owning a surf shop along with my brother, I had spent more than thirty years in the sunshine. Fair-haired and with ruddy, fair skin, I probably should have covered my body when I was out in the elements. But throughout the 1960s and well into the late 70s there was no such thing as sunscreen or sunblock. We used only body oils to enhance our tanning and browning experience. We were not attuned to the dangers of long-term sun exposure. I'd slap a bit of zinc oxide on my nose and on my bottom lip and head for the beach. I'd never heard of melanoma, much less worried about it.

Consequently, by the time I was forty years old, my bottom lip and my nose were the only two places on my body where I didn't have cancerous cells forming. Suddenly, by fifty years of age, it seemed as if the warranty on my body had expired.

It seemed as if the warranty on my body had expired.

In October 2004, at the same time that I was receiving weekly treatments for my back problems, I was also frequenting a skin specialist's office to have the cancerous cells removed. Most of the problematic cells were on my face and shoulders. Then one week, the skin specialist called and said, "You need to come in to the office ASAP."

I could tell by the tone of his voice that he wasn't kidding. "Why, Doc? What's up?"

"Remember that last week we took a biopsy on some of those troublesome cells?"

"Yeah..." I didn't want to remember.

"I found something."

"What do you mean, 'You found something'?"

The doc was reluctant to reveal too much information on the phone, but finally I convinced him to give me a hint as to why he was so adamant that I head to his office at that moment. "The cancer has gone internal," he said straightforwardly, "and we need to do some emergency surgery. I need to cut some things out, because the melanoma could be spreading at a rapid rate. We can take you to the hospital, but I have a surgical room here at the office. I think we can take care of you right here, but we need to do it now."

"You gotta be kidding."

"I'm not kidding, Brig. Pack a bag and get in here as soon as you can."

I told Lita, and we were both in shock. Understand, I'm a believer. I believe God created my body, and He knows how to fix it. While I have the greatest respect for people in the medical profession, I know that God is my healer, not a doctor. So when the doc said we had to operate and we had to operate now, I thought, *Oh, this was not what I was planning on doing today. This isn't how things are supposed to work.*

Nevertheless, we hurriedly got some things together and headed over to the doctor's office. We were a bit taken aback by the urgency of the situation but by no means scared. Panicked, maybe. Scared, no. Regardless,

I watched in disbelief as the surgical knife slit through my skin.

we didn't take the proper time to think and pray through our decisions. We simply reacted and followed the doctor's instructions. (If you get a negative diagnosis in your life about anything, I suggest you get a second opinion.)

Once I was on the operating table, the doctor administered some anesthetic so I could remain awake and watch what he was doing. Then he took out a purple marking pen and drew on my side, sketching an area about the size of my cell phone or a six- to eight-ounce filet.

"What's that?" I asked.

"We have to cut that much," the doctor replied. "The spot may be small, but melanoma often spreads and has tentacles that go wide and deep. We have to make sure we get all the growth so it doesn't continue to spread."

I watched in disbelief as the surgical knife slit through my skin. I couldn't feel anything because of the anesthetic, but he cut so deeply, I barely even bled. In a matter of minutes, he had cleaned out the cancerous cells lurking below my skin. I knew my face was white as snow. Lita's eyes looked as big as saucers. We both watched in amazement and horror.

As the doctor was stitching my side back together, he said, "Now, for the next one—"

"Whoa! The next one? What do you mean 'the next one'?"

"Brig, the cancer has spread and has gone in a few areas where the sun doesn't shine. We've got to go there also."

"Wait a minute," I said. "Sew me up. We're not doing this."

"You have to do something."

"Maybe so, but this isn't it."

Lita and I left the doctor's office, went home, and called our naturopathic doctor. When we told him what had just happened, the doctor was deeply concerned. "You didn't let them cut on you, did you?" he asked immediately.

"Well, yeah, I did."

"You will need to get here to Orlando as soon as possible."

That's all we needed to hear. Lita and I were in Orlando the next day.

When the doctor examined me, his facial expression told the story.

"It's pretty bad," he said soberly, "but we can take care of this naturally rather than through surgery." He prescribed an all-natural medicine protocol for me. He also suggested a diet loaded with fruits, vegetables, herbs, and supplements. I agreed to take them because I had seen the difference the natural nutritional approach had made in Lita's health.

"Your body needs more antioxidants," the doctor told me, "and we need to fight off this inflammation. That's all that cancer is, and we can beat this cancer from the inside out."

I nodded in agreement, thinking, *No problem. I can do that.*

"Your diet has to change, Brig," the doctor continued. "And we have to strengthen your immune system." The doctor suggested that I should especially start eating fruits and vegetables that were high in antioxidants as well as having good nutritional value.

Back home, we went to the grocery store and found apricots, pomegranates, prunes, and all sorts of other fruits and vegetables. I ate as much as I could stand. I quickly realized that peeling pomegranates was not something I wanted to do every day for the rest of my life. The next day, I called the doctor: "Doc, I have good and bad news."

"What's the good news?"

"The good news is that I found all those fruits and vegetables that you recommended. And I ate them today."

"Great! What's the bad news?"

"The bad news is that I am going to die! If eating prunes and pomegranates is what it's gonna take for me to live, then it looks like I'm gonna die. I'm not willing to do this. Real men don't eat that stuff!"

The doctor was a cool kind of guy, so he offered me an alternative. "Go online and see if you can find those same fruits and vegetables in some sort of puréed form. I'll give you the combinations that will make them more palatable, and you can drink the fruits and vegetables rather than eat them."

My son Paul helped me go online and Google puréed fruits and vegetables. I was a bit overwhelmed. There were more than ten thousand sources of puréed fruits and vegetables! Where was I to start? How would I know which were good or bad?

In late 2004 I called my friend Tim Wilson, who had been working with me in North Carolina on the development of a Believers Network. Tim is a great researcher and had the patience to find the products that might hold some special value for me. He was commissioned to find the fruits or veggies with the most nutritional value and those that had the highest antioxidants I could drink.

Within a few days, Tim called and said, "I've found three or four companies and products that I think you might be interested in checking out."

Tim and I discussed these products and companies. Always the consummate entrepreneurs, our discussion expanded regarding our doing some marketing for them if we found a product we really liked. We scheduled appointments to visit the companies that piqued our interest.

Within days, Tim, Lita, and I booked flights to Phoenix-Scottsdale, Arizona, and Salt Lake City, Utah. We visited four companies, interviewed their executives, and sampled their products. The first was a company in Scottsdale that was marketing an aloe-based product. Then we stopped in Phoenix to visit Vemma Corporation, a company highlighting an exotic fruit that claimed unique and special attributes. We then visited a company in Utah marketing the Tahitian Noni product. To be honest, none of the products that we sampled had the research to support their claims. Moreover, we disliked the taste of the three products we sampled.

Our last stop was to Monarch Health Sciences Corporation, primarily known as a distributor of diet and weight-loss supplements. They were just finishing up their research on a new nutritional beverage they called MonaVie, a blend of nineteen exotic fruits, with the acai berry leading as the crown jewel of the product.

The first three companies we visited were quite impressive. The owners of the companies were gracious and most accommodating to us. Their office buildings were modern and magnificent, with perfectly manicured lawns, and their production facilities were top notch. Then there was Monarch Health Sciences. Thank the Lord for meager beginnings, and please, oh please, don't ever judge a book by its cover. If we had, we wouldn't have even gone inside the place. A modest little 1970s edition two-story office building and warehouse contained the fledgling Monarch Health Sciences and its products. Lita, Tim, and I looked at one another as if to say, "What in the world are we doing here?" We almost turned around to exit the parking lot without even going inside the building.

"We're here," Lita said. "We might as well go in."

We went inside the dimly lit, drab office space of Randy Larsen, Henry

Marsh, and Dallin Larsen. Dallin was the cofounder, CEO, and president of the company. We guessed that he was also the chief cook and bottle washer too. It was a tiny operation, and I could tell from Lita's expression that we probably wouldn't be staying long.

But beware of these kinds of settings. There was a jewel in the place, and we were about to meet him.

We introduced ourselves to Henry and Randy, exchanged pleasantries, and then met Dallin. We were pleasantly surprised with his demeanor. He was warm, friendly, bright-eyed, and very articulate. There was a neat presence about this confident, blue-eyed, middle-aged guy.

Meeting Dallin Larsen would soon prove to be a divine appointment. Within a few minutes of our meeting, he began to outline his plans for the company's future. He told us a bit about their history, their past and present product line, and of course their new addition to their family of products: a unique nutritional beverage called MonaVie, a fruit juice that was a blend of nineteen exotic fruits and based around acai berries found in the rain forests of Brazil.

Meeting Dallin Larsen would soon prove to be a divine appointment.

Dallin was talking my language. One of the main reasons I had included Dallin's company on my list was his involvement with acai berries. I had been aware of this special berry from the Amazon for quite some time. I was first introduced to acai berries during my business trips to Brazil while building my Amway business there. The Brazilians—especially the folks living near the Amazon—were wild about this berry. They consumed it in many forms up to three times a day as a staple of their diet.

I also knew the berries were grown only atop a certain type of tree indigenous to the Amazon. It was no small feat to harvest anything from the Amazon, much less get it out of the country to an international market. "How did you guys get permission from the Brazilian government to do all this?" I asked.

Dallin gave us a sample of his new product, a delicious purple juice that seemed to have a slight grit to it.

"Wow, that's delicious!" I said. "If it is as good for you as it tastes, you've got something here."

Dallin explained that the texture was due to more than a dozen puréed fruits. He took us on a tour of his small production facility and explained the flash freeze-dried process they were using to capture the acai berry's nutritional benefits. "This is what makes the difference between our product and our competitors'," he told us. The patent was still pending on that unusual process, and we knew that once he could capture the legal rights to the process, no other acai product could compare. (MonaVie was granted the unique patent in 2009.)

Dallin also showed us the many vitamin supplements and weight-loss products they were marketing. We were not impressed with the line of weight-loss products and supplements he showed us, but this special purple juice piqued our interest.

Lita and I were not interested in visiting Monarch Health Sciences in order to get involved in the business side of it. Tim and I had some interest, since we are both networking entrepreneurs, but we weren't there to get involved with some guys from Salt Lake City we didn't know. My primary interest was to find a product

This special purple juice piqued our interest.

that would bring me back to better health. I had three great kids at home and a wonderful wife. I didn't want my life to end at such a young and tender age. Sure, I had read in the Bible that Adam had lived for 930 years, Noah for 950 years, and Moses had lived for 120 years. All I wanted was to at least get into my sixties and enjoy life with my family and dear friends. I had worked hard and wanted to be free to do whatever God wanted me to do. I liked Dallin, but we were more focused at the moment on what this product could do for me.

Dallin did not know my background, nor did he know of my recent closure with the Amway business or my networking experience. He had no idea of my passion to reach people through what I referred to as the Marketplace Ministry, to which Lita and I had felt called. He seemed to be a straight-up kind of a guy, and we were impressed with his company and this new product he was taking to market.

Lita and I also were impressed with Dallin's sincerity and his passion for his product, as well as his passion for the networking industry. When Dallin shared with us his own experiences in network marketing, having endured some of the same sort of disappointments that we had, we knew that we had found a kindred spirit. Later, as we got to know each other a bit better, I discovered that Dallin also possessed a keen ability to pick up

A divine appointment with divine new friends and associates:
Karree and Dallin Larsen, founder and president of MonaVie

on my Brigisms, those principles and sayings that have become such a part
of me.

"If I ever do another network," I told Dallin, "it will be the last thing
for the last time."

"Last thing, last time," Dallin mused. "I like that."

"Yep, it's time for me to move from success to significance," I said, reit-
erating a theme of Bob Buford's book *Half Time.*

"Success to significance," Dallin repeated. "Yes, that's the goal."

I took home a case of four bottles of Dallin's juice. On Monday morning, I poured myself a large glass of this purple juice. At the time, the bottle
didn't have any instructions on the label as it does now. The recommended
usage was two ounces in the morning and two ounces in the evening. Since
I liked the taste of the juice, I drank an entire bottle—twenty-four
ounces—in two days. Hey, it was *fruit* juice, and it tasted delicious. (I believe that anything worth doing is worth overdoing!)

I experienced two unusual results almost immediately. Within forty-
eight hours, I felt no back pain. Remember, I was living with chronic pain
from a pinched sciatic nerve and had been going to a chiropractor's office
weekly for eight months with little success. So this result was totally
unexpected.

But I hadn't bought the juice for my back pain. I had sought out
Dallin Larsen's product to help build up my immune system and provide
my body with the antioxidants I needed to help my system fight off the

cancer that was gnawing at my body. Yet within forty-eight hours my back pain was mysteriously gone!

Keep in mind that I am a man of faith. I believe that Jesus not only healed people in biblical times, but that His power is available to heal people today. Lita and I had been praying that God would heal my body, so when I awakened two days later and didn't feel the incessant pain in my back, I immediately started praising God.

"Lita! Guess what?" I said as I shook her next to me. "God healed me!"

"You're nuts," Lita groaned and rolled away from me.

"No, I'm serious!" I shouted. "Look at this!" I bounded out of bed and started bouncing all over the room. "I'm dancin'! I'm walking! I don't feel any pain!"

Lita sat up in bed and looked at me in amazement. She acknowledged that something really had happened to me.

We were both astounded by what was going on. I certainly gave no credit to the juice for what had happened. Anything that tasted that good in that short time period could not have anything to do with my new and improved condition. Or could it?

THAT WAS on a Wednesday, and I functioned that entire day without any pain. I gave my mom a bottle of Dallin's product. Our kids tasted the juice and liked it in smoothies, so they downed another bottle. I gave my fourth bottle to one of my neighbors. By Friday I was out of the product, although I had already ordered another shipment that was due to arrive at any time.

In less than ninety minutes my back pain was gone.

That same day, I began to notice a few kinks in my back again. The pain wasn't as bad as previously, but occasionally it caused me to flinch. I knew from studying the Bible that God doesn't heal and then unheal a person later, so I wondered, *What's going on here?*

I had not attributed any healing virtues to the juice.[8] In fact, I prepared to visit the chiropractor again.

About one o'clock that Friday afternoon a delivery service showed up with three cases of the MonaVie juice. I didn't even bother to chill it. I quickly opened a bottle and slugged down about eight ounces. In less than ninety minutes my back pain was gone. On a scale of one to ten, with ten meaning intense pain, I had gone from a seven to a zero!

I sat down on the steps and was sipping some more juice when Lita saw the puzzled expression on my face and asked, "What are you doing? What's happening?"

"Baby, sit down," I said, patting the stair beside me.

"What's wrong?"

"My back pain is completely gone."

"You gotta be kidding!"

I explained to her what had just happened over the last hour and a half. I shared with her that I felt my back pain dissipate after drinking the juice. I reached out for Lita's hand and drew her down to the step beside me. "Sit down. Guess what?"

"What?" she eyed me cautiously. Of course she was happy for me and thrilled to see me relieved of my awful discomfort. But it was my next statement that really got her attention.

I looked her in the eye and said, "We're going to be rich!"

Lita laughed and said, "Brig, we're already rich."

"No, I mean *really* rich, the kind of rich that makes even believers jealous of it! I believe we have found something very special, and we owe it to the multitudes to tell them about this. With this unique product and my big mouth, you know what we can do."

She laughed again and playfully pushed me away as she got up and went back to the kitchen, but I could tell that she knew I was serious. And I was! This was one of those moments when you just plain know that you know. Opportunity and readiness had just met.

I was also intrigued. I wanted to understand why this elixir called MonaVie had this effect on me, so I called one of the lead doctors on Monarch's medical board, Dr. Ralph F. Carson, the doctor who had studied and researched the acai berry and other natural foods. I told Dr. Carson what I had experienced. "Why would that happen?" I asked.

He didn't seem surprised. I could tell Dr. Carson was cautious about making any healing claims for the product, but he briefly outlined the benefits of the glucosamine in the juice and suggested that as an explanation.

"But Doc, I've been taking large doses of glucosamine in capsules the size of horse tablets! And I have yet to see any pain reduction in the months I have been taking them."

"Brig, drinking the juice and getting the glucosamine in a liquid form, sublingually, is a much quicker and more effective way of entering your system. It is like a direct shot to the pain. That is probably why you have experienced such marvelous results."

"Okay," I said. "I'll keep drinking it, and let's see what happens."

CHAPTER **16**

Restored Hope

I KNEW I HAD found something special. I held a bottle of MonaVie in my hands, eyeing it suspiciously, wondering whether it was a miracle elixir or snake oil—or something else. While staring at the bottle, I mentally reviewed my back pain and recounted the attempts I had made to alleviate it. When I went to find treatment for my ailing lower back condition, I received three options.

One, I could undergo surgery to fuse the two worn vertebrae together. That was out—no more skiing, surfing, or snowboarding as I knew it. The second option involved a German technology that I likened to a modern-day stretch rack. The doctors suggested three to six months of treatments that would cost a small fortune, and they couldn't (or wouldn't) guarantee that the technology would achieve the results for which I was hoping. Moreover, there was a backlog of patients and a three-month wait to even get scheduled to use the equipment. (And you know how I feel about waiting!) The third option was to continue the chiropractic route, taking some medication and receiving treatments four to five days a week and just doing therapy so it would alleviate some of the pain. All the while, I would be unable to do any kind of exercising or participate in the sports that I so much enjoyed.

I decided to go with the third option, all the while believing for a miracle. Even as I sat there pain-free after trying MonaVie, I wondered how many other folks were in similar predicaments. Clearly, I was not the only person who suffered from such excruciating back pain. Maybe this juice could help some other people too.

✦   ✦   ✦

DESPITE BEING enthralled with Dallin Larsen's sincerity, Lita remained skeptical enough to do her homework. She sent a sample of the juice to our naturopathic doctor, and he responded enthusiastically. "How did you get a live product in a bottle?" he asked.

I didn't know what he meant by that, but Lita understood that the doctor was impressed with the enzyme content of the juice. The doctor also mentioned that this product was good for everyone from ages eight to eighty-eight and any and all blood types. Now I was really excited. I like it when you find something of value that can be marketed to the masses. Yeah!

"Let's do this," Lita said to me, referring to Dallin's juice.

That's all I needed to hear. We agreed that if Dallin could move the company's focus to the juice, we'd invest our time and energy in promoting it.

Lita and I had discussed all sorts of other business options, most of which were the traditional models. All would demand substantial time and investments of money, not to mention the risks we'd face with each and every one of them. When we actually analyzed and compared all of our options, it

I knew I had found something special.

was plain to see that the networking industry was once again the out-and-out winner. It required little to no investment on our part, no great learning curve, working on our own schedule, and allowed us to choose with whom we would do business. Perfect. Not to mention many well-known economists were predicting the next two hottest trends: health and wellness and home-based businesses. I had hit the jackpot, so to speak. The real estate boom, the dot-com era, and now health and wellness. The baby boomers were dictating the trend, demanding, as usual, products that are fast, cheap, and good. I felt as though the MonaVie product could be all that and more for folks who were looking for a natural alternative to the high costs of traditional medicine. Why not this product? Why not now? A vast number of folks were looking to supplement their incomes as the economy began to dip. Why not us? We were looking. We were ready to take the plunge.

I've heard it said that opportunity strikes maybe twice in a person's lifetime, and where opportunity and readiness meet is a place that determines success. Lita and I felt as though we were in the right place at the right time with the right product.

We decided to get involved with Dallin and Monarch Health Sciences, but all the while we would lobby him to simplify his business model and focus fully on marketing the juice alone. We told him our intentions and enrolled in the business. We very simply let him know that we believed he had something in MonaVie that was quite special. I also declared to him that if the anointing of God was still on my life to do this again, this would be huge. If not, he would not hear much from me in the future.

We set a goal to involve a number of folks quickly and to build our business as swiftly as we could. Our plan was to develop some momentum and then just fuel the fire in those folks. We certainly got the attention of the owners by underpromising on our commitments and overdelivering on our results.

It would have been easy to go home and share this newfound opportunity with some of the top performers I'd known from my former business organization, but Lita and I decided not to go that route. Instead, we returned to Florida with a different game plan. If this product was as good as I thought it was, then we would attract people into the business on the merits of the product alone.

We formed a strategy: Drink It, Feel It, and Share It. We decided to place the product with friends, neighbors, and some of our acquaintances and let them decide on their involvement based on their results from drinking the product. Of course we also called some of our closest friends, folks with whom we had long-standing close relationships, and most of them got involved in the business based almost entirely on our friendship and the credibility we had with them. Lita and I were going to do this, so some of our friends decided they were going to do it with us before they knew any details on the product or the business. We were excited about what we had found, and that excitement was contagious. Our enthusiasm actually moved our friends to get into business with us. That is trust, and that sort of trust does not come easily to anyone. You have to demonstrate and extend that kind of trust before you can expect that kind of faith and trust from someone else.

Lita and I signed up a few folks just by sharing our excitement about what the product had done for us and what it might do for them. Thirty-nine dollars and a couple of cases of product? No big deal. Some folks got in simply to appease us. That was fine. "Drink the product," I encouraged them, "and if you see any results, let me know." I knew in time if they would drink the product, things would happen for them.

We decided to share MonaVie with anyone who might be looking for better health—physically or financially. We started with some of our neighbors since we had only recently moved into a new neighborhood. These were people we barely knew. We gave a bottle each to about a dozen folks as housewarming gifts, along with a message of welcome to the neighborhood. All of the neighbors wanted to know who we were and what we did for a living, so it was a natural approach. Seven of the twelve neighbors responded within the week, telling Lita or me stories about what the product had done for them and inquiring how they could get more of it.

So Lita and I simply invited those seven people to our home for what we called a home tasting party. There was no hype or sales pitch about the product or the business. We simply shared basic information on the product, where it came from, and how to get more of it. The folks attending our home tasting each shared how their bodies were reacting to the juice. They enthusiastically testified to the results they were experiencing since being introduced to MonaVie. Everyone seemed excited about the product and what it possibly could do for others. Right then and there, all seven individuals decided to register and get involved in the business.

> **"Drink the product, and if you see results, let me know."**

With the handful of friends that I influenced to get into the business, along with my neighbors, we were off and running within a few weeks. We had created a wave of excitement.

The following week, that original 7 people returned with some prospects, and we had 26 folks in our home. Each of them had shared the benefits of drinking the product with their friends before bringing them to our home to learn more about the opportunity. That's the way networking works: one person tells another who tells another. Those 26 folks at our house soon multiplied into 68 prospects and then 126 prospects. The idea of having MonaVie tasting parties, inviting a group of people to sample the product and hear about the business opportunity, was born.

I told Lita, "Baby, it looks like the anointing of increase is still on us. We're going to make this happen in a big way. It's going to take some time and some work, but we have to tell the world about this."

WE COULD hardly believe the results people were experiencing after drinking the product. Everyone, it seemed, had some amazing story about what the MonaVie product had done for them. The company made no healing claims for its product; the tasty nutritional blend was nothing more than fruits in a bottle. In fact, the company discouraged distributors from giving testimonies about healing. Some of the testimonies were so audacious I was careful not to repeat them. But I couldn't deny that the majority of folks were experiencing some amazing effects: more energy, more and better focus, sleeping better, improved skin conditions, and all sorts of pain dissipating from their bodies. Indeed, their faces seemed to glow. Their eyes were bright with enthusiasm for this product and, in some instances, for life itself again. MonaVie, with acai berries and other fruits, was causing a major stir. People were drinking it, feeling it, and sharing it. Lita and I continually were amazed. We knew we had our hands on something very special. This was going to be *huge!*

This was going to be *huge!*

Within a relatively short period of time, we had created quite a buzz about the MonaVie product and the opportunity in Jacksonville and the north Florida area. We enrolled a couple thousand people in our organization at an astonishing rate. Good news travels fast, and success really does breed success.

Lita and I decided we needed to capitalize on this. We were putting in some serious sweat equity, and we realized that we had struck gold in this opportunity. We approached Dallin to consider allowing us and several associates to acquire a piece of the rock, so to speak. We suggested he offer stock to some of the pioneers in their business as a reward for blazing the trail. True to the character of Dallin and his management team, they agreed to our suggestion.

In the meantime, Lita and I mortgaged a beach property to get some quick cash and decided to lobby for a larger position with the company. We had far outproduced the original twenty thousand distributors who had enrolled prior to us, so there was certainly a case in our favor to consider such a suggestion.

After some deliberation and discussion, the Monarch corporate board accepted our contributions and made available a special stock offering to all of their top producers that first year and granted each of us some rather gracious stock options. Lita and I took the plunge and went all in.

Now with some skin in the game and an incentive to really grow the company, we focused on moving forward. We rolled up our sleeves, put our heads down, and went to work, holding tasting parties at every opportunity we could.

I ALSO went to work designing some support tools to assist the new distributors that were engaged in building their businesses. I knew the value of having that kind of information available to all the new prospects coming in. I had an innate ability to take something complicated and make it simple enough for others to understand.

We had done this before, and we knew that having a systematic way of building the business would help others to progress much more swiftly. We say it this way: reliable information permits progress. We began communicating everyone's efforts. Systems are always birthed out of necessity in any industry for the sake of order. But unlike most support systems that merely teach how to build the business, we knew the importance of teaching people about the value of attitude and building up the whole person.

Within two years of joining forces with MonaVie, in early 2007 I formed a company known as R3Global, a support system that would make available all the teaching and training materials needed to understand the what, why, and how of building a successful network. R3Global was characterized by three principles: restoration, revival, and restitution. Why those three elements?

As I thought about developing this new system, my mind went back to an experience in Puerto Rico in 2000, where God had led me to the biblical account of Isaac's digging new wells. At that time, God had promised that if I were obedient, diligent, and faithful in what He was leading me to do, He would restore, revive, and bring restitution to me. I didn't understand then what God was revealing to me. Now, seven years later, it all made sense. God was restoring Lita and me—our physical bodies as well as our reputations and our finances. He was reviving us spiritually as well as reviving our relationships with friends and former business associates, and yes, He wanted to bring financial blessing to us, not simply pay us back for what we had lost, but bring restitution, in which we were even more blessed than we had been previously!

I saw clearly that, for Lita and me, MonaVie was our third well: the broad place with room enough for all. The blessings God wanted to pour out on us were not for our family alone; they were for the untold numbers of people we wanted to share this with and through. One thing about an abundant mentality: there is no lack in God's kingdom but there is plenty for all. Your success would not impede mine, and mine would not interfere with yours. Quite the opposite, by working together, we all could be blessed.

I saw R3Global as our fourth well, the one in which God promised Isaac that He would bless him and his descendants. In that fourth well, I recognized the fulfillment of God's promise to Lita and me, that we would finish what we started years earlier: to touch the world for Him through us in our business. This is how the body of Christ is built, one person reaching out to another with their gifts and talents and doing it as unto the Lord. By doing this, we would draw on His favor, all the while equipping the saints as we went. This is where the power of one comes in. One times God is infinite. When He and you are in agreement, who can stand against you? Don't you think that when your motive and intent are correct and pure to honor Him and help his people that God will get involved and bless you? He will, if you will just invite him to lead, guide, and direct you. The world has yet to see what God can do through the person who cares more about others and less about getting the credit. Humility is a wonderful virtue when you want to build a people business.

One person reaching one, who then reaches out to another is the law of exponential growth that I've been so enamored with since the first time I was introduced to the concept. Seeing it applied in a practical way and seeing the power of that agreement in business had taken us to great heights of success before. Now we knew that using that concept of exponential growth for the purpose of building the kingdom of God would take us to a whole new level. We knew that what we did with this would be limitless. It would only be limited by our willingness to share with others.

As for the three R's, I envisioned God doing a mighty work of *restoration* through R3Global and MonaVie, not just for my family and me, but for anyone who would choose to join us. I believed that just as God had blessed Isaac and restored Israel in our generation, He could do something similar in our lives, pumping new life into us and even restoring our hopes, dreams, health, relationships, and finances. I was convinced that as we purposed to prosper spiritually, we also would prosper in all other areas of our lives.

On a personal level, I believed God would restore my relationships with many of the people whom Lita and I loved. I also believed He would restore my position in my chosen career, relational marketing. In doing so, my joy and peace would also be restored, not to mention my health, just as He had restored Lita's health.

The second R in R3 stands for *revival.* I believe God showed me, as He restored us in all areas, that He would bring revival in the process. Revival means new life. I truly believe God would use us in and through our businesses to bring that opportunity to the folks we would share with, one at a time. I truly desire to see people live life to the fullest.

By sharing the good news with them as we built our businesses, we would be offering so much more than just another business opportunity. I envisioned our being a part of a real revival, not just a sign on a church or billboard, but the type of spiritual renovation that transforms the fabric of society, the kind of revival that our world so desperately needs. People are afraid, confused, angry, disappointed, frustrated, depressed, and hopeless. Who, in that state of being, wouldn't want a chance at a new life? A great awakening precedes a great revival. People in our society are getting a wakeup call as to where their security lies. I sincerely believe the timing of what we are doing couldn't be better.

Restitution, the third R in R3Global, is something that took a bit of explanation for some to understand. Who has not lost something or someone they valued? Have you lost something that was rightfully yours through some ordeal that was not of your making? The loss of a close relationship before its time is come hurts and hurts deeply. Restitution causes lost things to come back to you, making the situation better than it was before. How? Doing it the way God directs us to do it. The Bible says: "Do not resist an evil person. If someone strikes you on the right cheek, turn to him the other also. And if someone wants to sue you and take your tunic, let him have your cloak as well."[9] Wow! This takes faith to obey and do with the right attitude and spirit. We all have experienced these situations in our lives and usually failed miserably at applying these principles.

Over time I have come to see the absolute necessity of following God's instruction manual, the Bible. Instead of repeating the same cycle of hurt, frustration, and even anger, we have learned over time to respond in the way God has instructed us, and that has taught us an invaluable lesson. We don't bicker and complain about those horrid situations; we pray, turn them over to the Lord, and believe that He will intervene in those certain cases.

There is a sevenfold principle in connection with restoration (and vengeance as well). The Bible says, "Yet when he [the thief] is found, he must restore sevenfold."[10]

I believe God does this. When the devil comes to kill, steal, and destroy, God has set forever in eternity that you must get back sevenfold. He will restore you in a better way than you were at first, and then He will increase and multiply what was stolen. That's our God, and He is good! Who doesn't want restitution in all things?

There was a proviso to that promise, though: God would do His part as long as I did not bear grudges or hold any animosity in my heart toward the people who have wronged me.

This is where we needed faith to carry us through. If you want God's blessing in your life, you must learn to forgive, which means that you have to bless those people who offended or hurt you; you must speak well of

---

SUCCESS PRINCIPLE FOR LIFE

As long as you continue to hold grudges and nurse unforgiveness in your heart toward those who have wronged you, you cannot fully receive God's blessings in your life. To have open arms ready to hold the fullest capacity of what God wants to give you, there must be a letting go of anger, pride, and every form of bitterness. We have to become the kind of vessels that can contain this kind of overflow.

them. You can't do that on your own willpower, at least not for long. You'll need God's help.

WHILE THE three R's were the spiritual roots out of which R3Global would grow, I designed the system to support individual distributors in seven practical areas called the Seven Pillars:

1. **Teaching**: Making available reliable information and knowledge to replicate the model of success we had built. Providing the teaching in whatever format was desired, including personal presentations, books, manuals, audio materials, CDs, DVDs, digital downloads, and live and archived webcasts. A key to success in a networking business is to teach teachers to teach other teachers how to teach.

2. **Training**: I often say, "You teach people, but you train dogs." Real training in network marketing is taking someone by the hand and walking him through a step-by-step process to understand how to get the desired results. In other words, you teach them by showing them. Repetition is the father of learning. Show someone how to set a goal, how to build a list of prospects, and how to contact and invite people to become part of the business. In networking, people will learn from what you tell and show them.

3. **Motivation**: Everyone needs encouragement, so motivation is a key factor we focus on in order to move a person emotionally. People make emotional decisions to do what they do. Rarely do they make a totally logical decision to become involved in network marketing. People are motivated by seeing and hearing from others who faced challenges in their lives and overcame them. People love the underdogs who make it. We teach "read, listen, and participate" to succeed. Folks get motivated when they are constantly exposing themselves to positive information that reinforces their belief in themselves: "I can do it!" We will use audio materials, DVDs, Internet resources, webcasts, magazine articles, and our own magazine, *The Treasure Chest*, to applaud people in the business who are doing well and to keep the goal in front of any of our distributors who are struggling. Recognition is essential in motivating folks. Men die for it and babies cry for it. Recognition is a valuable tool in our arsenal to produce winners.

4. **Inspiration**: Motivation is an "outside job," so to speak, but inspiration is an inside job, reaching and touching the heart of an individual. Leadership is nothing more than inspired influence. You've probably

heard the oft-quoted, "People don't care how much you know until they know how much you care." This is true. So I created New Life Network to provide support for the emotional and spiritual aspects of a person. This is a game changer for me in this industry. Lita and I care tremendously for every person with whom God gives us favor and for whom He gives us responsibility. We care about their eternal soul. So we minister to that person's needs by providing resources in every area of personal concern: communications, time management, marital relationships, raising children, dealing with addictions, abuse, finances, and even mental health. We are a resource center for these precious folks. We also provide a platform for folks to share their stories of overcoming and becoming so they can inspire others to do the same. If there is one ingredient that we credit for the long-term success we have seen, it is inspiration. We are not ashamed to help folks to develop a real working relationship with, in, and through Jesus Christ.

5. **Promotional Items**: Branding is a key element to taking and showing your pride of ownership. Brand recognition is a way we use to promote our product and business to our future prospects. The more exposure we get, the more folks will become curious about our product and business. It's called advertising. For instance, we have branded MonaVie and R3G on everything imaginable, including such traditional items as clothing. Then we took branding to an extreme to reach a broader market by branding everyday items: pens, cups, padfolios, calendars, and luggage. All kinds of useful novelty items carry our name. We have learned to exploit this area by doing custom cards, flyers, car decals, and even full wraps for any vehicle, trailer, or RV. I am fanatical about promoting what we believe in. Most folks will wear and tout items that they never get rewarded for using. Major brands use you to promote their wares and reward you with nothing, except to stroke your pride. But this is your business. You promote your product, so you get the rewards.

6. **Communication**: In a people business—which is what networking is—communication is king. We live in the information age. People want real time and current information that helps them to stay informed so they can make good decisions. If we can't reach out and touch and fully connect with our distributors, we will lose them. Consequently, we use every form of communication to make and keep those connections. We make wide use of real-time communication tools so our organization can stay fresh and current. We use and make available to every distributor voice

and visual tools, including fully interactive websites, virtual teaching and training platforms, every social media available, electronic voice mail, conference call lines, webinar platforms, webcasts done from our studios, and newsletters in print and electronic forms. People want to feel connected, and we do it.

7. **A Calendar of Events**: We have created what we call "the Grid," our matrix and our infrastructure. We grid the United States and Canada and various other countries. We gather and process information regarding active distributors in each of these grids and form a matrix showing us the activity status of each area and who is creating it. We also developed an Infrastructure of Functions that supports the distributors in their gridded regional areas. We sanction and promote events locally, regionally, and nationally. These are highly formatted events that cover everything from new distributor orientations to opportunity meetings to major weekend events. These are designed to help both new and seasoned distributors to be better exposed to successful distributors in the business. These events promote synergy and a real spirit of unity as folks get to see a bigger picture of the team we created. All for one and one for all is how we build. From the beginning, we loaded our calendar with exciting, fun-filled, information-packed events that our distributors could attend. I recognized how important it is for distributors to participate in these events, not simply to glean new ideas and find new business tools, but for the camaraderie and the fellowship with like-minded individuals and families.

Our goal was to provide people with a one-stop shop so to speak, or as I like to refer to it, a complete and total support system. That system provides sound information, inspiration, and knowledge to help each distributor build confidence, character, and positive attitudes. In essence, it is a personal development system that helps everyone to prosper and see personal growth. The greatest room for improvement is self-improvement. I know that if I build the whole person, he or she will build the business. Relational marketing is all about building the relationship. You could say it

---

BRIGISM

The greatest room for improvement is self-improvement.

this way: build a friendship, and the friend will build the business. We learned that by investing in people we gained more than we bargained for:

Money is a great servant, but it is a horrible master.

balanced, successful, happy people who appreciate our commitment beyond the bottom line. Again, we are in the people business. People are the real treasure that brings eternal value to this whole effort. The system helps us to secure a legacy that will outlive us and give all who buy into it residual, ongoing growth and success. With a proven support system in place, anybody can build a successful business and learn how to manage and maintain it so it can gain a life of its own. That's what I call an ongoing and residual effect. So providing support to the whole person—body, soul, and spirit—has been our mission. As the spirit-man goes, so goes life and business.

There was an entirely different spirit in our R3G organization than in my previous network marketing experience. Yet we still encouraged people to be financially prosperous. They usually get into business with us initially for the money. It's a business, after all. They want the goodies that money can buy, both the tangible things and the intangible. But usually, once people are in the business for a while, they fall in love with the people, and what were once merely business relationships often turn into deep, lifelong friendships.

Of course, everybody wants a friend. But I have discovered that folks will stay long term and build their business because of a cause, something they internalize and make personal to them. Everybody wants to be a part of something that's bigger than themselves. They want to be a part of a cause that impacts others.

Once they make the trek to the people and the cause, the business moves from their heads to their hearts, and wonderful things begin to happen for them. Often, folks find their purpose and even their destiny, something that gives them an opportunity to really live and not just survive, to get out of themselves long enough to see the need in so many others that they can help. True freedom seems to be at the root of the reasoning to do this: freedom to choose. I'm convinced that there is no personal freedom in life without financial freedom. If you're in financial bondage, you are a servant to the lender and have very limited freedom. Money will dictate every decision you make. Money is a great servant, but it is a horrible master.

I want to promote a balance—mentally, physically, spiritually, socially—in the lives of our distributors with their families and businesses. I want to help them accomplish a more value-based lifestyle that will be more satisfying ultimately.

Lita and I encourage people to look to the Lord for their success rather than us. "We're just normal people," Lita says repeatedly. "Anybody can do what we are doing." We are not the message; we are merely the messengers. What one can do, another can do too.

And indeed, they have! This speaks volumes about the validity of this value-based support system: putting God first, family second, country and business third.

To date, we have more than forty-five Black Diamonds in MonaVie, with more than five hundred Diamonds, and the number increases each year. The Diamonds levels earn between $200,000 and 660,000 a year, and the Black Diamonds make an average income of $1.2 million to $1.4 million each year.[11] The surprising key here is that most of these folks attained this level of income within twelve to thirty-six months. In a down economy, that's not too shabby for a part-time income earned by everyday folks, most of whom have never built a networking

> **We are not the message; we are merely the messengers.**

business. Many have gone on to much higher levels and greater incomes. The vast majority of those distributors are part of the R3Global network, even though several other support systems exist within the MonaVie network of distributors.

Besides the folks who have grown wealthy in the MonaVie business, there are untold numbers of people who are prospering in their lives and their other lines of work, due to the basic principles they were taught through our support system. They heap accolades upon the R3G support system, because the wisdom they acquired through R3G has translated into success in all the other areas of their lives.

We emphasize that success, while available to all, is not automatic. People are born equal with the right to become unequal. Success is a matter of choice, not chance. MonaVie is a business, and if you want to succeed in it, you have to work hard and smart. You have do the right things and avoid the wrong. "Feed what you want to grow, and starve what you want to die," I tell people. We have already delineated most of the right steps, and it is relatively easy for anyone to replicate them, but they still require discipline and work. My formula for success is simple: Why + How over Attitude x Action + Time equals Success. Work like it depends on you and pray like it depends on God; that's a winning combination based on the scripture: "I can do all things through Christ who strengthens me."[12]

We certainly make no claims that simply because a person is a Christian that God will make them a success in any business. God made all of us free moral agents; we choose to do things our way or His. His ways are higher and have magnificent consequences when we learn to apply His wisdom. We do teach people, however, that their values will dictate their priorities and intentions. A value-based life is much more satisfying.

Feed what you want to grow, and starve what you want to die.

I KNEW early on that if we were going to be successful in MonaVie, the spiritual aspect of our business had to be strong. We were seasoned and wise enough to know that unless we build with our foundation on the Lord, we labor in vain.[13]

I called Ed and Cheryl Henderson in Georgia and said, "I want to see you. I have something important I need to share with you." That's all the information I gave them, but the Hendersons welcomed my visit.

Since the demise of our former networking marketing business and the debacle with the North Carolina ministry, New Life Network had been idle. Occasionally, Cheryl had said to Ed, "Let's get rid of all these books and ministry materials. We're not using them, and we could give them to somebody who could do some good."

"No, let's wait and see what God has in mind," Ed said. At the time, he had no idea that I had found something special with this new venture I was considering.

I sat down with Ed and Cheryl in their kitchen and told them about that circumstances that had led me to meet Dallin Larsen. "I've found what I think is going to be the great venture in my life," I told them. "I believe I have a route to actually continue what we started, but now we can go much further. I don't believe I can do it without you. I am going to need your assistance to accomplish this. New Life will have a new home."

I explained how I found the MonaVie company and product and the people behind it. I informed them that this company was in Salt Lake City and that Dallin Larsen was open to my particular method of incorporating my faith into the building of the business. He didn't feel threatened in any way by my strong convictions and zeal for the Lord. I shared about the product and the manner in which I was incorporating the systematic way of teaching people how to build their businesses. I also gave them insight as to how people were positively responding to our emphasis on R3: restoration, revival, and restitution.

Ed and Cheryl not only received my information but embraced the message personally. I sensed strongly that God had given me a renewed spirit about the networking industry and that He was going to restore us to our original positions and then take us far beyond to finish what He had started in us. I also let Ed and Cheryl know that I felt that we were about to enter into a *providential partnership* with Dallin and his team.

As I talked, I could see the reticence in Ed and Cheryl's eyes, and I didn't blame them. After all, the shock and disappointment of putting our blood, sweat, and tears into two ventures over a twenty-year period only to have the doors slam shut on us was devastating to say the least. It was no doubt heartbreaking and hurtful to see our ministry shut down. So it was back to work for them to make a living.

Ed had found a fulfilling job with U.S. Investigation Services, a company that did background searches and security clearance investigations for the military. Cheryl was a top sales person and interior decorator for a fine furniture company. They had settled into an entirely different routine than what they had been accustomed to as ministers with New Life Network.

Ed and Cheryl expressed their delight that I had found some new direction, but they remained cautious, because they were fully entrenched in their new positions. I could tell they were still in a recovery mode from our last letdown. They were always ones to ponder and cautiously consider things and to count the costs. I fully respected that about them and knew they would prayerfully consider my invitation to come back into the ministry aspect of my business venture.

One can learn more through trials than triumphs. Trust me on this: Ed and Cheryl and Lita and I can attest to great lessons we have learned through those trials. Fire refines or burns up, and we had been tempered in that refining process.

Ed and Cheryl didn't jump in as I had anticipated, but I had primed the pump. I wanted them to see, feel, and experience my excitement and enthusiasm about this new venture. I made a deposit in them and knew that, if God was in this, they would respond in time.

I told Cheryl with all the conviction I could muster, "We're going to finish what we started." The Bible says, "He who began a good work in you will carry it on to completion."[14] I also know that God is always willing to reveal His will to one who is willing to do it. Ed and Cheryl are those kind of folks. Like Lita and me, Ed and Cheryl are both driven to reach the masses for the sake of Christ.

Ed and Cheryl asked for some time to think and pray about their decision, and I agreed, but I knew in my heart that they were already working on how we could co-labor once again in this great commission. Meanwhile, they researched MonaVie online and learned more about the product. More than anything about the business, the one question Cheryl and Ed asked repeatedly was, "Are you and Lita in agreement about this? Do you both agree that you want us to come back? Are you in agreement that this business is what you feel God wants you to do?" As much as Ed and Cheryl trusted the gifts in me, they wanted to make sure that we were all on the same track, especially Lita and me.

Cheryl dove in and started reorganizing and relaunching New Life Network, both from a ministry standpoint and from a financial base. Ed continued to work at his job until New Life had enough resources to support salaries again. As MonaVie and R3Global grew, so did New Life Network. Before long, Ed joined Cheryl in full-time ministry to the network of spiritually hungry distributors.

Where there are people, there are challenges, and we were drawing lots of new folks into our organization. The needs of networkers are many and diverse. Ed and Cheryl were immediately busy with ministry opportunities, including everything from marriage and family matters to personal finances and a host of other perennial issues that New Life Network helps people to cope with and overcome.

They also are on the forefront when emergencies strike our friends in the business. Ed Aristizabal, a Black Diamond in the business, phoned me one day, and as soon as I heard his voice, I sensed a deep concern. He said, "Shelly's had a brain aneurism." I was shocked. Shelly was a vibrant mother and wife in her early forties, full of life and energy. As I do when confronted with these situations, I listened, gathered my thoughts, and then offered to pray for Shelly and Ed. As usual, I followed up by immediately calling Ed and Cheryl to rally New Life Network to prayer. We knew that the statistics were against us, that more than 90 percent of the people who suffer that type of aneurism do not survive. But we took authority over that situation and believed God for a miracle.

Not only did Shelly survive, but before long, she was active in her business again. About a month and a half after the aneurism, Ed told me the rest of the story. At the time of the aneurism, Shelly had been in the perfect place for this medical emergency: she was meeting with a bunch of doctors. She was a mere five minutes from a group of doctors who specialize in treating aneurisms. Had she been farther away, the story might have turned out much differently.

To Lita and me, and to all of us at R3Global, New Life Network is one of the most vital components of the makeup of R3Global as the total support system. Any success we have experienced in this people-helping-people industry is due in large part to the role New Life Network plays in ministering to our friends and associates. Ed and Cheryl are friends for life, and Lita and I are grateful for their believing in us and for sharing our vision as we co-labor to win the masses to Christ and raise them up to make a positive difference in this life.

CHAPTER **17**

Having Fun Again

WHEN I STARTED WITH MonaVie in January 2005, one of the first people I thought about inviting to join me was my friend Charlie Kalb. I first met Charlie in 1986 at a restaurant with some mutual friends. I was explaining a new business opportunity, and as Charlie now tells the story, he spent the first hour of our meeting telling me how great he was. Unquestionably, he commanded respect in the community as a successful Realtor, the vice president of the Rotary Club, a leading member of the Jaycees, and a mover and a shaker in a half dozen other organizations.

After a while, I looked at Charlie and commented politely but apparently with much more precision than I then realized, "You know, Charlie, if you'd take your eyes off yourself and put your eyes on other people, and be willing to help other people get what they want, you could be big in this thing."

Charlie looked back at me in amazement, as though that thought had never before occurred to him. A few weeks later, we got together again. Charlie and I struck up a friendship that has lasted for more than thirty years. We were able to shoot straight with each other from the start. I've always encouraged people in business with me to do three things if they want to be successful: read, listen, and participate. Read informative and inspiring books, listen to leaders who can point you in the right direction, and participate in functions so you can interact and rub shoulders with other like-minded people to create synergy, using all your senses to validate and support your con-scious decision to succeed. I learned the simple acronym GIGO long ago. It stands for "garbage in, garbage out." But if you put in good things, good things will come out. You are the sum total of the books you read and the people with whom you associate. I was a long-haired hippie-type and a beer-drinking surfer dude because that's who I hung around. I changed my circumstances when I decided to change who I allowed into my life. Reading, listening, and participating is the process for someone who wants to transform his thinking, which translates into a changed life.

> **If you'd take your eyes off yourself and be willing to help others, you could be big.**

"IF I were to read something," Charlie ventured during one of our first conversations, "what should I be reading?"

I put my hand on his shoulder, looked him straight in the eye, and said, "For you, I'd recommend the Bible."

Charlie appeared perplexed. "Well, there are lots of books in the Bible. Which do you recommend for me?"

"Proverbs," I replied without hesitation. "Because it is the instruction manual for life."

Charlie admitted later that although he was almost offended by my di-rectness, for some reason, he went home, found a Bible, blew the dust off it, and began to read. And his life began to change.

Charlie and his wife, Debbie, lived outside of Lake City, Florida, where in the mid-1980s housing loan interest rates went through the roof, and suddenly Charlie was close to losing his real estate business and everything he had worked to acquire during the previous fifteen years. He had been riding high, but now the props had been knocked out from under him, due to no fault of his own. No wonder Charlie's first impres-sions of me were not positive. I was having too much fun! He had worked hard all his life, yet he was sitting in that restaurant with a bleeding ulcer and his hair falling out, and I was bubbling over with enthusiasm. Charlie told me later that my jovial effervescence didn't encourage him. It made him mad!

Charlie's ego and pride were the hurdles he would have to overcome. I've heard it said that ego is a strange disease that makes everyone sick except the person who has it. I knew that Charlie's pride would contribute to his demise if he chose to hang on to it. Pride always comes before a fall. But I loved Charlie and wanted the best for him. I understood that starting a business after age forty, in the second half of his life, was not something he was too excited about. But I persisted.

"Charlie, I believe in you," I told him. "I believe you can succeed in this business."

He later told me that those words meant the world to him, because due to the downturn in the economy and the circumstances he was facing, he wasn't really sure that he believed in himself anymore. His blustery bravado and braggadocian behavior was simply a facade to hide the fact that he was afraid he might not be able to keep his family afloat much longer. With two teenagers to support, as well as Charlie's parents who lived on the same property, his burdens weighed heavily on his shoulders. He signed on with me in the network marketing business.

Debbie owned and operated her own beauty shop, and as Charlie's business crumbled around them, she worked harder to pay the bills. Charlie knew he was going to have to do something else besides real estate to support his family, but Debbie was too shell-shocked to get excited about another business venture. She didn't want to risk anything else. Her risk tolerance level had dropped off the scale. For the first few months that Charlie signed on, Debbie didn't want any part of it. But Charlie recognized that there was something special about how this business was progressing.

I knew that Charlie was hungry for a real relationship with someone who would shoot straight with him and offer a friendship that would work both ways. He poked around at enough meetings I was doing to gather sufficient insight to satisfy his curiosity about his doing this. When he finally settled in his mind that this business was really no different than what he had been doing his whole life—interacting with people and influencing them to consider something he believed in—his eyes opened to the possibility that he could make the business work for others and for himself. When he got

I was having too much fun!

started, he went for it. He set his goals, formulated a plan of action, and implemented it methodically.

Once Charlie was convinced, he was very convincing to everyone with whom he shared the business opportunity. By the end of Charlie's first year in the business, he was earning a good six-figure income, part time. He was working four or five nights a week, two or three hours each evening. Most people earn a living from nine to five. We teach that you can make a life and earn your freedom from five o'clock on. Charlie was truly a worker bee when it came to doing presentations. He racked up miles going up and down the East Coast, doing home meetings to support the folks he had sponsored. Most of those miles were traveled after working his day job until five o'clock each afternoon! Along the way, Charlie and his entire family put their faith in Jesus Christ and found a new joy in living. Before long, Debbie left her beauty salon behind and joined Charlie in his business.

Friends doing what friends do: flying in my King Air with my buddies Charlie Kalb and Frank Soucinek in the late 1980s

Lita and I invited Debbie and Charlie to visit New Life Church in Jacksonville. Charlie had attended a Lutheran church as a boy, and Debbie had grown up going to a Baptist church, so the enthusiastic worship style of New Life was a bit of a shock to their system. But they liked it! And they were intrigued by Pastor Paul Zink's teaching. Rather than condemnation for not being good enough, they heard about God's love and His deep desire to set them free from sin and draw them ever closer in a relationship with Him. They went back to Lake City and started a New Testament–style house church in the living room of their house! The church began with five couples (including Charlie's family) and grew quickly into a large congregation.

Over the next ten years, Charlie and I were like brothers. He had a gift for organizing and directing people, so he became the function director for all of my major conventions. He was so smooth in his execution of running any size function. His attention to detail was amazing to me. (That is not my gift, by the way.) I have

Most people earn a living from nine to five, but you can make a life from five o'clock on.

learned in this industry that you have to attract talent and place them in positions where they can feel that they are a part of something that matters. Somebody said, "I have learned to staff my weaknesses," and that is certainly true of me.

Charlie gained enormous respect from me; he never asked for anything for faithfully executing these duties on my behalf. He was a blessing and a necessary part of the great team we built. I always like to reward that kind of service to me and others, so I welcomed Charlie to travel with me whenever he chose to do so. We were constantly together, and we definitely traveled in style. We flew around the country in a Super King Air 300 propjet. Our ground transportation was in limos and luxury vehicles. Our East Coast road trips were done in a custom Prevost motor home. We stayed in the finest five-star resorts and hotels wherever we went. And Charlie and I simply enjoyed each other's company. We had fun, encouraged each other's faith, and had a sweet spiritual fellowship. He's been a friend who has stuck closer than a brother to me.

Charlie and I had some great talks too, solving the problems of the world as we traveled together. One night we headed from Atlanta to North Carolina with me behind the wheel of the Prevost and Charlie relaxing in the copilot's seat. We got so engaged in our conversation that we blew right past our exit and kept on driving. We drove three states away before we realized we had missed our turn!

Charlie often reminds me that he always had to make sure someone was with me when I traveled without him, otherwise I'd get lost. I'm like the cowboy who gets on a horse and rides off in six different directions. Many times people have asked me where we are going. I would answer, "I don't know, but we sure are making good time."

Once I ran a promotion for my organization and rewarded them with a cruise to the Bahamas, which departed out of Fort Lauderdale. I drove myself from Jacksonville Beach to Fort Lauderdale, but details are not my strong suit. I couldn't find my way to the ship, so Charlie somehow convinced the captain of this two-thousand-passenger cruise to delay departure for two and half hours, because I was lost in Miami and meandered all the way to Key Largo. Had I not chartered most of the cabins on the ship, the captain would have no doubt left me behind. When I drove up to the dock, I could hear the cheers of the people already on board, watching from above on the decks. Well, at least *I* thought they were cheering!

From the earliest days of our friendship, Charlie and I dreamed of our families working together in business. So when my friend Frank Soucinek told Charlie that I was looking at building another networking business, Charlie was expecting my telephone call. After all, Debbie and Charlie had been close to Lita and me throughout the building and the ultimate demise of our first networking venture.

Charlie was one of my closest confidants through the extremely tough times at the end of my Amway career. Charlie saw the good, the bad, and the ugly side of what politics did to our dream life. It's said that you really don't get to know someone when things are going well, but you do when everything hits the fan. That's when you get to know who someone is and what they are made of. During that horrendous time in Lita's and my lives, Charlie became a true inner-circle friend, someone whom I trusted completely. He epitomized one of my favorite sayings: "A friend is someone who is walking in when everyone else is walking out." He hung in there with me until the bitter end in 2000, when I separated myself from my twenty-one-year networking family and decided to move on.

Charlie remained in the business halfheartedly with some friends and associates for three or four years. He went back to selling real estate while

---

B R I G I S M

A friend is someone who is walking in when
everyone else is walking out.

Lita and I moved to North Carolina. We didn't stay in contact as much during that time, but I knew somehow we would be together again. I missed our strong Christian fellowship.

Early in 2005, I called Charlie and said, "I'm looking at something where we can help some people and make some money. Are you open to it?"

"No, I'm not interested in helping anybody else right now," Charlie replied flatly. "It's good to catch up with you, Brig, but Debbie and I have decided we've had enough of network marketing."

"I'm looking at something where we can help some people and make some money."

I was disappointed by Charlie's response but not discouraged. After all, he didn't say he wasn't interested in making money. So about six weeks later, I called him back. "Hey, Charlie, I'm looking at this thing. It's going to be huge."

Charlie looked at Debbie while I was still on the phone with him. "What do you think?" he asked her.

"Nope, not interested," she said.

Charlie spoke kindly to me. "I appreciate your calling, Brig, but we're not interested."

In May of that year, I called Charlie for the third time. I didn't know it, but Charlie recognized by then that his real estate business was stymied and stagnant. He was looking for something else to help support his family. "Hey, Charlie, this is Brig," I called as usual. "I'm looking at something, and I'm not going to do it without you. That's it. It's only thirty-nine dollars to get in, and if you don't have the money, I'll put it up for you."

"Okay, it's your money," Charlie quipped.

I could see Charlie smirking on the other end of the phone. I paid his enrollment fee into MonaVie, and he has yet to pay me back!

It took some patience and understanding on my part to wait on Charlie to get excited about the business, and it also took some persistence. Someone quipped that failure is the path of least persistence. It took six months or more, but Charlie finally engaged after seeing and hearing of the unprecedented success Lita and I were experiencing. Showing him the copies of our bonuses helped, but more important for Charlie was seeing and meeting the corporate leadership. When Charlie met Dallin Larsen, for instance, Charlie recognized there was something different in Dallin's attitude toward building a great business. Seeing

Dallin's heart toward others got Charlie's attention. Besides, Dallin and I were a winning combination, and Charlie knew it.

Charlie said, "If Brig were a racehorse, I would bet on him. He knows how to win." So Charlie decided to engage and began building his business on June 15, 2005.

Since then, he and Debbie have made millions of dollars in the business. Charlie says, "I still haven't repaid Brig that money!" But of course he has—exponentially! If you ask Charlie why he got back into business with me, he won't begin by talking about the benefits of the product or even the money he thought he could make. Charlie will talk about relationships—it is relational marketing after all—and how he wanted to renew our relationship. Working together in our newfound venture guaranteed that we'd be having fun once again.

I convinced Charlie and Debbie to go along with Lita and me to MonaVie's first ever international convention in Utah. Charlie says I duped him into going, because I told him we were going for a vacation and he found himself at a convention. But it was meant to be.

While there, Charlie met Dallin Larsen and was impressed not so much with the CEO of the company but with Dallin the person. Charlie closely observed Dallin's demeanor during the first day of the convention. Dallin stayed glued to his front-row seat, overseeing each and every speaker and activity of that convention. He wasn't acting like some self-important VIP; he was warm and friendly to everyone around him and sensitive to each person in that crowd who approached him. That got Charlie's attention big-time.

Charlie approached me on Friday night to tell me he was leaving the convention early, because he had seen enough. I was initially taken aback by that, thinking that something was wrong. But Charlie quickly dispelled that notion by saying that he'd seen all he needed to see. Charlie was convinced that Dallin cared for me and the distributors of this new venture he was launching. Charlie had wanted to know that I wasn't setting myself up for another fall with the wrong people, people who were self-centered and had wrong, ulterior motives. Charlie is a good judge of character, and he judged this one right on.

On the way home, Charlie engaged big-time. He set his goals and developed both an action plan and a plan to implement immediately. He came out of the chutes on fire!

He and Debbie put some parameters around their entry into the business, so it wouldn't take over their lives. They had a good plan for how they wanted to approach building the business. Rather than going back to the people in their former networking business and attempting to recruit them, on the plane trip back to Florida, Charlie made a list of thirty people who respected him and would trust his judgment on this new opportunity.

Back home, he went into his office on Monday and informed his real estate team that he was going to be changing direction and doing something a bit different. On Tuesday night, Charlie called eight people and signed them up in the business. On Wednesday night, he called eight more and recruited them as well. By the end of the week, the volume he had created netted him a first commission in excess of seven hundred dollars for that week alone. And he hadn't even tasted the juice yet! I had given him a bottle of the juice to try, but Charlie had given it to his mother. The people he was drawing into the business didn't really know much about the nutritional beverage; they only knew that Charlie was excited about the business possibilities. Shucks, Charlie didn't know much about the product, either! But his friends trusted Charlie's judgment; they weren't signing up because they had discovered a great product—although they would—they signed up because of their relationship with Charlie and Debbie. They were people into whose lives he had sown, and they knew he wouldn't mislead them or use them in any way. Once again, friends will always do what friends do. As Charlie and I often say, "This is relational marketing, people helping people. We are not in the juice business; we're in the *people* business." Juice doesn't move people; people move juice!

> **Charlie made a list of thirty people who respected him and would trust his judgment on this new opportunity.**

Charlie and Debbie's business skyrocketed. The following week they made a thousand dollars, and every month after, as their organization grew, their income increased. It grew exponentially for the next two years. Charlie may have started a little later than some others, but his wisdom, combined with his great work ethic, secured him a spot as one of the top seven income earners in the MonaVie business. Talk about a comeback! Charlie and I marveled as our organization recruited more than two million people, created a cumulative volume in excess of $2 billion in sales, and became the fastest company to have achieved $1 billion in sales—all in less than four years.

Charlie and Debbie reached a point in their business where they were earning over a hundred thousand dollars a week consistently by their third year in the business. Charlie insists that he wasn't doing anything special, that what he did, anyone could do. "All I was doing was identifying people who were willing to help themselves," he observed. Its not about people who you think will do this;

> **We are not in the juice business; we're in the *people business.***

its about finding a person who has a dream that he is willing to do something about. It's about hungry people looking for other people who are hungry for more in life.

Recently, I asked Charlie to describe the secrets to his rapid success. "Singleness of product made things simple," Charlie replied. "Some people may see that as a drawback, that MonaVie had only one product. But for me, it lent itself to the business being simple." Of course, it was a unique blend, and it did have a patent-pending process that ensured exclusivity. It was as good or better than anything on the market, so it was a clear and concise message that we could herald and then teach. MonaVie has since developed several other products, but we still focus on keeping things simple.

A second key to his success in Charlie's view is the binary compensation plan, rather than a unilevel plan. In networking, binary means building two legs versus many. People can become profitable quickly, because it only requires you to bring in two people. Everybody knows two folks who want better health, both physically and financially. Building a business in a binary matrix allows you to benefit not only from all those folks you personally sponsor but all those that they recruit also. This is the leveraging of your efforts through others. You benefit directly from the fruits of your own labors, but you also benefit and can actually profit-share in other people's success, even though you may not know them personally.

"The binary plan is magical," Charlie said. "It's the magic of one person touching two. Everyone knows two people."

"This is one of the simplest things I've ever done," Charlie said. "There are two basic things that have to happen for this to work: sponsor people and move the product." Since most of the people you sponsor are them-

Success and money buys conveniences like private airplanes. Flying
privately sure beats those security lines and scanners!

selves consumers of the product, you can actually focus on one activity: sponsoring people who use the product and want the benefits of it.

"It was relatively simple to build," said Charlie. "We've never coerced or deceived anyone into listening to our presentation or trying our product. We actually led with the product. 'Have you heard of MonaVie? Have you tasted it?' We drank it with them; they experienced some positive results after drinking it, and we shared our own experience with them. We have actually built this business on the merits of the product alone. It was that good. If the product didn't gain their attention up front, the feeling we got every Friday at three o'clock certainly did. That's when commissions were paid. Better health financially interested the majority that got in with us. We didn't have to hide the name of the company, and we were on the cutting edge of the health and wellness industry with an outstanding nutritional product."

This is one of the simplest things I've ever done.

What about dealing with rejection? "Any man should be used to rejection," Charlie jokes. "I got used to rejection in the real estate business. Sure it hurts, especially when it is someone you care about who turns you down. But I learned that they are not telling you no; they are telling themselves no. If you lose a real estate listing, you have to go out and talk to three to four more people for every one that you land. It's similar with any business. Some people will want in, and others won't. That's okay. Keep moving forward." We use the "SW-SW-SW-SW model: some will, some won't, so what? some will! It takes only a few who say "yes!" to build a substantial income.

CHARLIE AND Debbie regard MonaVie and R3Global as the vehicle and the platform they use to help other husbands and wives improve their relationships. They speak to thousands of people each year about how they can build their businesses, and Charlie and Debbie provide great tips for financial success, but their real passion is to help people have better marriages and families. "All the money you earn and all the accolades you receive are worthless if you lose your family in the process," Charlie says. God has honored their efforts to help families, and at the same time Charlie and Debbie have become financially free. Their son-in-law and all of our kids and grandkids are supportive or directly involved in our business. This has been a dream come true for both the Kalb and Hart families. How special is that?

AS CHARLIE and Debbie's business took off and grew, so did Lita's and my business. That's the way it works. The folks we work with are in business for themselves but not by themselves, so we all benefit from one another's efforts. Too bad the world doesn't fully understand the benefits of that structure and philosophy. It would be a much better world in which to live: people helping people to help people.

> **I teach folks not to sell but to tell.**

I love sharing with others the things that excite me or bring some kind of benefit to my life. We all do that every day of our lives. I don't try to sell anybody anything. In my business I teach folks not to sell but to tell. Share about your experience with products or services that piqued your interest.

It's similar to sharing a good movie, good book, a great restaurant, or any other product, service, or place that excites or blesses you. You just tell someone about it. That person will either respond positively with interest and want to know more about the product or not. That's not too deep, is it?

That's my industry: interactive distribution. You interact with people and end up doing some form of distribution to them. People buy into those things that you're excited about. You are simply sharing, not selling. In my business, you get paid for sharing. It's the difference between amateur networking and professional networking. One gets paid; the other gets his ego stroked. Big difference. Ego doesn't pay the bills.

When we meet people, the conversation inevitably turns to talking about what you do in life, your career, your job, or your business. Most people start by discussing the weather, sports, current events, or other people, and then finances or money issues come up. In conversations such as these, I listen for a need, and once I hear a person who wants something more, that person is a prospect for my business. It's been said that small minds talk about other people, mediocre minds talk about current events, but great minds talk about the future. That's the person I look for: the dreamer.

When I approach folks to see if they are looking, I qualify them by stimulating a conversation with what I call the FORM format. I discuss their *family, occupation, recreation,* and then *motive* or *money.* After listening to them and acknowledging their life concerns and interests, I normally chill until they ask me what I do. Or I may throw out some bait to see how they respond.

"I have stumbled into a gold mine. There is more than enough for me and my family, so I'm looking for some folks who would like to help me dig," I'll say with a twinkle in my eye. Basically I want to know whether they have anything against making some more money.

People who are looking for more in life really don't care what it is, as long as it is legal, honest, moral, and ethical. So my gold mine approach often determines the hunger factor.

"Well, hey! I'll help you dig!" they usually respond.

"Sign right here," I say. "You hold the pen, and I'll move the paper."

I like to keep things light, as people tend to take life much too seriously. It's how you make folks feel that gets to them. Make them feel good about themselves and they will like you. The people I get to like me often go into business with me.

I try to keep folks laughing at themselves and life. I will say, "Don't take life too seriously. You aren't going to get out of it alive anyway." Or, "If

---

BRIGISM

Don't take life too seriously. You aren't going to
get out of it alive anyway.

---

you are concerned only about yourself and no one else, always looking out for number one makes you step in number two!" You gotta make them laugh, because the Scripture says: "A cheerful heart is good medicine."[15]

The key to succeeding in relational marketing, however, is not the selling of particular products. Most people miss the opportunity because they assume that it's all about selling something. We are in the business of sifting and sorting, taking folks from suspects to prospects. We are people who are looking for people who are looking for something more. We teach to share it, not sell it.

I emphasize that people move product; product doesn't move people. Sponsor people, and people will move the product. Clearly, my approach is contrary to the traditional means of building a business. I emphasize that we are in the people business. I have distributors take an oath with me: "I promise I will never try to sell anything!" I teach them to let the product sell itself. If it is all that we say it is, the product will sell itself.

The key to the success of any good networking business is that you must be marketing a product or service that (1) everybody uses, (2) is easy to learn to use, and (3) is depleted (used up) and bought again. That sort of product or service will create the residual effect and ongoing sales. With MonaVie, our two billion dollars in sales within five years proves one thing: we aren't

We are looking for people who are sick and tired of being sick and tired.

that good, but the product is. So we tell distributors, let the product sell itself. Allow folks to sample it as often as possible.

The way to succeed in my industry is to focus your attention on building people and then developing relationships with them. They will build the business. If you have as good or better a product than someone else has, and you provide a better service to them than others, they will beat a path to your door. I chose to build the networks I have been in because they had superior products and extraordinary compensation plans. What the product can't do for some, the income opportunity will. Bottom line: we look for people who are sick and tired of being sick and tired and just hacking out a living. We find people who want to live life, not just survive.

The business I represent just might be the vehicle to someone's hopes and dreams. It is a business with no financial ceiling, so the opportunity for success can be unlimited. Actually, it is limited only by how you see it and by how many other folks you are willing to share it with. With more than six and a half billion people on the planet, and the population rising every day, I see a world of opportunity. People are all looking for something more. Of course, that doesn't mean they will all want to be involved in a network marketing business. But as I said previously, you only need a few to develop financial independence and freedom. In our business, I teach that three legs that you build will get you free and six legs will get you rich.

> One thing common about good and bad times is that neither lasts for long.

Early on, I came up with a simple marketing plan that I referred to as ITS: invite, taste, share. Invite people to taste the product, and then just share your MonaVie experience with them. I teach, "Never say never." Some of the best and most successful distributors I have in my organization are those who initially told me they'd never get involved in the networking industry.

"How can that be?" I hear you asking. Simple. Things change for folks. Life is constantly in flux. One thing common about good times or bad is that neither lasts for long! So some folks are ready now, some later, and some never. Go with the ones who are ready now, and stay in touch with those for whom the timing isn't yet quite right. Some people come in weeks later, some months, and some years later. You can only control what you do, so focus on who wants in now. All the others are watching. Trust me, they are watching. Go ahead and succeed without them, and you will be amazed at the respect you will earn. Many will join you in the future.

In the early days of MonaVie, we sometimes had difficulty maintaining quality control of the product. The MonaVie product consists of nineteen puréed fruits, which means the flesh, skin, and meat of the fruit, as well as the seeds, are all crushed and mixed together into a liquid form. The process that we used early on didn't have the standards and quality control we now have. The processing plants in Brazil and in the United States were developing and refining the flash-freezing process to capture the nutrients in the fruits. But in the beginning, each batch of juice seemed to hold a few surprises for us—and sometimes for some of our clients.

Occasionally, when someone was pouring the juice, the fatty acids would clog together and form small lumps in the beverage. When pouring it for our tastings, we would jest about how the fragments were leafs and twigs that got through the process. It was embarrassing, to say the least. Rather than being upset or allowing potential enrollees to be offended by the extraneous material, Holly Roush, a Black Diamond, along with her husband, Corbin, quickly learned how to turn the negative into a positive.

> "You got a leaf! Oh, they love that in California!"

"Oh, look," Holly exclaimed when someone at one of her tasting parties discovered portions of a leaf in their juice. "You got a leaf! Oh, they love that in California!"

Today, MonaVie has developed unsurpassed quality control procedures and has acquired patents on the flash-freeze process itself. I personally know the commitment that the management team at MonaVie has made to doing things with absolute excellence. That commitment to developing and producing superior products for the distributor base allows us as independent distributors to focus on what we do best: identify, qualify, recruit, engage, and teach the process of building so we can build, manage, and maintain our businesses to be both robust and profitable.

We aren't doctors and don't claim to be "juiceologists," explaining what is in the MonaVie juice or why it is so beneficial for anyone to drink. I know it has nineteen forgotten fruits in it, including acai berries, but for me to explain what it does or why it is so good for you would be like asking me what's in an apple. I don't have to know all the scientific data, and neither does anyone else in the business. We just have to know where to access it. Our websites offer all the information anyone needs to make an educated decision about the benefits of the product. We basically testify to the benefits of drinking this premiere blend to get the essential vitamins and nutrients our bodies need to function at its optimum level.

Truth is, facts and logic don't sponsor folks; they simply support the reason people believe in the product. For me, it is a simple choice: either eat the seven to thirteen servings of fruit each day that the Food and Drug Administration says is required for you to get the nutrients your body

BRIGISM

I want to die young at an old age.

needs and requires to stay fit and healthy, or drink two to four ounces of MonaVie to get the same and even better nutrients.

Most people will never go through the arduous process of finding, purchasing, and preparing seven to thirteen servings of fruit each day. Baby boomers like me want our nutrition fast, cheap, and good. MonaVie gives me the results fast, inexpensively, and in a form that is good for me. Fruits in your diet are better than all the alternatives out there. I tell people to drink it, or you may just die earlier that you want to.

Some folks say the cost—two to four dollars a day—is too expensive. I respond that you *invest* two to four dollars a day in your health. Some people spend eight to ten dollars a day on expensive coffee products. No antioxidants in that. Our product is inexpensive compared to things on which you spend money that have no lasting value. But people find the money and time to do what they choose to do. There's that choice thing again! To me, choosing to spend a few dollars a day is not expensive. Heart bypass surgery, diabetes medications, or the many medicinal regimens—now those things are expensive! I teach that I would rather apologize once up front for a higher price than spend years apologizing for poor quality. Getting ahead of the curve and taking a proactive approach to better health is the way to go. Prevention is always better than treating illness.

My goal is to die young at an old age. Quality of life? Who *doesn't* want to live a happier, healthier, and more prosperous life? As far as I know, everyone who is in their right mind should have a goal like this! That is one of the reasons I chose this particular product and company to take to market. I believe in better health: physically, financially, emotionally, and spiritually. What a great message to herald!

CHAPTER **18**

Friends Do What
Friends Do

ONE OF MY FAVORITE sayings in sharing my business with others is: "Friends do what friends do." For a good illustration of that principle, all you have to do is look at Frank and Cindy Soucinek.

On the way home from our first meeting with Dallin Larsen, Lita and I called Frank and Cindy, two of our most loyal and sincere friends. Frank and I had been friends since we met in Lake City, Florida, in the mid-1980s at an open opportunity meeting at which I was speaking. A successful businessman in the area had invited Frank to the meeting where he could meet a "wild and crazy wealthy guy expanding his business."

When I entered the room, Frank noticed the knots on my shoes, which he later realized were made from ostrich skin. "There's the wealthy guy," Frank nudged Cindy.

After my presentation that night, Frank was convinced of two things: (1) I believed in what I was doing, and (2) I genuinely cared about people. Frank was most impressed that I stayed after the meeting for about two and a half hours to talk personally with every person in the room who wanted to speak with me. When we proceeded to a local restaurant near the facility, Frank and Cindy followed with the group.

After observing from a distance, Frank approached me and introduced himself. He had listened closely to how I had talked to people about everything from their business cash flow to their eternal destination. I could tell he had something on his mind. Frank and I talked for a bit, and then he started questioning me about the subject of salvation and how a person could enter heaven. I made a few comments concerning how that works. Frank looked back at me confidently and said, "Well, I'm a pretty good person."

> **A lot of good people go to hell.**

"I'm sure you are," I assured him, looking him straight in the eyes. "But a lot of good people go to hell. Would you like to do something about changing that?" I wasn't concerned about recruiting Frank into the business; I was concerned for his eternal soul. "You can spend eternity where it's hot, or you can spend eternity in air-conditioning. Which would you prefer?"

Frank quickly picked up on my simple analogy. He bowed his head right there and invited Christ into his life.

Understand, my ability to lead people to Christ is due to the power of the Holy Spirit and the favor of God on my life, not my own brilliance or persuasiveness. God is more concerned with our *availability* than He is our *ability*. I merely make myself available for anyone ready to make a change. God had a plan for Frank and Cindy's life long before they ever met me, and God simply used me to awaken them to His Spirit and what He wanted to do in and through their lives. The Scripture says, "Let your light so shine before men, that they may see your good works and glorify your Father in heaven."[16] I use every ounce of the success with which God has blessed me to attract folks to the message He has given me. The Scripture also says that He is the vine and we are the branches, and apart of him we can do nothing.[17] I rely on the Holy Spirit to lead, guide, and direct me in conversations and actions with people. And we are a good team!

Incidentally, this also proves that God can and will use anybody and any circumstance to reveal Himself, if we just let Him. For me, that means He uses the simple things of this world to confound the wise.

✦ ✦ ✦

FOR THE next two weeks, everywhere I went to conduct business meetings, Frank and Cindy were there, watching and listening to me. Each evening, after the meeting, I noticed Frank standing close behind me, almost as though he was my bodyguard. More important, he was watching me to make sure I was the real deal, that my words and actions were consistent.

Cindy had grown up attending church and had become a Christian as a young girl, but she had allowed her relationship to slip away and hadn't been living for the Lord when she and Frank began attending my meetings. At the close of one of my larger weekend functions that we conducted in hotels, Cindy renewed her commitment to Christ.

As she and Frank began to get their spiritual bearings, they drove from Lake City to New Life Church in Jacksonville every Sunday to attend church services with Lita and me. They loved the joyful environment, and they especially liked listening to Pastor Paul Zink's messages. Like many folks, when they experienced the living Word of God, they felt as though they were drinking out of a fresh stream. They hungered and thirsted for righteousness, and they just soaked it up. How refreshing it was for Lita and me as we watched Frank and Cindy grow in grace and wisdom.

As Frank and Cindy traveled from meeting to meeting with Lita and me, they noticed that some people were more interested in making money than maintaining their personal character. Frank and Cindy expressed their concerns to me, and I recognized the truth in what they were saying. "That's how we all started," I explained. "We came to listen to an opportunity to help ourselves financially in the business. Most of us were initially motivated by our own self-interest."

In time, as folks discern that you are not looking for anything from them except their success, they learn to trust and drop their guards a bit. I have learned that until folks give you the right to speak into their lives, you are trespassing, and they will block you out. That is why a vital element to my prayer life is to ask for two key things from God: His wisdom and His favor.

Leadership is nothing more than inspired influence. I want to inspire folks to seek what really has value and influence them to do the same for others. I have watched as God performs miracles in these areas.

I reminded Frank and Cindy that Jesus said that it is not the healthy who need a doctor; it's the sick. We also were once blind and couldn't see the error of our ways, but God opened our eyes, and now we see.

"I love to give people a break," I explained to Frank and Cindy. "I was shown that kind of grace before I became a Christian, and I need to extend that same sort of grace and mercy to others. I know that light overcomes darkness, not the other way around. Lita and I just love folks into the kingdom, and our business prospers in the process." I told them, "Let's get the man healed, then when the financial blessings come, the person will have the character to be a good steward of his acquired resources."

Frank and Cindy understood that being patient and tolerant with folks is really all about transformation, seeing them transformed into the image and likeness of Christ. For some people, that takes more time than others.

Frank and Cindy were attached at the hip with Lita and me from the early days of our Amway career, when we were just beginning to understand real prosperity. Frank watched as my Chevrolet Astro van was replaced by a Mercedes-Benz, and then as we grew into motor homes and then high-end motor coaches. Frank was with me the day I took delivery of my first Rolls-Royce, a gorgeous baby blue modern chariot. In fact, Frank drove the Rolls before I did, chauffeuring us to Savannah to do a meeting.

> **Jesus said that it's not the healthy who need a doctor; it's the sick.**

People love to see the underdog achieve and beat the odds. I was a pickup truck guy and always keep one in my fleet to this day, but those expensive trinkets really get people fired up with hope and belief! I used the material success to encourage others that they could achieve what Lita and I had. It worked magnificently. The fancy cars and motor coaches were high-end tools I used to instill a dream in others that they could have anything in life for which they were willing to dream and work.

Many folks tend to repeat what other folks around them say or believe. "I'll never have one of those."

I quickly agree with them. "You're right! You never will if you don't think you can. But that is not true either. You can do or have anything you set your mind to do. So it's your choice. What you say is what you will get." The Bible reminds us that the power of life and death is in the tongue.[18] Sooner or later, you will get whatever you confess over yourself. God Himself won't put something on you that you don't desire. He is a gentleman. He will respect your beliefs and desires, right or wrong. He gives you the option to believe or to not believe for something.

I did my best to be a good steward of what God placed in our hands. I sought to use our success to inspire and influence others to believe for more in life. The things we acquired were only a means to an end. We achieved very high levels of success financially, and we lived as we taught others: always reward yourself for your achievements.

People are often surprised to learn that for all our flamboyance, when it comes to the tools we use to inspire others in business, Lita and I are actually quite conservative money managers. I teach a 10-10-10-30-40 rule for being debt free and to maintain financial freedom: tithe 10 percent of your income, save 10 percent, blow 10 percent, reinvest 30 percent back into your business, and live on the remaining 40 percent. Live fully within your means. Learn to say no to things that don't help to build you and your business. Develop your networking business, but keep your day job as long as you can, and that income can pay your taxes.

Lita and I love to teach people the benefits of delayed gratification and the pure joy of being debt free. We made all of our purchases of depreciating assets in cash, or as we like to say, "Make one payment!" If you can't afford something ten times over, don't buy it. It will end up owning you. I have learned you can own anything in life as long as it doesn't own you. Frank and Cindy have been good students of these principles, and they also now enjoy the benefits of living debt free.

Frank can also attest to the fact that we rarely sell things as we have moved up in the standards of living we have enjoyed. We learned the value of *sowing* things rather than just selling them. God directs that we can receive a thirty-, sixty-, one-hundred-fold return on our gifts, according to our faith. We have seen the absolute validity of this in our lives. As God directs, we have enjoyed sowing anything and everything from high-end motorcycles, luxury automobiles, motor coaches, and even airplanes to those who have a need and a desire for them. God just puts these people in our lives and on our hearts. Through the process of praying about keeping something, selling it, or sowing it, we get most excited when we get instructions to sow, because we know the consequences of our faith and obedience in such matters. Whatever we

We are blessed to be a blessing. Pay it forward.

sow will come back in greater form, and it has! You can't outgive God. Start by giving from what you have, and see what I mean. You have to learn to give before you can receive. That's one reason why we teach people to give their way out of debt: give your time, your words, your life, *and* your substance.

Frank and Cindy, as well as many others, have witnessed the blessing of this principle of sowing and reaping, and they are proponents of this today. We believe we are blessed to be a blessing. Pay it forward.

When Frank and Cindy went through some difficulty in their marriage, Lita and I stuck with them, praying for them, not willing to give up on them as individuals or as a couple. And we refused to let them quit on each other. We encouraged them to work with Ed and Cheryl Henderson to find some good marriage counseling through New Life Network. Frank and Cindy weathered the storm and came out stronger in their marriage. They watched our children grow up, and they walked with us through our difficult times in our personal and business relationships. We have a history with Frank and Cindy. They know Lita and me intimately, through good times and bad, and we know them.

On the way back from meeting with Dallin Larsen, I was babbling away, describing on the phone to Frank what we had discovered in MonaVie and attempting to convey the potential business opportunity to him. Frank wasn't interested, so finally Lita jumped on the call and said, "Frank, just wait until you meet Dallin Larsen. He's the real deal."

Another couple that has been so dear to Lita and me since early on in our marriage, as well as the networking chapters of our lives, is Don and Lu Crews. They lived in Cocoa Beach with their four kids. Of course they treated Lita and me as their adopted kids!

I met Don in Fort Lauderdale at an open opportunity meeting at which I was speaking in my early Amway days. He owned and operated an engineering and commercial construction business, and I considered him to be quite successful in that day. Lu recalls that Don came home and said, "That guy must be on drugs. No one could be that excited naturally!"

Lu, you will recall, was the person who came to Lita's rescue when she was so ill in the mid-1990s. Lu is so loving and kind. With her Jewish roots, she is the consummate mother to her kids and us. Lita and I consider Don and Lu our extended mom and dad.

When you talk about a colorful individual, Don Crews comes to mind: loud, brash, outspoken, but with a bark that is worse than his bite.

Don is the youngest old guy I know. His wit and common sense is priceless. He is the ultimate Florida Gators fan. He loves to travel, but he has a fear of flying, and he cracks me up when he talks about it. Nevertheless, he and Lu taught Lita and me how to travel and how to travel well. They introduced us to areas in the country that are spectacular. They also taught us how to relax and have fun in life. Don taught me how to snow ski, water ski, and sail a boat. We laugh, love, and enjoy life together.

One of our first ski trips together was to Snowshoe, West Virginia. Don and Lu were skiing ahead of me, when I suddenly whisked by them, out of control. The next thing they heard was my yelling at the top of my lungs. I had skied off the trail and into deep powder. All they could see when they got to me were two ski tips sticking out of the snow! We laughed so hard while I tried getting out of that deep snow. We thought we were going to have to call the ski patrol to get me out.

Right from the start, Don and Lu worked their way into our hearts and lives. The first time Lita and I invited Don and Lu to stay with us in Jacksonville Beach, we were still newlyweds. So new, in fact, that when Don and Lu arrived, some delivery men were just then delivering the bed they were going to sleep on that night. In the morning, Don was going to make breakfast, but there were no pans in the house. Don went out and not only bought the bacon and eggs but also the pan to cook them in!

I had the opportunity of sharing my business with Don and Lu, and we hit it off from day one. I was intrigued by this guy and gal. They were as free-spirited and opinionated about life's issues as I was. Don was a little left of center when I met him, but God in His grace and mercy gave me the privilege of leading Don and Lu to the Lord early in our relationship. We have been nearly inseparable for the past thirty years, fully involved in each other's families. True friends are hard to come by, and Don and Lu were (and are) some of our dearest. Lita and I are much richer folks because of our relationship with Don and Lu and their family. We have been through thick and thin together, and they have supported us in every crazy adventure and wild idea I decided to pursue.

Don and Lu became involved in the Amway business with me. They didn't do that well in the business, but we enjoyed each other's company, and Don always encouraged me. Later, we bought and sold real estate, some good, some not so good. We invested in some rather speculative ventures, a few that made money, others that didn't. One of our ventures was particularly disastrous. We invested a bunch of hard-earned dollars hoping to strike it rich in eastern Kentucky by drilling shallow oil wells. Don and I are optimists, which is a good character trait that can sometimes work against you. We had no clue that we were being duped in those oil wells. We went out to the oil fields and the "good ol' boy" with whom we hoped to partner spun a tale for us, describing how he had been so successful in doing this. We bought in hook, line, and sinker—mostly sinker. Our new partner opened that valve and let the Kentucky black gold flow through the large pipe and spigot. We were so naive, we were mesmerized by his presentation. Don and I wrote checks for money we didn't even have, thinking the best. *We're gonna be rich!*

Sometimes we all miss the mark a bit. I won't bore you with all the dirty details, but let's just say, Don and I got taken big-time. I don't even want to tell you what our financially conservative wives said about that oil mess.

But Don and Lu and Lita and I got through that sticky situation and our friendship stayed intact. In fact, it got better. You can either laugh or cry when you make stupid mistakes. You can either get bitter about disappointing situations in life, or you can get better. We got nothing but better. We decided to laugh—and we had a lot to laugh about! The Bible says, "A friend loves at all times, and a brother is born for adversity."[19] Don and Lu have been those kinds of friends to Lita and me, and to this day we still look forward to sharing all sorts of new and exciting adventures. Shoot, what's next? We like living on the edge without falling off. It keeps life exciting.

So there was no question in my mind about what I was going to do after I found MonaVie, my next networking adventure. First, I called Frank and Cindy, and minutes later I called Don and Lu to introduce them to what they would be doing with me for the next season of our lives.

Don knew the moment I called and started sharing that he was in trouble. He interrupted my spiel to ask, "Okay, Brig. What are we doing now? And how much is it going to cost me?"

That's when you know you have something very special in a relationship. It really didn't matter all that much to Don and Lu what it was that I was excited about. They were going to support Lita and me in anything we decided to do. We had a trust factor between us that very few people understand. I never ask people to trust me, but I do ask that they trust my judgment. Nowadays, Lita and I do our due diligence before jumping at anything. We refuse to get in a hurry when it comes to getting involved in new opportunities.

Don and Lu were among the first folks I actually signed up in the Mona-Vie business simply by calling them. They believed in Lita and me. Despite some of our past business debacles, they chose to focus on the possibilities, so they signed up. Most people tend to throw the baby out with the bathwater. Just because you ate a bad meal, doesn't mean you quit eating. Come on, try, try again. Persistence and consistency will pay off in time.

Don and Lu not only got in but they have done very well with us in the launching of the MonaVie business.

MEANWHILE, FRANK and Cindy already owned several businesses in Lake City, Florida, when I first approached them about joining us in our next networking venture. Besides being busy with their five children and their church, they owned a plumbing contract business, a land development business, they were building homes and swimming pools. They also had opened a private Christian school and had recently purchased a golf course. The Soucineks were doing well to say the least, and they weren't looking for anything else to take up their precious time.

Nevertheless, I went to visit them at their home. As we stretched out on the floor, as we had done so many times before, I told them what I had discovered in this new company and product out of Salt Lake City. I was so excited, I couldn't even hear Frank and Cindy telling me all the reasons why they didn't want to get involved in any other business, let alone another networking venture.

For every protest Frank came up with, I'd say, "Frank, we're gonna do this." I became a bit fanatical because I so wanted them to be a part of it. By the way, a fanatic is someone who doesn't change his mind or the subject. That's where I was with Frank. It didn't matter what he said. I knew that I knew he was going to get into the MonaVie business with me. I had already made my decision; his didn't matter! I was determined. He was my friend, and he was going to come along with me on this deal. I gave him all the good and logical reasoning why I thought this business had the makings of a huge opportunity for us to cash in on, but when that didn't work, I went right to the emotional side—right to the heart.

Cindy acknowledged the positive benefits of the product she and the kids had been drinking, but Frank was a holdout. The hurt and disappointment were still lingering from our first networking venture in years past. Finally, I let Frank have it with both barrels. I let him know that I was going to do this with or without him, but I desperately wanted him with us on this new journey. I reminded him about friends doing what friends do.

He was starting to realize how much I believed in what I had found, but my passion and conviction about MonaVie still weren't hitting the mark for Frank. I just couldn't seem to touch or find his hot button. I now know that people will never remember so much what you say to them or even do, but they will always remember how you made them feel. Emotions will always win over logic. I was making a serious deposit in Frank and Cindy's emotions about what we could do together.

At last, Frank and Cindy warmed slightly to the idea. "Okay, look," Frank said. "I believe that you're going to make it in this as you put your heart and energy into it. But we are just not interested in risking the time and energy it takes to build another business. We'll enroll and keep using the product to support you guys, because we are your friends. But that's the only reason. We don't want to do another network marketing business. We've never really seen any significant financial success in that before. And we said we would never do another network again. So just sign us up, and we'll get the two cases a month, and we'll drink the stuff to support you."

> **People will not so much remember what you did or said to them, but they will always remember how you made them feel.**

What Frank was saying illustrates an important principle of building a relational marketing business. Many people will get into the business simply because of their relationship with you. They may never be wildly successful in the business, and that's okay. Their goal is to help support you, and you should always be appreciative of that. I know I was. It meant the world to me to know that my friends still believed in me to some degree. I would take what I could get for now, knowing that, in time, Frank and Cindy would want to get involved as this business prospered for us.

I also know that you should never say never in life about almost anything. We have personally witnessed the fact that right behind that *never* may reside God's perfect will for your life.

So I placed Frank in the matrix and labored on without him for the first year or so. During those first fourteen months in the business, Frank earned from it exactly what he had predicted: nothing. Cindy and the kids drank the juice they bought.

Meanwhile, Lita and I had put our best efforts into getting our Mona-Vie business launched and moving forward. We were recruiting folks into the business from living our everyday lives

Never say never. Behind that *never* may reside God's perfect will for your life.

and doing what we normally did—running errands, shopping, chauffeuring our kids around—all the while being aware of the folks around us who might become interested in what we were doing. We shared with anyone who showed an interest in wanting better health. That was the door opener.

From the beginning, the company offered generous incentives and bonuses for creating business volume. Within the first six months, Lita and I had achieved the highest levels they had set for the elite builders. We hit and surpassed every level the company had built into the compensation plan within the first year. This thing was on a roll!

So within the first year we earned incentive trips to exotic destinations such as Costa Rica, Hawaii, Park City (Utah), and a Caribbean cruise. By that time, a number of our acquaintances and friends had heard about this new and exciting venture, so many of them joined us in building the MonaVie business. A good number of them were experiencing substantial success and were quickly advancing through the higher ranks.

The Diamond level in the business was, at one point, the quintessential and most coveted success level to shoot for. The annual income level for these Diamonds was around $200,000 to $250,000. Amazingly, most of the folks qualifying for this level of success were new to networking; MonaVie was their first venture into the networking industry.

While Lita and I were having a ball, getting to know our newfound friends and associates and sharing in their exotic trips, Frank and Cindy were watching from a distance. Herein lies the best part of their story.

During that time, I'd occasionally call Frank and say, "Hey, this thing is cranking, and we're making a ton of money."

"Great. Love ya," Frank replied. Click. The phone disconnected. Frank remained unimpressed.

But what money and position could not do, relationship and friendship did. The dozens of qualified Diamonds with whom we were now hanging out were becoming the central theme of our everyday discussions,

Having fun with Frank is part of the formula for enjoying life.

especially the trips we were taking with them. Frank and Cindy felt disconnected, and it bothered them. For the first time in years, they weren't a central part of our lives.

Now, it wasn't that Frank and Cindy couldn't afford to go on luxury
trips. The truth was, they didn't *qualify* to go, and they weren't invited.
These were reward and incentive trips provided by the company for those
who had achieved the Diamond level in the business.

Remember, everyone has a dream. Part of Frank's dream was not to be
left out. He wanted to be a part of the fun we were experiencing with a
whole new group of folks. At times, I actually felt he was a bit jealous of
the others monopolizing much of our time.

It worked! Frank realized that the only way to rectify that situation
was to get involved and start building his position in the business. When
he finally found his hot button and his reason why, he and Cindy poured
themselves into building their MonaVie business to the Diamond level.
Cindy wanted a new home and all the furnishings to go along with it.
Frank just wanted to be with the gang.

Everybody's hot button is different, and you don't know what they
want unless you ask.

Frank was too busy to do tasting parties, so he simply pointed people
to my website. "Watch those first few video clips online, and I'll call you
back in an hour," he'd tell prospective enrollees. He was on a mission,

and as we've said many times, "When you know your why in life, you'll figure out the how." Frank was driven. He and Cindy enrolled thirty to forty folks so fast it was crazy. Those folks started replicating what Frank was doing, and it caused a wave of growth that drove Frank and Cindy (and others!) to the Diamond and Black Diamond levels. In a matter of months, Frank and Cindy were hobnobbing with the biggest producers in the organization.

> **When you know your why in life, you'll figure out the how.**

Past success doesn't always guarantee future success, but in Frank's case, determination, focus, a concentrated effort, and pure persistence paid off. Frank and Cindy haven't missed any of the executive incentive trips since. Yep, we are hanging out again.

It's true: where there is a will, there is a way. As busy as Frank was, he found the time and the energy and the way to make his MonaVie efforts successful. I know that people either make excuses or money in life, but you can't make both. Anyone who finds his or her dream can find the way to accomplish something great.

Frank has been one of my greatest supporters in the business, but more important, he's been a friend who is closer than a brother. He and Cindy have traveled with Lita and me all around this big world, having fun, laughing, crying, and just plain sharing life in its fullest together. Frank has a servant's heart and has been a strong spiritual support to Lita and me, as well as to Dallin and Karree Larsen.

There is nothing more satisfying than to be with people you respect and just plain enjoy their company. Lita and I have realized how valuable and precious it is to have friends we can trust with everything we have and everybody we love. We especially love being around folks who have need of nothing from us but our friendship. The sweet fellowship we share with Frank and Cindy is a precious commodity these days.

It is a simple but often forgotten rule of life: you must give into relationships if you hope to have them, much less be able to draw from them. Frank and Cindy and Lita and I made good deposits in our relationships, and now they are returning the favor big-time. Not long ago, we had lunch together along with our families while we were snow skiing in Park City. As we enjoyed the breathtaking scenery from atop the mountain, I leaned over to our son Daniel and pointed at Frank and Cindy. "Tell them what I said," and I nudged Daniel on the arm.

Daniel said, "Dad told me that if I ever find one good friend like you, I'll have done something very special."

I've heard it said that if you live your life, and at the end of it you have two good friends, you are a rich man. I am blessed to have more than my share of good friendships, but I'm working on a few more!

CHAPTER **19**

Providential Partnerships

WHEN STEVE AND GINA Merritt's business began earning twenty thousand dollars a week, Steve called me. "Hey, Brig," he said, "I just realized something. Did you know that every time we make another twenty thousand dollars a week, that's another million dollars a year?"

I smiled into the phone at Steve's naive enthusiasm. Truth is, Steve and Gina were so busy and excited about building their business, they hadn't really considered just how much money they were making. And they were making a lot! Every seven days, MonaVie was depositing in their account between ten and twenty thousand dollars. That's the minimum that Black Diamonds earn with MonaVie.

Before long, Steve and Gina were making forty thousand dollars a week, then sixty thousand dollars. Steve called again. "Brig, that sixty thousand dollars a week turns into three million dollars a year!"

"I know it," I laughed along with him. "And guess what? When you are earning eighty thousand a week, that's four million."

At this writing, Steve is earning more than a hundred thousand dollars each week. Not bad for a guy who started with only one bottle a month.

Today, Steve jokes that a person doesn't need several college degrees to succeed in network marketing. "I was the guy who facetiously threatened my high school principal and said, 'If you don't pass me, I'm comin' back!' He passed me."

Steve was a hardworking, no-nonsense guy just getting by in any way he could. He just went with the flow in life, lighthearted and fun, but he was always open to an opportunity to get ahead. To prove the point, Steve would walk dogs in hurricanes for some of his more prominent neighbors just to make good use of his time while riding the storms out. (Steve and I don't claim to be the sharpest knives in the drawer.)

In November 2005, my friend Charlie Kalb sponsored Bob and Linda Robinson, and Bob sponsored Steve and Gina Merritt in the MonaVie business. The Merritts lived in Lantana, Florida, where Gina worked as a flight attendant for Delta Airlines and Steve was a former world champion barefoot water-skier working as an independent sales representative for a promotional company. Their why—their reason—for getting into a networking business was simple. They wanted to bring Gina home from working full time with the airline. Gina had been flying several days a week for twenty-four years, and Steve wanted to bring her home.

Bob Robinson, like most of the folks who get involved in the business, wasn't real astute to the details or specifics of the business itself. He got involved because of his relationship with Charlie. He just allowed Charlie to enroll him without going through the details. So when he sponsored Steve and Gina in the business, he didn't have a clue as to how to actually walk them through the sign-up process. Steve and Gina figured it out on their own. Bob did his best to explain what the product was and how the business worked. He stumbled through a rather confusing presentation and finally shrugged in exasperation. "You know, Gina, the real reason I'm involved in this business is that Charlie is in and is making some crazy money with it. He says we can do the same, and I trust his judgment."

Gina caught the vision. "Bobby!" she practically shrieked. "I work with Delta Airlines, and I got hit with a 50 percent pay cut about eight months ago. Wait a minute. How much does it cost to get in?"

"It's thirty-nine dollars to get in, and you should buy a couple of cases of juice."

"We can do it!" Gina exclaimed. She was excited about the possibility of earning an extra three hundred dollars per month. She had no idea of the incredible journey upon which she and Steve were embarking. Steve didn't catch the vision as quickly. He basically enrolled with Bobby to get him off his back. Yes, they were friends, but Steve had some reservations about engaging in another networking style of business. I personally called to encourage Steve, as did Charlie Kalb, but the calls went straight to Steve's voice mail and he deleted them. He really felt like he didn't want to risk the time and effort it was going take to start up another network marketing business. But there were a few things he had to consider before saying no. He was forty years of age, and he and Gina were struggling financially. Their jobs were not fulfilling, and they owed Steve's mom a hundred thousand dollars. So with a bit of skepticism and a lot of doubt regarding their decision, they bit the bullet and did what friends do: they went ahead and enrolled with Bobby for thirty-nine dollars. They recall that when they put the enrollment fee and first order on their credit card, they crossed their fingers and prayed the one-hundred-dollar transaction would go through. What a great story, as they tell it now!

With four kids, the Merritts' budget didn't allow for any sizable financial outlay, so they began their business by purchasing only one bottle of MonaVie per month. Steve was still out on the road most of the week, so when the bottle of MonaVie arrived at their home, Gina decided to sample it. "I loved the taste of the juice so much," she recalls, "that I drank the entire bottle before Steve got home that week. I didn't know that I only needed to drink two ounces in the morning and two ounces at night. The next two months, when the juice arrived, I did the same thing, so for the first three months we were in the business, Steve never tasted the juice!"

Steve's aha moment came when he received an e-mail from Charlie Kalb announcing that MonaVie had rewarded him with a luxury motor coach. That news got Steve's attention, as Steve had always wanted a motor home for Gina and the kids to travel in to various water sports competitions. (It's always the dream that finally gets a person's attention.)

Charlie's motto was, "I'm not looking for money; money is looking for me. I'm not looking for people; people are looking for me." At the time, Charlie was making about four thousand dollars a week. Steve was now motivated to at least look into how Charlie could earn so much in such a short period of time. Curiosity got the best of him, so he decided to drive five hours to Jacksonville to see what this was really all about.

I was the guest speaker that night, and I saw Steve in the back of the room. I acknowledged him and did my best to encourage him to engage. What Steve saw and experienced there became his tipping point. He realized that he could not only do this, but he determined then and there to head home fully committed and on fire to make this business happen.

At the conclusion of the meeting, Charlie approached Steve and said, "Which night would be better for a tasting party at your house? Tuesday or Thursday?" Charlie didn't ask Steve whether or not he wanted to have a tasting party. He just booked it.

At their first tasting party, they presented a short introduction, Charlie told his MonaVie experience and gave everyone a sample of the juice, they watched a video, and he explained the opportunity to others. Steve and Gina invited their friends from the neighborhood, their church, anyone they could tell. Almost all promised to attend. At the party, only eight people actually showed up, including Steve's parents. Of the eight folks who showed up, two fell asleep during the presentation. "Apparently, I had only four friends," Steve says with a laugh today. But it was no laughing matter then. "I need to find some folks who want more in life," Steve decided.

I'm not looking for money; money is looking for me.

"We were what you would call 'innocently ignorant' to what we actually had our hands on. But one thing we knew, we could do what they were asking us to do, and that was enough. We were naive enough to believe that we could attain the levels that Charlie and Brig had gone to. We wanted to be one of those Black Diamonds," Steve remembers.

Steve and Gina's enthusiasm was contagious. Steve recalls, "It stemmed from the fact that we had to do something about our financial situation, and this is what showed up. We decided to do it with all the energy we could muster. We had our doubts, but we decided not to give them the time of day. We couldn't afford for this business not to work for us. We figured it worked for Brig, Charlie, and a host of others, so we knew it would work for us as long as we worked it.

"We had no credibility of our own, so we borrowed Charlie's and Brig's, sharing the success they had seen and how anyone else could do the same if they chose to. The more tasting parties we hosted, the more we were convinced that we could attract the folks we needed in order to really make this happen. We focused our attention on the things we could do, not on what we couldn't do. So we could host tastings and invite people, and that is exactly what we decided to do. We went for it!"

The Merritts poured themselves into exposing new folks to the product and opportunity every night of the week. The two creative things they could do to earn income were to sponsor folks and move the juice. They were laser-focused and didn't let anything or anyone interfere with their action plan for the next four months. "We decided to turn off our television and do as many tasting parties as we could in a four-month period," said Steve. They did over 120 tastings in a three-month period, morning, noon, and night. Following the *MAP* book to the letter, Steve and Gina treated their business like a million-dollar venture right from the start. They worked like crazy, focusing on their business with intensity, and their plan worked.

They replaced Gina's income within six weeks! Within 125 days the Merritts reached the highest and most elite level in the MonaVie business at that time: Executive Black Diamond. It took them four months of dedicated effort to achieve this prestigious level, but with it came millionaire status. They were now earning upwards of a hundred thousand dollars a week. Steve attributes their rapid success to three things: "Sticking to the basics, doing them often, and doing them well. We followed without question the pattern the Harts had developed for us. We just got on the tracks and powered our business by doing what they had done to achieve those levels of success. We realized it was nothing more than exposing new people to the product and the plan. Some would engage now, others would engage later. We ran with the ones that engaged now and just stayed available to the ones that didn't get on board initially. It was kind of like following the leader. We bought into following the system they had developed. Why question what was working? We just intensified the efforts. We followed the *MAP* (the Maximum Action Plan) book, sticking to the ten-step pattern. If it wasn't in the *MAP* book, we didn't even consider doing it.

"Now the same pattern is working for all of those we invited in. The duplication factor is what has blown our minds in this. It really is simple, teachable, and duplicable. That's why we now have a business that has gained a life of its own. We did it, and now others are doing the same. We threw the pebble in the pond, and the ripple effect continues. Praise the Lord!"

Steve and Gina also remind me of another important principle they so closely followed: two incomes are better than one. In other words, don't leave your full-time job until you have replaced it three times over. Why? Multiple streams of income are always better than one. Sticking with your job also adheres to a law of networking: do only what is replicable by the masses of folks coming in. Do what you want them to do. As much as the

Merritts wanted to have Gina at home, they were well beyond ten times their income status with their part-time business before they even considered retiring from their full-time jobs.

Staying at their place of employment afforded them two important elements in building their business: (1) they were in situations to contact and meet new people with whom they could share their newfound business opportunity, and (2) they decided to reinvest much of their initial earnings back into building their business. They invested in inventory of more product, in the support tools, or "ammo" as Gina calls them. They also invested by traveling to do meetings for their organization and by attending the functions and events. They practiced another basic principle of success: delayed gratification. Thus they could build a much larger base and a more secure financial income.

A common mistake made by many who are new to networking is thinking that they need to leave their jobs so they can put more time into the building of their networking business. Not true. The majority of people work nine-to-five jobs and aren't available to meet with you until after normal business hours. It's a myth that being full time in this industry is necessary to earn a large income from it. It's all about establishing a firm base of distributors that all do a little bit, and then replicate that model. Do that and the success will come.

Leaving your regular employment is a wrong example to the new folks considering the business. They often see that as an excuse to not get involved. "I can't do this business, because I don't have the time." But time can be used in many ways. Some people make a living from nine to five; fortunes are made in our industry after five o'clock in the afternoon.

"But isn't that the idea," I hear you saying, "to put yourself in a position so you have some options?"

Yes, but most folks have never owned and operated their own businesses, and it's quite a different situation. An employee mentality is all about showing up when someone else dictates to you what you have to do, when you are to do it, and how you must do it. When you are in business for yourself, you must have the discipline to be able to organize and manage your time and resources.

Just because someone dislikes his job and can't wait to be out of there is no reason to quit. In fact, that is often one of the reasons we encourage them to stay at it. The unwanted job can be the motivating factor that helps someone overcome his fears and do what it takes to become proficient at network marketing. Use that negative situation as your reason to find the time and the wherewithal to accomplish your goals.

Remember, anything that has real value and meaning in life takes time to accomplish. There is no such thing as getting rich quick, but there are ways to develop greater income streams quicker than traditional routes. Don't rush it. Steve and Gina took their time and didn't leave their jobs until they couldn't afford not to leave. The size of their organization and the responsibilities they had were the factors they considered when they decided to go full time in their new and profitable venture.

Steve and Gina Merritt are New Crowns in MonaVie,
following in our footsteps.

In four and half years Steve and Gina climbed the ladder of success to the highest levels offered by the company. With every new rank they achieved, they were awarded cash bonuses and perks like nothing they had ever known or experienced previously. The Merritts earned a Mercedes-Benz at the Black Diamond level, a one-hundred-thousand-dollar bonus and motor coach at the Royal level, jet credits aboard the corporate jet and a three-hundred-thousand-dollar bonus at the Presidential level, and a six-hundred-thousand-dollar bonus and a weeklong cruise on their own private yacht at the Imperial level. Steve and Gina accomplished all of these levels in record times in the industry.

In January 2009, Steve and Gina continued their climb to success and

At a recent R3Global get-together, we took this picture of the numerous MonaVie Black Diamonds (or Millionaires Club) who utilized our system.

became the second couple in MonaVie's history to reach and achieve the prestigious level of Crown Black Diamond in the business. I must confess, when Lita and I achieved the Crown Black Diamond level, it was through-the-roof exciting for my family and me, but helping another couple to achieve this goal was far more rewarding to us than doing it ourselves. This is what turns us on. It's almost as rewarding as watching our own kids achieve great things. To celebrate and reward them for their outstanding success, in front of thousands of people at the R3Global Teaching and Planning Conference in Orlando, MonaVie CEO Dallin Larsen presented the Merritts with a bonus check for one million dollars. In addition to the money, Dallin also presented Steve and Gina with the option of choosing one of five exotic automobiles: a Ferrari, a Bentley, an Aston Martin, a Rolls-Royce, or a Lamborghini. Steve walked away with the keys and the title to a gorgeous brand-new green Lamborghini Murcielago.

"What a way to bring in the New Year!" Steve exclaimed.

Gina quipped, "On my tenth anniversary working for Delta, I received a lapel pin. When I reached twenty years, they gave me a catalog and said to pick something out. When I reached the twenty-four-year mark, they gave me a bottle of airline wine with a ribbon around it. After only four and half years, MonaVie gave us two million dollars in bonuses, a brand-new Mercedes, a motor coach, yacht trips, jet credits, a dozen exotic trips, and a Lamborghini sports car!"

Success hasn't changed Steve but for the better. He still jests to some of his neighbors that he'll still be available to walk their dogs during up-coming hurricanes.

I love what Steve does when other networkers approach him to get in their businesses. Steve is quick to ask, "So what do you guys have to offer? Do you have a trip to outer space? Yeah, I didn't think so. Take a look at this!"

He hasn't found a reward plan yet that can compare to ours.

Lita and I and the Merritts have qualified for and been rewarded with incentive trips to Costa Rica, three trips to Hawaii, two trips to the Bahamas, a two-week Caribbean cruise, a weeklong trip to Ireland, and a spectacular leadership trip to Bora Bora. Steve and Gina continue to press onward and upward as they herald the message of freedom through MonaVie and R3Global. They continue to borrow our credibility in order to sponsor folks to this day—I remind them that they aren't doing so bad themselves.

Early on, I saw tremendous potential in Steve and Gina and have done my best to mentor them to achieve whatever goals they choose to set. They are like sponges when it comes to learning about this business and the industry itself. Over the years, Steve and Gina have become some of Lita's and my favorite business-building associates and friends. When they earned their weeklong imperial yacht trip, they invited us to go along with them. Of course, that's how we roll. When we earned our trip, we committed to share ours with them, and they committed to do the same with us. It's wonderful to have these great experiences, but it's just plain magical when you can share them with folks you love and care about. Dallin and Karree Larsen flew in to join us for a couple of days during both the Merritt and Hart imperial yacht trips. Ain't it great?

Making and sharing memories as key members of our R3Global team, Steve and Gina are fantastic examples of how to start from scratch in a network marketing business and become wildly successful through dedication, perseverance, sacrifice, and hard work. They have developed the leadership skills that will take them to even higher levels of success. They are models to those who can and will follow in their footsteps into fulfilling careers in the relational marketing industry.

I DIDN'T know Corbin and Holly Roush, a young couple with three children under twelve, when they first got into the MonaVie business, or I should say, when Holly started her MonaVie business in September 2005. Corbin had a successful corporate career and looked with no small disdain at Holly's fledgling juice business. Holly didn't blame him. She didn't have a clue how to successfully build a network marketing business. She just trusted the judgment of her brother-in-law, who just so happened to be a top-forty money earner in the PGA that year. Bo Van Pelt had called and was excited about the prospects of this natural fruit juice called MonaVie. He felt that this was a fit for his "overzealous sister-in-law." Like many other folks, Holly was influenced to get into the business because of a relationship with a person in whom she had trust. Bo had nothing at all to gain from this, so Holly felt safe in the exploration of this newfound adventure. Looking back, Holly recalls, "When I first started the business, I knew nothing about how to do it! I had never seen or been to a tasting party, and I didn't know what an up-line or down-line was and had no clue about what a system was or just how important it was in building your business. I got on Brig's website one day and found out that he was going to be in Dallas, doing an open opportunity meeting. All I knew was that I had to see what this guy was doing so I could gain some insight into what this was really all about. I was drawn to the success he had seen and I wanted the same. I grabbed two of my friends, Julie Christner and Laura Lester, and we drove four hours from Tulsa to see Brig and to find out what this was really all about."

Holly and Corbin Roush are Presidential Black Diamonds in MonaVie, and their family is the reason why.

Holly didn't know what she was going to find when she arrived in Dallas, but what she discovered changed her life and the lives of her family members.

"We walked into the hotel conference room, and there were only about twenty people there. Most people would have run, thinking no one wants to do this. But I was jumping out of my skin thinking, *No one is doing this business. There are only twenty people here, and I brought three. This is going to be huge!*"

Holly sat in that room and took everything in. At some point in the meeting, I made a comment that I was looking to help at least ten people become millionaires. Holly remembers that moment. "I was raising my hand, thinking, *Pick me! Pick me!*"

Holly is the epitome of what you look for in folks who are going to do something great in life. She reminds me of the story of two shoe salesmen sent to China because their companies wanted to explore the possibilities of expanding into the international markets. Both boarded flights the same day but one hour apart. When the first salesman landed, he gathered his wares and headed out into the streets. But he paused to notice something very strange: no one was wearing shoes. Perplexed at first, dismayed in a few moments, and quite discouraged within minutes of his discovery, he raced to a nearby phone and called his corporate headquarters and left this message: "Landed in China. Am coming back home immediately. Absolutely no opportunity here. Don't send any shoes. No one wears shoes here! Won't work." The negative salesman boarded a plane and returned to the States.

I love sharing with others how we all can succeed big by utilizing principles from the Bible.

Meanwhile, the other salesman landed in the same airport, gathered his wares, and headed through the airport to the exact same street his predecessor did. He had a quite similar reaction as he looked at the people out in the streets. Almost as swiftly as his counterpart, he raced to the phone, dialed his office, and left this message: "Landed in China. Am going to extend my stay indefinitely. Greatest opportunity I've ever seen. No one wearing shoes here! Send all the shoes we have! We're going to be rich!"

Both salesmen saw the same things, but one decided to see opportunity and the other had vision for none. No doubt, they both got what they saw.

This is a good time to ask, What does your future look like? Possibility thinking is a wonderful thing. All things do come to those who truly believe.

That's the lesson, of course, and you will notice this same truth as you read Holly's story. There were a number of issues that Holly had to face immediately as she embarked on her newfound opportunity, but that didn't hinder her as she decided to focus on the things that were in her favor. Everyone will face challenges in life, especially when opportunity knocks. But once again it all comes down to vision and how you decide to respond to it. Holly had the same options that you have. How do you see the glass? Half empty or half full?

With Holly's enthusiasm, it was no surprise to me when Holly and her two friends, Julie and Laura, became the first big MonaVie success stories in their hometown of Tulsa. We're not talking about the mediocre kind of success; we are talking about these moms blazing a trail to millionaire status and beyond in record time. They achieved goals that were previously unheard of in this industry. They gained the attention and respect of not only the townspeople but, more important, their husbands!

God certainly has His way of allowing us to be humbled in life. There came a time in Corbin's life (Holly's negative-thinking husband!) when his corporate job turned sour. Corbin was the victim of cutbacks and downsizing, even though he was a trusted friend of the owner and the highest producing salesperson in his company. Nevertheless, Corbin was unexpectedly called in and informed that his pay was to be cut by three-fourths, yet he would continue in his position, producing as he had, with a smile on his face, or else. Wow, what a blow.

Meanwhile, unknown to Corbin at the time, in her part-time venture, Holly had achieved a level of financial success whereby she was earning twice as much as Corbin was making. What a glorious day when Holly sent him back to his company to inform his boss and "friend" that he had decided not to continue his employment with the company. Corbin

The invitations on Sunday mornings are among the most precious moments at our functions, because so many people change their lives for the better.

walked out with his dignity in place and decided to join Holly in her little juice business. Since the two began collaborating together, their business has skyrocketed. There was nothing like agreement to bring synergy in their efforts.

They blasted through all the ranks up to the Presidential Black Diamond level. It was extrasweet when they collected bonuses of one hundred thousand dollars, three hundred thousand dollars, and six hundred thousand dollars in two years—in addition to their commissions. It's been said that the best revenge is sweet and outrageous success. If that is so, then Corbin not only recovered gracefully but has experienced the satisfaction of overcoming and becoming.

Of course, Holly and Corbin have enjoyed the money and the perks, but if you ask Corbin what this particular business and industry of networking has meant to their family, he's quick to express appreciation for the time he now has with their three sons, coaching them in football, and being a full-time husband and dad.

IF YOU launch out with the vision God has instilled in you, He doesn't expect you to figure out all the messy details. He knows what you need before you even ask. The Bible says: "Trust in the Lord with all your heart,

Lita and I share from our hearts at R3Global functions, teaching folks
how to live a happier, healthier, and more prosperous life.

and lean not on your own understanding; in all your ways acknowledge
him, and he will make your paths straight."[20] That's straight into His perfect and divine will for your life, even if it requires Him to set up divine
appointments so you can meet the right folks who have the gifts and talents that you need to build your dream. All the while, they are being fulfilled in theirs. I call that the triple win—I win, they win, and the people
we serve win.

Be open to divine appointments in the least expected places. Just take
one step at a time and follow peace; you'll get there. Keep your antennas
up. Be on the lookout for those kinds of folks with whom you just seem to
have an instant connection, a kind of immediate chemistry. Go about living your life, and realize that they do show up and you have to be attentive
to them when they do. Looking for these kinds of relationships charges
your atmosphere with an air of expectancy. Almost like a law of attraction,
God brings them into your life to fulfill the mission He has for you. Man,
is that exciting! Something to look forward to!

I began hosting weekend events to take the show on the road. I liken
these events to the gathering of believers to reinforce our mission: to teach,
train, motivate, and help them to believe in what we are doing together
and to believe in themselves. I base these conferences on the biblical in-

struction: "Let us not give up meeting together, as some are in the habit of doing, but let us encourage one another—and all the more as you see the Day approaching."[21]

I am big on getting folks together and watching as the magic happens, as they are exposed to other folks' success stories. This is the listen-and-participate side of plugging into a system. I create the venues and give each person the right to earn a place onstage, which becomes their platform to share their story. Interestingly, the teaching and training resources we have do very well, as they should. These folks teach and instruct from proven experience, not theory. But when individuals and couples share their stories of who they are, where they came from, and what they did to overcome and become, those resources are in much greater demand. Why? Because they touch people where they are, they reach the hearts of folks, because they are relating to the folks who want to believe in themselves. People get encouraged when they see others they personally relate to.

At our R3Global events, we provide plenty of practical business principles combined with fascinating testimonials from individuals and couples who started their businesses from little to nothing and have built ultraprofitable businesses for themselves. As always, everything we plan and do in these events culminates in helping the folks move the business from their heads to their hearts. That is when and where the magic happens.

Of course, we still offer Sunday morning worship services, where we give opportunities for every person attending to get their spirit-man in order. I decided long ago in my quest to reach people that I wanted to influence them with lasting effects. By sowing into these folks' lives, we are building something that no one can tear apart. No weapon formed against us can prosper. We get our hearts mended together for

If I can do it, so can you.
Why not you? Why not now?

righteous purposes, and these relationships become inseparable. This is where covenant comes in. We commit to a common vision, each other, and more important, to the Lord God Himself. The Bible says: "If God is for us, who can be against us?"[22]

It's important to get to know the people you're in business with so there is not only agreement but unity and then synergy. When people come together, they see the vision, buy into the vision, and come into agreement. The point of agreement is the point of power. People leave equipped and empowered to fulfill the vision.

The point of agreement is the point of power.

Divine partnerships are wonderful, and God has them predetermined them for you as you're faithful, diligent, and obedient.

CHAPTER **20**

Sneak Attack

Aftter we made a fresh start with our new and prospering relational marketing business, we enjoyed marvelous material success and fantastic spiritual blessings, but life wasn't all easy. It never is. The Enemy doesn't roll over and play dead simply because we make a fresh commitment. On the contrary, he battles back even harder, trying to reclaim what he thought he had securely imprisoned. And the Enemy of our souls doesn't fight fairly! He will hit you when and where you least expect it and in your most vulnerable place. As the Enemy does in the lives of many people, he found a way to get at Lita and me by striking someone we loved more than life itself: our oldest son, Daniel.

There is a truth in life that says, "Those who do not point you higher will by default drag you lower," and Lita and I saw that principle played out in Daniel's life. While we were living in North Carolina, he had a good core of friends on his soccer team, and his active schedule kept him busy.

When we moved back to Florida, however, Daniel became involved with the wrong crowd and his attitude soured. He wasn't belligerent, but he tended to be lethargic, lacking a sense of purpose or goals. His usually upbeat personality seemed dulled, and the friends with whom he spent most of his time were not a positive influence. Daniel always had a heart for underdogs, and that can be an admirable trait, but at a time when he needed some positive peer pressure, he chose friends who were going nowhere. Although Daniel was the life of the party, he was not influencing his friends to step up to another level; instead, he was allowing his buddies to drag him down to theirs and lower. Despite being an intelligent young man, Daniel's grades at school edged downward. Since this was a difficult time for our entire family, I attributed Daniel's change in temperament to the tension we all had felt before moving from the North Carolina mountain community back to our beach house in Florida.

I understood Daniel's lackadaisical attitude. Like me, Daniel has a strong "play gene," and we love to go, go, and go some more. But increasingly I felt certain that something more serious was going on. Having had some experience with drugs myself, I recognized when someone was using illegal substances, and it looked to me that Daniel was heading in that direction. I tried to talk with him about the dangers of drugs and how he needed to avoid people and places that placed him in potentially tempting situations. I knew all too well the subtle snares that lay waiting for someone prone toward addiction. One would think that because of my experience with drugs, I could talk freely with Daniel about the pitfalls and that my son would readily see the folly of his actions, but it was much more difficult than I ever dreamed possible. How do you tell your children not to do what you *did*?

Did we see any early warning flags or other signs of trouble? No more than any other parent who loves their son or daughter. We believed the best about our son. And Daniel was a good actor. He convinced us that everything was okay. When we discovered that things were not okay and that Daniel was headed toward serious trouble, our first thought was, *Where have we failed?* We did everything right. We raised our children in a strong Christian home, an environment filled with positive influences. We built their self-esteem by encouraging them to believe that they could achieve anything they set their minds to do. We gave them everything we thought they needed and many things they did not. So how or why does a child decide to go against everything his family believes? Everyone has an answer, but none of them seem adequate when the child is yours. That's the way we felt when we discovered that Daniel was using illegal drugs.

> **How or why does a child decide to go against everything his family believes?**

Accusing thoughts pummeled my mind. *Where did we go wrong? How could this happen? It must be my fault.* We understood that other kids could get off track, but not ours!

And then there were the spiritual questions: "God, how could You let this happen? We've been trying to serve You and help others to find You. Couldn't You have prevented this? Couldn't You have kept our child safe from harm?" Of course, it didn't help much to think that God did not keep His own Son from harm but allowed Him to be crucified as part of the plan to save the world. But at the moment, we weren't interested in saving the world; we were interested in saving our son's life. I felt like a failure as a father and as a Christian.

Repeatedly, Lita and I tried to tell Daniel, "This is your life. This isn't a dress rehearsal. This is the only chance you get. You don't want to mess it up by making bad choices."

Daniel listened but he didn't hear. Instead, he checked out emotionally. He wouldn't talk about what he was feeling, much less what he was experiencing with his friends. He virtually shut down all communication with us. When he was home, he mostly stayed in his room, and he slept inordinate amounts of time. With our busy lifestyle, friends and guests visited frequently in our home, but Daniel tuned them out as well, choosing not to interact with our friends and spending minimal time with our guests. That wasn't like Daniel. He was a gregarious kid, and he used to love being around our friends. Now, he wanted no part of them—or us.

Lita and I prayed for Daniel until we wept. We set boundaries, rules, and curfews. We took away privileges and put him in various schools. We did everything, *anything* we thought might help. But the more we did, the more Daniel sealed himself away from us.

I'm convinced that at least part of Daniel's downward slide was due to a lack of vision. The Bible says: "Where there is no vision, the people perish."[23] But a better application for what Daniel was going through was, "Without a vision or discipline, the people are unrestrained (set loose to pursue their own way without rules or self-control). But happy is he who keeps the law."

Daniel didn't know what he wanted to do, where he wanted to go in life, or what dreams he wanted to pursue. He had fallen away from the faith that he knew, and without the discipline in his life to follow the Lord, he was drifting. When anyone drifts, you rarely drift forward, only backward. Lita and I were careful not to overinfluence or force our kids into our business, because I fully understood the maturity level one needs be-fore embarking on a successful run at relational marketing. I certainly want them to succeed, but I want them, not me, to choose the direction and timing. My responsibility, as I see it, is to equip them and provide the best tools available for them to achieve in whatever field they choose to follow. You can't make anyone do what they don't want to do, not even your own children.

Lita and I never pressured Daniel to learn the relational marketing business, although we encouraged him to do things that would help him succeed at whatever he wanted to do. Never did we try to live our lives through our children. We understood that our role as parents was to pre-pare and equip our children for whatever God had for them. If that meant they were in business with us, great! If not, as long as they were doing what God wanted them to do, we knew they would prosper.

But it really bothered Lita and me as we saw Daniel continuing to make poor decisions. He couldn't or wouldn't comprehend that some of his choices could have ramifications for the rest of his life. We believed God had so much more for Daniel than what he was experiencing. We knew that Daniel had great God-given potential within him, and to watch him squander the favor God had poured into his life ripped our hearts to shreds.

The trouble came to a head when Brittany came to us and said, "Some-thing is going on with Daniel. He left the house the other night after every-one else went to bed."

When I asked Daniel about it, he lied. Before long, we realized that wasn't the only thing he was lying about to us. Shortly after that, Daniel was driving with his brother Paul in the car when the police pulled him over and found that Daniel had been using an illegal substance.

We went to court, and Daniel stood before the judge. As I sat in that courthouse, I had a sinking feeling. *Oh, boy, I've been here before.*

The judge recognized that Daniel was not a hardened drug-user, but he was no less firm with him. "You have two choices," he told Daniel. "You can abide by what your parents are suggesting, which is to go to a place where you can get your life straightened out, or you can go to jail. Understand, if you go into a program and rebel against it, you *will* go straight to jail."

With the judge's approval, Lita and I arranged for Daniel to attend a military school in Georgia. Daniel was not excited about going, to say the least, but we paid the tuition and got him ready to go. The day we were to take him to the military school, he ran away and we couldn't find him for two days. When we finally found him, Lita was livid. More than anything, other than Daniel's physical and spiritual well-being, Lita wanted to keep Daniel out of the legal system. No parent wants to see their child go to jail. Yet Daniel seemed bent on destructive choices.

We sought advice from Cheryl and Ed Henderson as well as others familiar with drug treatment centers. But some of the drug rehabilitation centers we investigated were either too lenient, making excuses for the addicts' behavior, or too stringent, treating the addicted person like a criminal. We felt confident that Daniel was still tenderhearted and teachable, that he hadn't progressed in his drug usage or the callousness of his heart to the point that he was incorrigible.

Dean Sikes had been a friend of our family since 1989. We knew Dean's heart for young people who were experiencing challenges in their lives, so we felt confident in asking for his help. Dean had managed music artist Phil Driscoll, who has been a family friend for more than thirty years. In January 1993 Dean began a ministry working with students, speaking mostly in high schools. We had seen firsthand some of the results of Dean's ministry to young people as well as to families in crisis.

When Lita and I were at our wits' end in trying to help Daniel muster the power to resist the lure of drugs, I called Dean and asked if he knew of a healthy place with a spiritual environment where Daniel could get help. He recommended the Paul Anderson Youth Home in Vidalia, Georgia. Since 1961, the Anderson youth home has been a Christian residential home for troubled youth. Their desire is to see troubled teenagers transformed and to provide help for parents like us in crisis. When we visited, we strongly felt that this was a place where Daniel could flourish. Founded by the former world weight-lifting champion whose name was on the door, the Paul Anderson Home was a loving but highly disciplined, structured environment. The boys awaken early, exercise, tend to specific chores at which they work hard, and then attend school on the premises. Even Daniel agreed that the in-house program offered what he needed. He was ready to change.

That was an important part of Daniel's stepping forward, because as anyone who has ever battled an addiction knows, nobody can force you to make the right decisions. Nothing changes until you are ready to change. You have to want to get well. Daniel did, so we decided to send him to the

Paul Anderson Youth Home. It was a heartrending day when we dropped off our oldest son at the home and then drove away, tears streaming down our faces. But Lita and I believed that Daniel's future, and possibly his life, were at stake. Of course, family members were welcome to visit, but this was limited to every six weeks at the beginning of the program, so it was hard for us to be so far away from Daniel. Lita and I traveled to Georgia for family days and summit meetings with the Paul Anderson staff that worked with Daniel.

Daniel grew to love and respect those guys and gals who gave of their lives to help influence him and others for the better. What a calling. Daniel now had a couple of mentors he aligned with for the next eighteen months. Drew Read and Eric Love are two of the men at that home that God used to give my son back to me.

During the time Daniel was at the Paul Anderson home, Lita and I did not try to hide it. We didn't want to say or do anything to embarrass Daniel, but we knew we could disarm one of the Enemy's most powerful weapons by publicly admitting the problem.

I even mentioned Daniel's situation from the platform at our events and asked the people there to pray for him. Many did. Many others came to us in tears, saying, "We need **Nothing changes until you are ready to change.**

help with our kids too," or, "We have a child who has gotten involved in destructive behaviors, and we are at our wits' end." These were not pagan families. These were often fine Christian parents whose kids had gotten in trouble. We were surprised to discover that the needs were far greater than we had thought.

Many of the families in our business were grappling with some of the same issues that Lita and I were facing. We funneled people to New Life Network and were quick to recommend the Paul Anderson Home, which we have supported ever since. Our willingness to be candid and vulnerable about Daniel opened the door for others to admit that they were struggling with similar situations in their families.

Brittany was the quintessential older sister, bouncing between being a little mother and an irate sister. Her responses ran the emotional gamut from "Oh, I'm so worried about Daniel. I miss him so much. I hope he's doing okay," to "He shouldn't have done that in the first place!" Paul was younger, but he knew that Daniel was in trouble and it had affected our entire family. "I'm not going to do that, Mom," he promised Lita.

Walking through the rehab program with Daniel strengthened the faith of every family member. We prayed for Daniel constantly and tried to be encouraging, without making excuses for him that would undermine what the Paul Anderson program was trying to accomplish. We recognized, as Daniel did now, that he had to take responsibility for his actions. It was a tough lesson for all of us, but it made us stronger.

My prodigal son Daniel shared his testimony with my organization and kept it real.

The program at Paul Anderson was strict but not overly rigid. It was designed to deal with the whole person, incorporating physical activities such as weight lifting along with spiritual development. At first, Daniel wanted out, but he gradually made the turn and began to grow stronger physically, emotionally, and spiritually. He realized the error of his previous ways, and he became a stellar student at Paul Anderson. He recommitted his life to God and began to dream again. "I still don't know what I'm going to do," he said, "but it's okay. I know God has a plan."

When it came time for graduation, Daniel was chosen to give a testimony about his life. With Lita and me sitting in the audience, he apologized publicly for his past indiscretions and asked for forgiveness and prayers.

The time away gave Daniel a chance to grow up, to reflect, to realize that there were consequences for his actions. When he came home to us after eighteen months at the Paul Anderson Youth Home, Daniel was a changed young man.

It was a glorious day for me when I was able to tell Dean Sikes, "I want to thank you. I got my son back."

Since then, a number of other kids from R3Global families have gone through the program at the Paul Anderson Youth Home, and we have become active supporters of the work there. We've learned that the Enemy attacks any vulnerable areas in our lives, and if our kids feel neglected, rejected, or unimportant, that makes them an open target. The Paul Anderson Youth Home staff cautioned us, "Don't be in denial and don't underestimate your child's ability to deceive."

On a personal level, Dean Sikes has helped me to sort through some lessons I wish I would have considered more seriously prior to Daniel's dalliance with drugs. The Bible says, "Reliable communication permits progress."[24] One of the greatest lessons we learned through our experience was that you must keep the lines of communication open. You can't talk *at* each other; you must talk to one another. For reasons that seemed logical at the time, we had allowed ourselves to become isolated from one another, passing in our home like ships in the night, casually acknowledging each other but not interacting deeply.

Although I didn't recognize it, Daniel may have been reaching out for a father and perhaps was longing for my affirmation as much as I once grasped at any morsel of approval my dad might drop in my direction. While I recognized that I didn't want to perpetuate the patterns my dad had established, it is still hard to give what you have never received. I had to come to grips with the fact that my dad could only give me what he had been given, and if I wanted to give more to my son, I had to draw my own worth and approval from my heavenly Father. Only then could I be a good father to Daniel. I had to open up and admit that to Daniel, but even more important, I had to admit that to myself. Dean reminded me, there's a big difference between being a good dad and being a good father. A dad gives his child what the child wants; a father gives his child what the child needs.

I experienced something similar with Brittany and discovered that she harbored some deep-seated anger toward me for being gone from home so much and missing so much of her early life. We had an intense relationship for a number of years, but thankfully, as I became more of a father to Brittany than merely a dad, our relationship improved. Today, Brittany and I have a strong relationship, and she is following her dreams with my full support. I'm so proud of her! She has a very strong creative gift. I'm amazed at how she can make something out of nothing. She's faithful, diligent, and focused. She found her niche while studying a year abroad at a creative arts school. Now she works as a fashion intern in Southern California. I expect to see her in high demand as she continues to utilize her visual communication degree. I wouldn't be surprised if someday soon you might hear of her work in dressing the stars of Hollywood or the windows in the heart of the Big Apple.

As the youngest of our children, Paul benefits from the wisdom we've learned from our mistakes with his older siblings. He has a sensitive heart, is the consummate gentleman, and gets along with everyone. We're proud he's an excellent student and has a quiet strength about him. Paul is a semipro skateboarder who travels to compete coast-to-coast on a regular basis. He may well have a worldwide platform from which he can positively influence people, and Lita and I will be cheering for him from the front row. We love that he's chasing his dream!

As for Daniel, we're happy to say he's back to his true self. He has an eternal smile, and he sees the bigger picture and gets the job done better than it's ever been done before. I love his entrepreneurial spirit and positive outlook. We couldn't be more proud of Daniel today.

The devil bid high for our kids, but he lost. We're excited to see what God is going to do in and through all of our children's lives. We stand on the Scriptures: "Train up a child in the way he should go: and when he is old, he will not depart from it."[25]

Since your children are always your children, no matter how old they grow, you might want to heed this scripture. Sow into them so you can stand on this promise. It works. Praise the Lord! When your children are doing well, life is good.

CHAPTER **21**

Do Your Giving While You're Living

LIFE IS CERTAINLY A lot more than material success and money. Don't get me wrong; I enjoy living well, and I've been wonderfully blessed. But if money is the only reason you do something, it's insufficient motivation, and believe it or not, it won't satisfy. If money brings any satisfaction at all, it comes when you give it away, when you use your financial resources to help others. God doesn't have a problem blessing His people. E. V. Hill said, "If God can get it *through* you, He can get it *to* you." The Bible is replete with illustrations of people who prospered enormously, even in the midst of hard times. But God doesn't open the windows of heaven and pour out blessings on selfish people. He blesses givers.

Giving is a condition of the heart. You either are a giver or you aren't, and God knows your heart. Who in their right mind wouldn't want to be a blessing to those they see in need? It's the greatest feeling I can attest to in my life. We were all meant to do good to others, and that's how we follow the greatest commandment of all: "Love thy neighbor as thyself."[26] Whether we are giving of our substance or in good deeds, both have intrinsic value.

I don't want money to control me ever again. That's financial bondage, and I've been there. Since our spiritual heart surgery, we have been healed, delivered, and set free from hardheartedness and especially from stinginess. Getting free enough to become givers is one of the greatest transitions we have made, and one with some of the greatest consequences. Scripture says, "Give, and it will be given to you. A good measure, pressed down, shaken together and running over, will be poured into your lap."[27]

Please understand, money is not inherently evil. It's the *love* of money that is the root of all evil, not money itself. That's why I say I *love* God, I *love* my wife and kids, I *love* you, but I only *like* money. Why? Because of the things we can do with it. It represents our sweat equity, a part of our DNA, so to speak.

Lita and I love to give, so when we know we're about to receive a large bonus check, we normally have a strong impression about where we plan on sowing a bit of that reward. Lita and I have learned that the amount doesn't matter. It's a matter of obedience, doing it the way the Lord instructs.

Another scripture has been very meaningful to me when it comes to giving. God's Word instructs us, "Remember this: Whoever sows sparingly will also reap sparingly, and whoever sows generously will also reap generously."[28] Another passage will help you to understand where I am coming from: "Be not deceived; God is not mocked: for whatsoever a man soweth, that shall he also reap."[29]

Lita and I are nothing more than vessels that have been used of God to accomplish His will in this earth. We teach what God has instructed us to do in our lives, and we are just passing it on. Why? Because it works! If the Lord leads us to give something big or small to someone, we do it and God can (and does!) give us more.

For example, our dear friend Mylon LeFevre was staying at our Florida home while our family was traveling. Knowing that Mylon loves cars and motorcycles almost as much as I do, I left instructions with Steve Whyte, who oversees our property and vehicles, to have the keys to all our vehicles ready for Mylon. "Drive whatever you want," I told Mylon. "If you want to take the limo or one of the Mercedes or the Rolls-Royce one day, Steve will have them ready. If you want to drive the Mercedes SL 500, Steve will have that washed and ready to go too. Drive anything you want." I knew that Mylon would be like a kid in a candy store when he walked into our garage. That garage was my personal toy box, housing half a dozen custom Harleys and a dozen or so luxury automobiles.

Sure enough, Mylon ran the gamut and test drove nearly all the vehicles during his stay. When I returned, I asked him, "Did you enjoy driving the Rolls-Royce?"

"Oh, yeah, that was great," Mylon answered in his slow Georgia drawl.

"And how about the Harley?"

"Oh, yeah!" Mylon replied. I knew he loved Harley-Davidson motorcycles because he and I had taken several road trips on the hogs. There's something about men and loud, gnarly bikes.

"Which was your favorite?" I asked, honestly wanting to know.

"Well, of all your cars, I loved that little 500 SL Mercedes convertible the best. That baby is *sweet!*"

Mylon LeFevre is another providential partnership.

Lita and I love Mylon's spirit. A former rock 'n' roll musician, he once zipped around the world in private jets, from one show to the next with the likes of George Harrison, Eric Clapton, Mick Jagger, and the gang. (Mylon was just recently inducted into the Georgia Music Hall of Fame). Mylon had grown up in a gospel musical family, but he had rebelled against everything Christian, choosing a life of drugs and debauchery instead. Although Mylon gave up on God, God never gave up on Mylon. In the early 1980s, the prodigal son came home, and similar to the biblical story, Mylon asked for nothing when he returned. He took a job as a custodian at Mount Paran Church of God just so he could be around the teaching of the Bible. He was quick to admit that drugs and the rock-'n'-roll lifestyle had taken their toll on his mind, but as he studied the Bible, he was able to memorize huge chunks of scripture. More important, he was able to apply the biblical truths to his life. As Mylon got his life together with God, God gave him an opportunity to use his gift for writing songs, producing, and playing again, but this time in praise of his Savior and Lord, Jesus Christ.

Mylon put together a top-notch contemporary Christian rock band and toured the country as Mylon LeFevre and Broken Heart. The group was a huge success, but unfortunately, after plowing most of the earnings back into the ministry, Mylon had little remaining for himself.

After a major heart attack, Mylon continued to tour, but he turned his attention to his new calling of preaching and teaching. His gentle, Scripture-packed exhortations always inspired our R3Global audiences. Unpretentious and humble, Mylon never asked for a thing. So when he expressed such enthusiasm over the 500 SL, Lita and I had no question as to what we were going to do. Look out! Someone is about to get blessed!

The following week, a delivery man knocked on Mylon's front door in Atlanta. "I have a delivery here for a Mr. Mylon LeFevre."

"That's me," Mylon said as he followed the man outside. There on a car transporter was the beautiful black SL 500 that Mylon had enjoyed so much during his stay at our home. Mylon was blown away!

I love using material things to bless someone else. Giving is an outward expression of an inward feeling. We love Mylon, his heart, and his ministry. What an encouragement that car was to him.

At another time, Mylon and I were riding across the country on our Harleys when we stopped at a mom-and-pop restaurant to get a bite to eat. The waitress was a sweet lady, and when we got to talking with her, we discovered that she was struggling to make ends meet. We had a sandwich and some coffee and were ready to get back on the choppers and ride, and then I realized I hadn't quit thinking about this little mom and her plight. So the Lord, as He does, pricked my heart and set me up for another random act of kindness. I wanted to bless this little waitress.

(Here is where when folks tell me money is evil, I can't even relate. I need more, and so does everyone else that is willing to share with those less fortunate than themselves.)

Our entire bill barely came to twenty dollars, but I reached in for my "wad," as I call it, and was able to leave that sweet little lady and waitress a four-hundred-dollar tip. Mylon's eyes almost popped out, but he just smiled. He understood what I was doing.

I believe that God sets up situations like that for all of us. He puts us in situations not just to bless others but to test us and to try our hearts. The Bible says: "For where your treasure is, there your heart will be also."[30] We need to get our hearts aligned with our heavenly Father's. What a neat world it would be if everyone was trying to outbless everyone else!

Today might be a good time for you to start being aware of the opportunities that God is entrusting to you. Look out! You might just get blessed. I am set on teaching others to recognize and act on the giving opportunities the Lord puts in front of us. It doesn't take much: a smile, a simple word spoken to uplift or encourage, or just an act of kindness to show that you care. Simple, huh? But those random acts of kindness pay dividends you won't be able to put a price on. They will continue to show up in your life in things given to you by others. That's the way it goes.

Lita and I have come to understand that those opportunities may be doors to greater blessings if we respond properly. We're just the vessel to be used by God to accomplish something greater than the act of kindness or generosity itself. The Bible says, "One man gives freely, yet gains even more; another withholds unduly, but comes to poverty. A generous man will prosper; he who refreshes others will himself be refreshed."[31] Lita's and my general rule when it comes to giving is simple: don't hold back good when it's within your ability to give. There is also an order to things, kind of like a test. If you are faithful to respond and fulfill the small and insignificant assignments God puts in your path, He will certainly entrust you with other opportunities to be an even greater blessing. You'll get a promotion, and it will be the path to true and greater riches. Go back and continue to reread those scriptures, getting them embedded inside you so that you become a giving machine. Look out! You will get blessed. To date, we have yet to be able to outgive God. He is still winning! Yeah!

Don't hold back good when it's within your ability to give.

God never gives you an assignment without giving you the resources and the ability to carry it out. A lot of people want to do acts of kindness using other people's money and resources, but God has presented me with assignments that were specifically intended for me to use what He has given me to help someone else. I've experienced promotion that comes through doing such acts when I did them privately, swiftly, with no fanfare or improper motives, and without a hidden agenda or with any strings attached. That's what I call showing unconditional love in your giving.

When I first met Mylon, I fell in love with his heart. I probably related to him too, since we both grew up during the same era and shared a lot of the same taste in music. Like me, Mylon went through quite an ordeal in his transition from a fully ingrained, secular lifestyle to a new life in Christ. God allowed me to see Mylon's pain in the midst of this transition. He was going through a rough time in almost every area of his life. Although he was in quite a lot of turmoil, I saw an inner faith and strength in him, and

I knew he was sincere in his efforts to get to a point where he could consistently live out his commitment to Christ.

God seemed to knit Mylon's heart together with mine, and I entered into a covenant with him regarding his vision for reaching out to folks with his unique and powerful testimony. As fine a musician as Mylon is, he is an even more excellent communicator, and hence the transition from rock star to preacher and teacher.

God impressed on my heart and mind to enter into Mylon's suffering and to help him to get through it. I knew that Mylon needed money, and I had the resources to help, but that was not the way God wanted me to do it. He didn't want me to offer Mylon a bailout because I felt sorry for him. No, God wanted to teach me a few things as I shared Mylon's journey to restoration, revival, and restitution.

That's why, when we had an opportunity to sow into Mylon's personal life and ministry, it almost instantly became a blessing to Lita and me. Understand, I owned more cars than any one person should, so that first act of kindness was simply to bless Mylon. Period. Lita and I also believe in sowing our best, not our trash or throwaways.

Sow your best and God will bless you in kind. "God cannot be mocked. A man reaps what he sows."[32] Sow junk and rubbish, and you will get junk and rubbish back. To put it another way, if you plant orange seeds, you aren't going to get apple trees.

Whatever it is that Lita and I sow, we like to put it in top-notch condition before sowing it. We want everything we sow to be a blessing, not a burden or merely a relief to us, which would be giving with a wrong motive. For us, that's a heart issue.

In other words, if you are going to do something, do it right. Remember the Golden Rule: Do unto others as you would have them do unto you. God sees your acts of kindness, and when you bless someone else, God responds in like manner.

Not surprisingly, since we sowed that car into Mylon's life and other cars into other folks' lives, Lita and I have received many new cars in return.

God sees how you bless others, and He always blesses you even better. It is the law of sowing and reaping, but it involves the attitude of the giver's heart more than the price of your gift.

Any level of giving is honored by God when it is done in obedience and with a cheerful heart. I believe it is an honor to be asked of the Lord to do these things. Giving to those in need, regardless of the level, is like putting money in the bank with a far higher interest rate than any financial institution on earth! Our wealth is not in what we have but in what we have given.

Lita and I have sown all sorts of things—money, motorcycles, cars, airplanes, homes, and commercial buildings—into the lives of folks for whom we knew it would be a blessing. We also knew that those folks would use those gifts to advance God's kingdom here on earth, making this world a better place for all of us.

Mylon became the beneficiary of gifts he never expected, and that became an even greater blessing to us. God was pleased, and we were too.

I'm convinced that if we, as believers who represent the church, would be on alert for opportunities to do random acts of kindness, we wouldn't need welfare and government programs. When enough people buy into that philosophy, this whole deal down here will change for the better. If we all would do our part, we could put a big dent in poverty and lack here on earth. God's ways are so much higher than ours.

I don't tell these stories to toot our horn, but I do have a desire to change my world for the better, one person at a time. Imagine everyone doing a little bit to influence as many folks as possible to do good. What a difference we would make! What good is having material success if you don't use it to bless other people? You know as well as I do, you aren't going to take anything with you when you leave here. There aren't any Brinks trucks following hearses to the graveyard.

An old rhyme contains a lot of wisdom: "Do your giving while you're living; then you're knowing where it's going."

My goals and the themes for my businesses are making money, having fun, and helping a lot of people to do the same. We also believe in giving back. Right from the beginning, Dallin Larsen and I believed in rewarding people's efforts. "If you're willing to do two things," I told him, "we can outperform any other network marketing company and reach levels never before achieved in the industry's history."

"Okay, I'm game," Dallin said with a laugh. "What are the two things we must do?"

"First, pay the distributors their worth. The Scripture says, 'The labourer is worthy of his hire,'[33] so let's pay our distributors well and pay them promptly every week." From my previous network marketing experience, I knew how discouraging it could be to distributors when they were paid only a portion of what they actually deserved and paid only once a month. Any time a person's pay is delayed in any way, it zaps their motivation. Pay them well so they won't go anywhere else, and pay them now so they can learn to trust the company. Dallin and the corporate team broke the mold when they developed the most lucrative compensation plan in the industry's history. No wonder they attract and keep so many productive individuals in their company.

"Second," I added, "is to provide lots of recognition. Everyone likes to receive praise for their accomplishments. It's as powerful a motivator as money, and probably even more powerful." I've heard it said that men will die for it and babies will cry for it. Recognition!

Dallin agreed wholeheartedly with both proposals. He had started his career in network marketing as a distributor, so he understood not only the truth in my suggestions but the value of each and every one of the distributors. Without their buying into the vision of the company, no product would move and no profits would be made. So he fully understood that rewarding folks in a timely and healthy manner would earn their long-term loyalty and dedication. He envisioned and incorporated a series of production levels and pin levels to represent achievement levels: Star, Star 500, Star 1000, Bronze, Silver, Gold, Ruby, Emerald, and Diamond. Each of these pin levels, as they were achieved, represented a very lucrative and generous income.

Even as Lita and I flew home from our first meeting with Dallin, I could already see myself going through the ranks and achieving every one of those levels and earning the bonuses that went with them. I knew the drill: sponsor people, people move product, and the volume of product moved represents commissions paid. After all, that is why I went into the business with him. The higher the pin level, the more money a person could make. So my question was, "How high is up?"

I told Lita, "I actually don't understand all the details of attaining the levels Dallin has established, but whatever it takes to reach the highest levels, that's what we are shooting for. Diamond was the premier level that was set at the company's onset, and we knew how much volume that meant doing in a week's time. We simply translated that into how many people we needed to create that volume weekly in each leg of our business, and we went for it, putting in one person at a time and watching the volume increase each time we recruited new folks into the business. Lita and I knew that we were going to go Diamond, so we decided to do it in the least amount of time possible.

Now there are three things I know about money: (1) I would rather have it than not have it, (2) I would rather make more of it than less of it, and (3) I would rather have it sooner than later. How about you? If you can agree to those three simple truths, then you just might consider why not you? why not now? In the words of Larry the Cable Guy, Lita and I wanted to "Git 'er done!"

We figured if we were going to be a part of this deal, then we should go for the gusto. You only have one chance to get started quickly, so we reached an agreement and went for it. Was it blind faith? No, we knew exactly what we had to do to create the volume we needed in order to earn the money. We just didn't know what pin level they would assign to those levels when we hit them. We loved having a goal to shoot for, but we knew we could go above and beyond the levels the corporate management first saw—and we did!

I remember calling Dallin and saying, "You know, this isn't quite right. I'm a Diamond, but I'm doing ten times more volume than some of the other people who have achieved the same level. We're going to need to set some more goals and create some new levels that will reward the folks who want to go much further in the business."

"Okay, what exactly are you thinking?" Dallin asked cautiously.

"I think we need to create another three to six levels that simply reward the exponential volume that a Diamond creates beyond that original volume level. Anyone who goes Diamond and helps other people in his group to reach that same level needs a much greater reward," I said.

"What do you think we ought to do?"

"Let's establish three new levels of Diamonds, then a whole new category for those folks who help three legs to go Diamond. Let's call them Black Diamonds."

Dallin asked me to come up with what I thought was a fair and reasonable compensation and rewards for those new ranks. Think about that. When was the last time your boss asked for your opinion on how you could reward yourself and others in his business? I'll tell you: Never! But Dallin did, and that is one of the reasons he is another one of those providential partners. He is a humble man with a contrite heart who is also very wise. He knows that there is safety in a multitude of counselors and also wisdom. He is a fair and balanced kind of a guy.

I suggested to him a list of the new ranks and pin levels with the corresponding volumes required to achieve them. For the sake of simplicity, I will spare you the details of the volume requirements and describe the rewards I thought were worthy of these efforts. I'm describing these to you because I don't know of any company in the world that rewards folks like this company does.

When someone achieves the Diamond Level ($200,000 to $700,000 a year), they receive an all-expense-paid trip for two for a week in Maui, Hawaii. More than five hundred couples have received this reward to date. For Black Diamonds (earning approximately $1.2 million a year), the rewards are even greater: custom rings and pendants and a three-year paid lease on a black Mercedes-Benz (any model). More than forty-five distributors have received these rewards to date. It wasn't that I wanted or even needed another Mercedes, but when someone else gives you one for free, it drives differently than when you buy or lease it yourself.

I wanted Dallin to catch the power of incentives—the dream, the *dream,* the *Dream!*

"Good idea!" Dallin responded. "But I don't know if we can do that."

"Dallin, I've already run the numbers. They're right here. Here's the necessary volume. Here's what the car will cost." We both realized it was within the budget guidelines he had set already. In fact, we were at those levels when the company incorporated the new compensation and rewards structure.

Lita and I were a machine for the first three years. So Dallin delivered a brand-new 550 SL convertible to us that very first year. Yeehaw!

We have designated six other higher ranks and pin levels since that first year. We believe that no matter how successful people become, it is vital to allow them to continue to shoot for something beyond where they are. Otherwise, they tend to get complacent. They will stagnate and get out of the creative business-building stage. You must keep that carrot in front of the builders in any business. Give them more reasons to expand their horizons. It has nothing to do with greed; it has everything to do with having a vision beyond where you have been.

Soon the MonaVie rewards program exceeded anything in the networking industry and far beyond those in the traditional corporate world. Lita and I achieved five of the six higher awards levels in the first four years since the start of the company. We have helped dozens of others do the same in their businesses. That's how we gauge success—by how many oth-

MonaVie offers rewards worthy of the effort. For example, my new Murcielago. As new Crowns, Lita and I received one million dollars in cash and the exotic car.

ers we help to do the same. Since achieving the higher levels, we have been rewarded with luxury yacht trips each year, four exotic vacations each year, access to the company's jet so we can fly privately (through jet credits that we earn and use across the United States and internationally), trips aboard luxurious cruise ships, and bonus checks that accompanied each level we achieved: one hundred thousand dollars for hitting the Royal level, three hundred thousand dollars for achieving the Presidential level, six hundred thousand dollars for the Imperial level, and one million dollars for achieving the Crown level. The company also allowed us to pick one of five exotic cars: Bentley, Aston Martin, Ferrari, Rolls-Royce, or Lamborghini. We chose the Lamborghini. They gave us the keys and the title on top of the million-dollar bonus! Where is that happening in the work world today?

We received those rewards all in a three-year period. And the beat goes on. In our fourth year, Lita and I became the first Double Crowns in the company's history. For that level, they increased the ante and gave us a two-million-dollar bonus and an all-expense-paid trip for two around the world. Why wouldn't anybody look at my industry, knowing the rewards anyone can achieve? It makes no sense to me how a person can work for someone else for twenty to forty years and not receive anything, compared to what our industry does for folks. But they must have eyes to see and ears to hear.

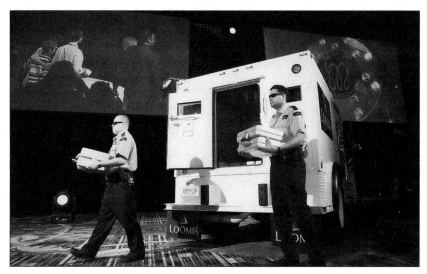

A million dollars in cash is delivered to us at the
2008 MonaVie International Convention.

Just for laughs, the company is now offering a Triple Crown reward to anyone beyond the level at which Lita and I now sit—an all-expense-paid trip aboard Richard Branson's Virgin Galactic spaceship, a reward trip that will literally take folks out of this world for a weightless adventure into space...and a three-million-dollar bonus. The trip doesn't interest Lita, but she is already wishing me well on the journey and is getting a big life insurance policy on me!

One of the main reasons we stay focused on the company we are with now is that they know how to reward their independent distributors at all levels, especially the top performers. Occasionally, people will try to recruit Lita and me for networks. When they do, I tell them about our rewards and incentives and then ask, "So what do you guys have?" Usually, they slink into the shadows, never to bother us again!

There are basically two kinds of people in this world: givers and takers. One of the many character traits I appreciated about Dallin Larsen when I first met him was the fact that he was a giver. Before the first bottle of MonaVie was ever sold, Dallin and I recognized that, like Abraham of old, we are blessed to be a blessing.

"If we really believe that," I suggested to Dallin, "and we want God's blessing on this company and business, why don't we give back to the very people and country that have given us this unique berry?" Dallin loved the idea. He and his wife, Karree, committed to provide financial assistance to some of the less fortunate people in the beautiful country of Brazil, specifically the orphan children in Rio de Janeiro. When Dallin inquired as to who we might contact to make this happen, I knew exactly who to call.

Doug Roland, a longtime friend from Jacksonville, was doing missionary and evangelistic work throughout South America and Brazil. Dallin and I called to present our idea to Doug, and he immediately suggested we talk with his friend Sergio Ponce in Rio.

We knew that if Dallin would visit and see the abject poverty and poor conditions in which these precious children were living, he would understand why we were so passionate about doing something there. Dallin talked with Sergio, and he and Karree visited him in Rio. But it was in the favelas, the wrenching slums of Rio, where Dallin and Karree's hearts were touched and broken for those kids. In 2006, less than a year after we had been in business, upon the Larsens' return to the States, the MORE Project—an acronym for MonaVie's Operation Rescue—was born.

Lita and I knew that if this company would adopt the project of helping these children and their families, the company would seal its fate and be bountifully blessed. Why? Because God says that we are not to forsake these little ones. In the Bible, we are told, "Religion that God our Father accepts as pure and faultless is this: to look after orphans and widows in their distress and to keep oneself from being polluted by the world."[34] That's keeping our eye on the prize and also staying humble of heart.

To me this was the real deal maker. This is the reason I believe that the MonaVie business has been so blessed and prosperous to this day.

As soon as the MORE Project was up and running, Lita and I committed to be regular supporters. As soon as we got R3Global up and running, Lita and I also committed our organization to be one of the major contributors as well.

Knowing that we couldn't help all of Brazil, we decided to focus our energy on the town of Vila Ipiranga, a mountainous community of about one hundred thousand people just outside Rio. We teamed with Sergio Ponce, his wife Silvia, and their entire family who had been ministering for years to the people in this part of the country, especially to these children and orphans. They had been fervently praying that God would send someone to help,

We are blessed to be a blessing.

because the task they faced was so overwhelming. When we called and offered to partner with them in this quest, by Sergio's account, we were an answer to his and his family's prayers. They not only shared our vision, they took on the task of being the overseers of the entire project there in Vila Ipiranga. Our first task was to provide for the most immediate needs, such as food, clothing, and personal support for as many of those kids and families as possible. But beyond that, we wanted to provide education, resources, and support so they could break the cycle of poverty. As the saying goes, if you give a man a fish, you feed him for a day, but if you teach him how to fish, you feed him for the rest of his life. Therefore, we helped these children and their families gain hope for a brighter future by providing the teaching and training they need so they can provide for their families. Bringing the family unit back together is absolutely key to restoring that hope they so desperately need.

In the process, we have every opportunity to share the love of Christ with them and to share the gospel as well. Through Christ they have the hope He offers, not simply for a better life here on earth, but also for life in heaven forever. Some of the Brazilian children have a rudimentary knowledge of Christianity, but most of them have never heard that they can have a loving, personal relationship with Christ. These kids get to see and experience the love of Christ in and through us as we simply minister to them.

We visited Brazil as part of the MORE Project. This is what it's all about.

To initially finance the MORE Project, the MonaVie Corporation committed to cover all the administrative costs. The rest of the expenses are paid by donations, and 100 percent of every contribution goes to directly support the work in Brazil. We receive a donation during every R3Global meeting to help feed, clothe, and educate the children in Brazil, but also to get people accustomed to giving. Lita and I match every dollar given, turning one dollar into two. In 2008, R3Global members donated more than $700,000 to the MORE Project. In 2009, we raised more than

He could be my next new distributor. We loved all these kids.

$3.2 million to help lift the quality of life for those beautiful families in Brazil. I tell people, "If you want to touch the world, come work with us." We want to teach people how to be more, do more, and give more. Incidentally, the more we give, the more we receive.

Support for the MORE Project children often comes from people who have plenty of reasons to be concerned about their own needs but who choose to reach out in some way to help others. One such young lady, eight-year-old Lilly Anderson, from Cumming, Georgia, near Atlanta, touched our hearts with her unselfish concern for the children in Brazil. Lilly has every reason to be self-absorbed, but she and her mom and dad—Jennifer and Joey—and her three-year-old sister, Audrey, are just the opposite.

In September 2009, when normally healthy, vibrant Lilly began to complain of persistent stomach pains, doctors discovered that she was anemic with a high protein count. After more exams, Lilly was diagnosed with neuroblastoma, a malignant, cancerous tumor that develops in nerve tissue. The doctors said that most likely Lilly had the condition from birth, and it began to manifest as she grew. By the time they discovered it, the tumor had progressed to stage four cancer.

Jennifer, Lilly's mom, is a MonaVie distributor who was introduced to the business through Debbie and Charlie Kalb. Knowing that there were high levels of antioxidants in MonaVie, Jennifer began fortifying Lilly's system with the juice. Lilly needed all the strength she could muster. Her frail, slender body underwent seven major rounds of chemotherapy, two surgeries, a spinal tap, and even stem-cell treatments. But she came through like a trooper!

Throughout Lilly's treatments, Charlie and Debbie kept in touch with the family. In November, Debbie called Dallin Larsen and told him about Lilly. Debbie had a special request: would the corporation allow Debbie to use some of her jet credits to fly Lilly to Orlando so she could attend the American Girl doll exhibition? Attending the show was one of Lilly's dreams.

"No," Dallin responded, much to Debbie's disappointment, and then he added, "But I'll do it."

Dallin authorized the MonaVie jet to pick up Jennifer and Lilly and one of her friends and whisk them to Orlando to attend the exhibition. Lilly was thrilled!

When she returned home, she wrote Dallin a beautiful thank-you note, which Dallin read in an emotion-packed webcast. That was the first time the MonaVie family at large heard about Lilly, and thousands of people began to pray for her complete recovery.

In November 2009, Lilly was back in St. Jude's Children's Hospital in Memphis for more treatments. Dallin and Karree Larsen were in Minnesota with Charlie and Debbie, conducting a meeting along with Corbin and Holly Roush, when they heard that Lilly was in the hospital again. The three couples flew to Memphis and, along with the two pilots, went to visit and encourage Lilly while she was hospitalized. Early in 2010, although she still had to undergo six months of antibody treatments, Lilly's doctors could find no trace of the cancer.

That's enough to get fired up about right there! But Lilly had seen some of the MonaVie videos on her mom's computer about our work in Brazil. So in the spring of 2010, Lilly decided she wanted to help some of the children with whom the MORE Project was involved. Lilly set up a lemonade stand outside the Anderson home, and she raised $121 for the children in Brazil.

In April 2010, Lilly came to the R3Global Eastern Regional Leadership Conference held at the World Congress Center in Atlanta. We told a bit of her story and brought her onstage. When the crowd heard about Lilly's gift of $121 and saw the beautiful little girl wearing a bandanna around her head, still bald from the chemo treatments, thousands of people rose to their feet and applauded Lilly's efforts. If I could have read the mind of the every member of that audience, I'm sure I would have sensed thousands of people thinking, "If Lilly can do something like that while she's recovering from cancer, what can I give? What *must* I do?" Lilly Anderson is an inspiration to all of us.

The MORE Project also inspired MonaVie and R3Global distributors Paul Mehan and Mike and Chrissy Bowman to ride their bicycles from Vancouver, British Columbia, all the way to our reunion in Orlando, Florida, a distance of more than forty-two hundred miles, over thirty-five days, while raising money to help support the work of the MORE Project. I'm convinced that the more we give, the more God will pour blessings into our lives. The people of this wonderful company and R3Global are proving that point on a daily basis.

MONAVIE HAS also been active indirectly in saving the lush rain forest along the Amazon River. Because we harvest the acai berries during three different seasons throughout the year, we save the trees from being targeted by other

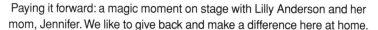

Paying it forward: a magic moment on stage with Lilly Anderson and her mom, Jennifer. We like to give back and make a difference here at home.

Dallin Larsen was named Ernst Young CEO of the Year in 2009. My friend and associate, I'm proud of you.

organizations that simply cut down the trees for the heart of palm that is used as a salad garnish in America. These companies pay fifty cents per tree for a single heart of palm—and the tree will never grow back! Thousands of acres are being harvested for those purposes, but we are making a difference there with a positive alternative. We're going and staying green. Year after year, the towering palm trees produce purple acai berries, one of nature's superfoods and one of the primary ingredients in MonaVie juices. The trees remain healthy and standing, producing more of God's superfood to help the next generation.

To us, it is all about being good caretakers of what God has given to us and being good stewards of the land. I love the fact that we give in many ways, and this is just another example of giving good information to the right people to help them make the right decisions that affect all of us. As I like to say, "Reliable information permits progress."

CHAPTER **22**

Live Until You Die,

and Die Empty!

BY THE END OF 2009, my new venture into the MonaVie business was now a billion-dollar business. The company was named by *Inc.* magazine as the fastest growing private company in the food and beverage category, and it was number 18 overall on the magazine's Top 500 list. No other network marketing business in the United States has ever grown so rapidly, built on one main product, with no major advertising campaigns. In fact, most of our advertising is done by word of mouth, one person telling another about the product and the opportunity. Since the company's inception in January 2005, well over two million people around the world have jumped on the MonaVie bandwagon and are on their way toward better health and nutrition. We are currently placing product in thirteen countries, with plans to expand to others within a few years.

MonaVie distributors posted more than two billion dollars in collective sales during the company's first five years, accomplishing this staggering feat with a base of fifty thousand to one hundred thousand active distributors in the United States and abroad. Leading the way were five hundred Diamonds and more than forty-five Black Diamonds. We plan to reach our next goal of five billion dollars by identifying another two thousand folks who want to go Diamond, and of that number, two hundred or more will achieve the Black Diamond level. Our long-range goal is 20/20: reaching for twenty billion dollars in sales per year within twenty years. The corporation is expanding and broadening its product line, while still holding to our vision of being the best health and wellness business for the world. Our new line of weight-management products hits the market as my book rolls off the press. Stay tuned for more exciting news about what we are about to do in this great industry.

We've worked diligently, but in truth, we can't and don't take any credit for this exceptional growth. We may do the physical work, but it is God who gives us the wisdom and favor that brings the growth and increase. We are privileged to be a part of what He is doing through us and through our business.

To date, we have remained in the food and beverage category of the marketplace, so we are not required to seek approval from the U.S. Food and Drug Administration (FDA). The MonaVie product is a blend of nineteen fruits; fruits are food, not drugs. The FDA puts its stamp of approval on all sorts of products we see advertised in the untold numbers of commercials on every channel on television. Have you noticed all the horrid side effects that you may encounter by using these man-made pharmaceuticals? Nope, the FDA is not the organization from whom we are looking for an endorsement.

When folks ask if our product is FDA approved, we simply say, "No, but it is GOD approved." God made the berries, and He gave us the wisdom to use them in this manner. When you want a good wake-up call, watch an afternoon or evening television show and note when these lotions, potions, and pills are offered as a quick fix for anything that ails you. Pay close attention to the possible side effects that may occur. If it weren't so sad, it would be ludicrous and hilariously funny. But it is sad that folks are looking for quick fixes and silver bullets, simply wanting things the easy way versus the diligent way. One of the reasons I have chosen to be in this industry is that the world will go back to all-natural remedies as people process and regain their understanding of doing things God's way versus our way. We are advocates of the preventative and all-natural route. Everything cycles, and this cycle holds the makings of unlimited opportunity in the health and wellness industry worldwide. Folks are looking for real answers to their health issues. We have the right industry, the right product, and the right people at the right place and at the right time. Most folks want to live a full and healthy life until they die. Some live and some just survive. You must be proactive to live that high life.

A FRIEND of mine told me that he had originally been turned off to network marketing because some professional athletes had approached him about getting into the business based solely on how much money he could make. That's unfortunate, because that is not R3Global's or my approach. We teach to lead with the product; in other words, let people sample the juice so folks can taste, see, and feel the benefits of this superior nutritional beverage.

Many people are initially interested primarily in the benefits of getting the nutrients through such a convenient and affordable manner. Drinking two to four ounces of this premiere blend of nineteen fruits is a positive alternative to finding, processing, and eating seven to thirteen servings of fruit yourself—daily! Ours is relatively inexpensive, fast, and good for you, all qualities that the baby boomers are looking for in a product they will consume and promote. Once people see those benefits and experience them for themselves, they often want to see the business side of our distribution program.

One of my goals through this company and R3Global is to take the message of better health—physically, financially, emotionally, spiritually—to the world, one person at a time. My ultimate goal is to replicate in others the success we have seen until small groups become large groups and large groups become massive groups worldwide. I want to fill coliseums around the world with people who are looking, who want to change their lives for the better, who want to make a difference in their personal lives, their family, their community, and their country and have a positive impact on their world. I am not hoping merely to convert people to a better way of living; I want to educate them so they can become more productive and effective in their lives, rather than just busy. I want them to enjoy this thing called life and their journey through it. I don't want people to be busy, I want them to be productive and effective in their lives.

My goal is to reach a massive number of people not simply *with* our business but *through* our business, with the platform God has given to me in order to achieve that goal. Of course I want to do something that is much more meaningful in the process; that is why I want to lead people into a truly satisfying relationship with the Lord. I desire to do something that has a lasting effect.

This is where the idea of moving from success to significance comes into play. I want to build a legacy that will affect the next generation and the generations to come. Not just in the here and now, but far beyond my life here on earth.

At least three highly respected, godly leaders have spoken those very words to Lita and me, declaring that we would reach masses of folks with a message of hope for them and the world. I love having a vision beyond myself. That way, God has to get involved for it to come to pass. I know that as I do my part, He certainly will do His. These declarations about our lives were spoken independently of each other and at different times and places. Each time those men of God spoke over us, they confirmed to me that my mission is to reach a massive number of people for Christ. I have since labeled it "the Great Rescue," launching out into the deep once more and going for the big catch. If you want to know what motivates me, there it is! Now, of course, this won't be done by my hand but by the Spirit of God.

> **God makes the impossible possible in and through you.**

When you have a grandiose vision beyond yourself, you have to understand that it will be accomplished "'not by might nor by power, but by my spirit,' says the LORD."[35] So relax and let God make the impossible possible in and through you. That's what He does best, and that's why He gets the honor and the glory. You just get to steward the money or the resources. It's all His, anyway.

In the process, I want to encourage, influence, and empower people to understand and have what I call ultimate success, which basically is knowing God's perfect and divine will in your life and then doing it. Faith without works is dead.

It's one thing to know what it is that God has purposed in your heart to do, but to make it happen is a whole other thing. That is why I developed the U-Can-II and the R3Global companies. They represent a support system for the people who want to accomplish their personal goals but don't know where to go to get that direction. My companies promote personal development for prosperity in the twenty-first century. Total success involves body, soul, and spirit. The Bible says: "For what shall it profit a man, if he shall gain the whole world, and lose his own soul?"[36] I want

The R3Global icon stands for ultimate success in body, soul, and spirit.

total success, the whole package. I want success in every area of my life, as do most people. But the success that comes from a submitted life to Christ is the kind of success that will follow a person into eternity. The person who hears, "Well done, good and faithful servant,"[37] is the person who has truly lived a successful life. That is ultimate success for each of us. Not much else will matter when we stand before our Maker—and we all will—to give an account of our lives. Whether one believes it or not is not the issue; it is true and it will happen. If you haul off and do nothing with your life, and then live for things with no eternal value or meaning, what do you think God is going to say to you? It is not a matter of *if* you lived your life; it's *who* you lived for and how you influenced others for His sake.

I did things on my own long enough to come to the end of myself. That's why I let people know that victory in life is not in the fight, but in the surrender. When I finally gave up on doing things my way and sought to do things God's way, my whole life began to make sense, and I experienced a sense of satisfaction beyond my comprehension. I truly experienced the peace that passes all understanding. Once you get on that track, nothing can compete or compare with it.

Lasting success doesn't have anything to do with money or materialism; all that stuff passes away. But the people you reach for Christ's sake will live on for eternity. So invest in things with a one-thousand-year mentality. What in your life will last that long? People who live for the Lord. I call that true leadership and inspired influence. You can't take anything with you except the people you influenced for His sake.

One of the things that still gets me excited is to stand on a stage (or anywhere for that matter) and tell a group of people, "I can show you how to succeed big-time in the next two to five years if you just do what I am

BRIGISM

The victory is not in the fight but in the surrender.

doing. But if you want true success in life, come on up and I'll introduce you to the One who can give you life and allow you to live it more abundantly. And you can have that in the next two to five *minutes!*" I love to pray with folks and be able to introduce my precious Lord to them in any setting. No time is a good time, so now is as good a time as any. If you hear His voice, don't harden your heart. I've tried living my life and chasing success without Him, and I didn't get the results I wanted. But with Him, I have no complaints, and I'm not going back, especially since I know for sure what He wants and desires for us. When I share with folks that God made all of us and made us in His image, I share with them that He has yet to create one failure. We were made in His image, and He is a winner!

If we fail, it is by choice, not by chance. It's our life and we get out of it what we decide to put into it. When you live a surrendered life to Christ, you must accept what God wants and wills for your life. So I start with one of God's promises, "'For I know the plans I have for you,' declares the LORD, 'plans to prosper you and not to harm you, plans to give you hope and a future.'"[38] Now, that's a promise!

My latest earned reward is a 2010 Rolls-Royce Phantom. What's better than getting one? Getting one for FREE!

I love sharing with folks why I so strongly believe in them and their hope for a bright future. "Because it's God's will for your life," I tell them. The Bible says, "Beloved, I wish above all things that thou mayest prosper and be in health, even as thy soul prospereth."[39] Isn't that amazing? That God would say "above *all things,*" He wills that you (yes, *you*) prosper and be in good health even as your soul prospers. Now your soul is what makes you like no other person in the world. It is your spiritual DNA, your mind, your will, and your emotions. So if you are going to prosper, you must get your mind, will, and emotions to a place of peace and not engage in a battle within yourself. I see it as giving yourself permission to succeed. No one else can do that for you, not even God Himself. He has already weighed in on your situation. He wills that you succeed. Now, it is you who are willing that it will be done. I tell people, "Will it, and it will be done for you."

God loves you. He is not mad at you, and He wants the best for you, just as any loving father would want for his kids. He is your Father in heaven, and He desires to see His children doing well. When I finally understood that, I prospered immediately in my soul. The rest was just a matter of doing something in this life to make a living that brought me peace and contentment. The relational marketing thing was the place I now know God had for me since before I was even born. That's the way He does things.

God is no respecter of persons, which means He shows no favoritism. I kid with folks and let them know that God loves all of us, but I happen

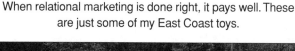

When relational marketing is done right, it pays well. These are just some of my East Coast toys.

to be one of his favorites! After the chuckles fade away, I let them know that He loves them as much as He loves me. If I can succeed to the level in life that I have, then God will do the same for anyone who desires it. Again, God is a gentleman, and if you don't desire Him in your life, He will not override your will to invade or become a part of your life. That would be trespassing, and He won't do it. But I ask folks, "Do you like where you are at this point in your life? If not, why not give God a chance at it with you? You will be amazed at just what might happen. He took me from the pit to the palace, from the jungle to the jet." He says, "The LORD will make you the head, not the tail. If you pay attention to the commands of the LORD your God that I give you this day and carefully follow them, you will always be at the top, never at the bottom."[40] If God can take me from the pit to the palace, and He is no respecter of persons, then He can do the same for you if you will let him. If I can do it, so can you!

PEOPLE SOMETIMES ask me, "You are so excited about the Lord, why don't you become a preacher?" That's simple: I'm not called to be a preacher. I'm called to be a businessman. In the Bible, there were kings and there were priests. My calling is that of a king; I may be the priest of my home, but not to the world. I support my friends who are called into that arena, and I am well pleased. I found God in the marketplace, in the business world, so it is not surprising to me that it is in the business world that I feel most comfortable telling others about Him. I call it marketplace ministry. Some people are in the business of ministry; I am in the ministry of business. I minister to folks in and through my business. I am one who was touched by seeing Christianity in practice with my own eyes. I saw people living it in the real world. I am of the belief that Christians should be the keyhole though which others see God. I want to teach people to walk the walk versus just talk the talk.

God put me in the very place where He has gifted me. Sure, a bunch of people come to know the Lord through our business, but I am still a businessperson. It's my desire, my passion, and where my gifting is. Whatever your business, if you are willing, God will use you as His representative as well.

Regardless of our job descriptions, we are instructed by Jesus to share the good news with the world and to help people become true disciples. He says to seek first the kingdom of God and His righteousness and all these other things will be added to us.[41] I've discovered that many in the marketplace are more open and eager to hear and do something about perpetuating the message of hope than most of the folks in traditional churches. Jesus said something about that: "It is not the healthy who need a doctor, but the sick."[42]

How do Lita and I balance our commitment to Christ and our ability to help people prosper through our business? The answer is simple. For some people their life calling is to the business of ministry. While everyone who is a true believer is called to be a minister in whatever occupation they may pursue, some men and women are specifically gifted and called to perform more professional ministry-oriented duties on a daily basis. Pastors, missionaries, and all sorts of nonprofit organizations exist today, and Lita and I encourage all of them who are presenting a biblical message and worldview.

But my life calling is different. I minister through my business. Relational network marketing has given us the opportunity to help people grow beyond anything they ever thought possible. I meet them where they are, and I help them to accomplish whatever it is that they desire. This is not about simply making money, but about becoming a better person, a better dad or mom, husband or wife, a better person in his or her community. We attempt to strengthen the whole person: body, mind, and spirit.

We are all called to take the gospel, the good news, into all the world. Living a happier, healthier, and more prosperous life is good news to a bunch of folks. Jesus asks us, as he asked Peter, "Do you love me?" Then He said, "Feed my sheep."[43] People need the good news; they need the hope that only God through His precious Son and His Word can bring. As believers, we are commissioned by the King of kings and Lord of lords. We are His ambassadors to go and share the truth in love throughout the world. Now, that's a mission I want in on! There's enough bad news being spread throughout the world. I want to bring some good news! All people everywhere need to be encouraged. How about you? Do you want to be encouraged? Then, first, go encourage someone else, and it will come back to you.

A dear brother in the Lord that I honor and respect reminded me that Francis of Assisi said, "Preach the gospel at all times, and if necessary, use words." Simply put, show the love of Christ to people; don't just tell them. We learned the game Show and Tell as kids; now as adults we sometimes need to be reminded that what we do speaks so loudly that others cannot hear what we are saying. Our actions must show the world God's love. Then, they may be willing to listen to our message.

Go. Show and tell one person at a time about this wonderful message of hope in and through Christ. And remember: Two-thirds of God is "go."

Because of our strong spiritual stands, I'm often asked, "Is MonaVie a Christian company?" In a word, the answer is "No." MonaVie is not a Christian organization.

My company, R3Global, although dedicated to God, is not necessarily a Christian business, either. It is simply a vehicle that I use as a believer to perpetuate the gospel. That is not a contradiction, nor do I have any ulterior motives, as some might suggest. I am a believer 24/7, not whenever it is convenient. I am anything but politically correct. How some people try to separate the spirit from the soul-man is beyond me. I can't do it, and I don't want to try. Jesus said, "If anyone is ashamed of me and my words, the Son of Man will be ashamed of him when he comes in his glory and in the glory of the Father and of the holy angels."[44] He also said, "He that denieth me before men shall be denied before the angels of God."[45] Companies aren't going to stand before God and give an account of their lives. They can't. People own those companies and decide who they are going to serve today. I want to honor God in every way possible with whomever I work with or for.

> **Some are called into the business of ministry; I am called to the ministry of business.**

I am a Christian who happens to make my living through network marketing. *People*—individuals—are Christians, not companies or organizations. One reason I believe so passionately in network marking is because it is a people business. In fact, I prefer the term *relational marketing*. It is all about building and nurturing the relationships we have with other people. People like to do business with people they both like and trust.

I simply teach about having a divine influence on people by bringing the fruit of the Spirit into everything we do: "love, joy, peace, patience, kindness, goodness, faithfulness, gentleness and self-control. Against such things there is no law."[46] Yeah, baby!

✦ ✦ ✦

OBVIOUSLY, NOT everyone who attends R3Global events (or Brig Hart events) buys into our values or even our ideas about living the Christian life. That's okay. We've decided that our job is to love people, present the gospel, and allow God to do the rest. He says, "So is my word that goes out from my mouth: It will not return to me empty, but will accomplish what I desire and achieve the purpose for which I sent it."[47] If I share the gospel in love with a proper motive and intent in my heart, that promise says it won't return void. It does its work in the hearts of the folks who are listening. If they have ears to hear, they hear; if not, they might come back at another time.

I don't want a title. I have a commission and an ordination of sorts from God Himself. That's all the motivation I need to encourage people, to empower them, and to commission them to change the world. I'm not afraid to step out, to do what God wants me to do. My attitude is, "Come on, devil. Greater is He who is in me than anything you can throw at me." Today is a bad day for Satan, because I woke up.

Our goal at R3Global, along with my association with MonaVie, is not simply to be the best company in the world, but to be the best company

I don't want a title.

for the world. Through networking, or relational marketing, I am convinced that I can succeed in my own life, and in the process, I want to help change our world for the better. And, yes, I believe that *you can too!*

Every so often, an interviewer will ask, "You've accomplished so much in your life. You've made millions of dollars, helped feed, clothe, and educate kids in Brazil, and spun off dozens of millionaires in business. So what's left? What do you still want to do?"

Understand this: success is not a destination; it's a journey. You don't ever arrive at success; you move on to the next assignment on your journey. The higher you climb up a mountain, the farther you see. I have many dreams and goals beyond where I am so far. There are so many folks who want and need to find their place in life, and I want to be a facilitator of that. Whether they get into business with me or not is not the issue. I want to make my mark on the society in which I live. I start with me, then my family, and then I launch out into the world, touching one person at a time. You never know who you are talking to or who you just might meet today or tomorrow. My life is about what is next. I am what you would call happily discontent. I am abased in all things, as the Bible speaks of it, but the God-nature in me is to be all that I can be while I am still on this earth. I want to fulfill my calling, my destiny, and I want to accomplish everything that God has in store for me.

I've heard it said that hell is when a person realizes the life they could have had versus the life they lived. I don't want anything of anyone else's. I just want all that God has assigned to me. I think big, so I know that He isn't done with me yet! You are going to live until you die, so why not really live until you die? I'll borrow the old slogan: Go for the Gusto! Or the old army recruitment slogan: Be All That You Can Be. Just go for it!

"Die empty," I respond to the interviewers. "I want to live life to the fullest and die empty. I want to die with no regrets. I want to get it all out there on the playing field and do everything I was born to do, and I want to help influence others to do the same. My good friend Myles Munroe says the wealthiest place on planet earth is not where the massive oil fields are or the diamond mines or the silver and gold mines. No, it's the cemetery! Why the cemetery? Because that's where all the unfulfilled dreams are buried. All the songs and books that were never written. All the artwork and other creative forms that were never performed. All the ideas and businesses that were never pursued or started. Sad, isn't it? I want to take nothing to the grave with me that God wants to express in and through me. I want to die empty, and I want to help others to do the same.

I call myself a hope broker. You can live without a lot of things. You can live without food for thirty days, without water for three days, without air for three minutes, but you can't live without hope for three seconds. So I broker hope to anyone who crosses our paths. I'm a looker who's looking for other lookers. Hope, remember, is nothing more than premature faith. Have faith that you can do anything you set your heart and mind to do.

My life hasn't always been peaceful, but the Prince of Peace resides in my heart and has always seen me through every situation I've faced. As I glance back on my life, I now realize that all the adversities that Lita and I experienced were for a purpose. If I hadn't grown up on the Eastern Shore of Maryland, I wouldn't have met some of the best friends a guy could have: Rex Willing, Ronnie Nelson, Greg Denson, Larry Parsons, and the rest of the gang. If I hadn't wrecked my dad's car, I probably wouldn't have gone into the Marine Corps. If our surf shops weren't going broke, I

BRIGISM

In every adversity is the seed of equal or greater benefit.

wouldn't have been willing to listen when Doug Grissom introduced me for the first time to multilevel and network marketing. Through the friends I met in Amway, I came to know the Lord. I wouldn't have met the love of my life, Miss Lita, or had my three beautiful children. If I hadn't suffered with melanoma and severe back pain, I probably would not have traveled to Salt Lake City to meet Dallin Larsen, and I might never have learned of MonaVie. Thank God for the good and bad times. In every adversity is the seed of equal or greater benefit. Tough times create tough people. Fire truly does refine and make one stronger.

You get the idea. What we regard as a drawback or a mistake, God often uses to get us ready to receive blessings beyond what we could ever think or imagine. It's a setup. Don't look at those valleys in your life as the end of it all. It's only the beginning. If you just keep moving and staying in the game, in every valley you will see another mountaintop. I like to say, "If you're going through hell, don't camp out there. Keep going!" This, too, shall pass, but you have to do something about it.

Lita and I aren't superhuman. But we have tapped into the One who helped to show us who we really are. By myself, I would still be that long-haired, hippie-type, beer-drinking, dope-smoking surfer without much of a hope or a future. But with God, well, you just read about what has happened in my life. Amazing isn't it?

We're just common, ordinary folks desiring to do extraordinary things in our lives, just like you! We've been through some tough things, but we

Accentuate the positive and eliminate the negative. don't give those difficulties a lot of attention. We look back only to learn, not to allow any of those negative experiences to hold us back. If God wanted us to look back in life, He would have put eyes in the back of our heads. Instead, we focus forward, toward the future. We accentuate the positive and eliminate the negative, or as some have said, *illuminate* the negative. Cast light on it, and suddenly those dark experiences don't seem so ominous anymore.

Occasionally, someone will ask, "What are your plans for the future?"

I see us doing the same sort of thing that we are doing now, but my role is changing. There will be new challenges, and in those we will meet new people with whom we will come into relationship. Each new challenge and relationship will bring another opportunity for us to grow and mature. I look forward to teaching, mentoring, and encouraging those folks that we will come into relationships with and developing new friendships. I consider myself an architect; I help people build their dreams. I desire to pull that dream out of folks and help them to facilitate it so they achieve the success they deserve.

U-Can-II and R3Global are the platforms I use to feed folks the resources they need to overcome and become. Who in this day doesn't want the restoration of their hopes and dreams, revival in the process, and restitution for all the things that have been taken from them? Who doesn't want to succeed and succeed big? Everyone on the planet needs to know how to achieve ultimate success in their lives, to be able to live the abundant life that the Lord promises to all who seek Him.

Consequently, my goal is to reach a broader base of people throughout the United States and even globally. Lita and I are wired to help people. We love the MonaVie business, the people in it, and what it stands for. But just like my other business encounters, they are only vehicles that provide a platform for me to do what I am called to do. Relational marketing is the purest form of free enterprise I have ever encountered. Anyone anywhere in the Free World can start with nothing but a hope and a dream and accomplish anything their heart desires. I am that person. I dared to dream a dream, and I decided to believe in that dream. Because we found our place in life through the industry of networking, we have been about the business of achieving many of our goals and dreams. By simply focusing our attention on helping other folks to achieve, we ourselves achieved, and we achieved in a big way. We helped ourselves by helping others.

I enjoy marketing our R3Global system and implementing its principles as a way of doing things that will produce positive results. I know our systematic way of building people's belief in themselves works. It not only works with MonaVie and the other businesses I have been associated with, but it will work for anyone or any business that sees the value in building people. Build people up and they will build your business.

We approach it with the support of a proven way of doing that through our system. The gist of that system is an acronym for that very word: **S**ave **Y**ourself **S**tress, **T**ime, **E**nergy, and **M**oney. How can you prove the system? By checking the fruit on the tree. If it produces good fruit, take it and enjoy it. If not, why would you even consider it?

Changing the way people feel about themselves is the starting point, and that takes faith. Many people who don't consider themselves people of faith still understand faith's importance. They can prosper in business if they follow the principles and patterns even if they are not believers. God's Word is His Word and it is true for all, regardless of whether we are believers or not. He doesn't require us to believe it, but if we do, it will work for whoever follows and applies it. I have seen financial blessings come to many more nonbelievers in my life than believers. But it all comes down to this: being faithful, diligent, and obedient to your calling. It's rather simple. If you do something as well as or better than anyone else, and you do a better job marketing it, you will be successful. But financial success and prosperity are two different things. Some people have a lot of money but lack peace. They die miserable.

Build people up and they will build your business.

Prosperity, although it may bring financial blessings, is a condition of the mind and heart. Many people are prosperous, but they are not wealthy in money. I know many folks who are fully content to be in the positions they're in because they have found God's peace concerning who they are and what they are doing.

Changing the way you think is a significant key to success. You become what you read, listen to, and participate with. It's called influence. Your mother said it best: "You become like those you hang out with." So find a model person to emulate, study that person, and do what he or she does. Trust me, you will become like them.

That is my ultimate purpose for writing this book. If you don't have a model that you can get near or relate to, use me. I am making everything and anything that has transformed me and my life available to anyone who desires the same results.

Remember: what one person can do, so can another. You just have to want to believe it for yourself. If I could do it for you, I would, but I can't. You must do that yourself. It's kind of like going to the bathroom; you're going to have to do that one on your own. I tell folks, you're in business for yourself but not by yourself. What you see in your mind's eye is what you can create in your life. See it there first, and you will soon see it elsewhere.

It all starts with a dream. Without a dream, a person is dead from the neck up. But MonaVie and R3Global cannot manufacture your dream. *You* have to provide that, then networking and relational marketing can become the vehicle through which you can accomplish those dreams. I have tremendous confidence in this great industry of networking to help

---

B R I G I S M

Without a dream, a person is dead from the neck up.

---

you make your dreams come true. When I'm describing our business to people who are considering getting involved, I tell them, "There are three essential components to a successful relational marketing business. One, you have to have a great product or service. Two, you need a quality distributor base. Three, you have to have a great support system." We have all three essential elements with MonaVie and R3Global, and that makes expanding our business relatively simple. The only missing element is YOU.

Quality individuals buy into the mission, message, methodology, and the motive of our hearts. Then we become partners in this great venture.

I travel all over the United States and in a number of foreign countries asking people some basic questions: "Can you get everything you want through what you are currently doing? If time and money were no issue in your life, what would you be doing?" "What else do you have where you can legally earn an extra two to five thousand dollars per week in the next three to twelve months in your spare time? Can it replicate itself so it increases and turns into long-term, passive income?" If you have something that will do that for you, wonderful! Hang on to it. But if you don't, why not consider a

True success is not measured in stuff.

career in an industry that is set to be the next big thing? In relational marketing, you can earn a little or a lot depending on your willingness to share the product and business opportunity with others. You have the freedom to set your own schedule, work at your own pace, and work with people whom you choose to work with who want to help you succeed and enjoy a life of adventure. What other business offers those benefits? If you don't do this, what else are you going to do to help fulfill your dreams?

Remember, true success is not measured in stuff; it is not a position. Success is the progressive realization of worthwhile goals and dreams. But it is even more than that. Ultimate success is hearing the commendation from Jesus, "Well done, good and faithful servant."[48] That affirmation of your success will ring throughout eternity.

My goal is to influence as many people as I can to consider a relationship with Christ. At first, that idea staggered me, but then I got to thinking about it. God has been teaching me the power of exponential growth for most of my life. He's been preparing me for the challenge. I know how this works. I don't need to go knocking on millions of doors. I just need to reach ten people and teach them how to reach ten. Each of them will teach another ten how to reach ten; that's a thousand people. Then each of those thousand people will reach ten; that's ten thousand. Those ten thousand will each reach ten, and that will be one hundred thousand. That one hundred thousand will each reach ten more; that's a million. Each of those million people will reach ten; that's ten million. That ten million will each help ten; that's one hundred million. Each of those will reach ten; that's a billion. And that billion people will help reach ten people; that is ten billion people, which is more than the population on the entire planet! Ten by ten, ten levels deep is every person in the world. Will everyone participate in doing good for others? No, but I only need a few who help a few just like the Lord did.

He touched twelve, who touched a few, who touched a few, and so on and so on. I got reached by someone who shared, and now I am reaching out to share with a few more. It's our duty and our calling. Two thousand years after Jesus did His part, the gospel continues to be perpetuated today through those folks who accepted, believed, and engaged in duplicating that message of hope. Now that's relational networking at its premium! See, it's been around for quite some time. God is the original networker. Nothing is more fulfilling than knowing that you are a part of this great commission to reach the world with the good news.

Don't tell me that I won't see my dream come true. I believe it can be done! And I believe that God will use a little berry from the Amazon and a cleaned-up surfer from Jacksonville to touch the world. If you want to help, all you have to do is say, "Here I am. I'm available. Please use me, Lord."

BRIGISM

You can have all the stuff in the world as long
as the stuff doesn't have you.

"Not me, Brig," I hear you saying. "I've never succeeded at much of anything."

Don't allow your past failures to define your future. With God's help, you can succeed far beyond anything you have ever imagined. I recall an incident recorded in the Bible in which Peter and some fellow fishermen had been fishing all night long and hadn't caught a thing. Jesus met them in the morning and encouraged them to launch out one more time. "Throw the nets on the right side," Jesus told them. No doubt, those professional fishermen thought, *What does that preacher know about our business?* But they obeyed nonetheless and the results were staggering: an enormous, overflowing, mind-boggling success. The fish were practically jumping into their boat, and more would have, but there was no more room![49] Those fishermen went from having nothing to overflowing prosperity. What happened? What changed?

Simply this: they trusted God and He became the center of their lives, including their business. That's what I want as well. I want to be known as a man who kept God first in my life, not with words only, but with my actions and attitudes, in every aspect of my life, especially my business. I've tried living life without Jesus and with Jesus. *With* Jesus is better! Once I was lost and now I am found, once I was blind and now I see.

Don't let fear dictate to you what you can or can't do. Fear and faith can coexist in the same thought, but it's your choice how to respond. Billy Sunday said, "Fear knocked at my door, faith answered and there was no one was there!"

I don't apologize for my values. I value God in my life. I love my wife and children, and I love my country too. I've had friends who shed their blood for our freedom. I have friends whose sons and daughters have lost limbs and some who have lost their lives protecting our freedom. So, for as long as I live, I will honor veterans and others who have served our country. I will not run away; I'm going to stand up and do what is right. I'm going to take off my hat

I don't apologize for my values.

and place my hand over my heart as I listen to the national anthem and pledge allegiance to our flag. Even though I'm not a good singer, I will sing with all my being, "God, Bless America!"

I made a promise to God many years ago, when I first came to know Christ. I said, "Lord, I know You will never forsake me, so I want You to know that I will never deny You. Whether You put me in front of one person or one hundred thousand people, I will proclaim Your goodness and Your glory. I will honor You and tell people about You as best I know how."

Charlie Kalb said, "Some people say they are afraid to bring people to meetings where Brig is speaking because they are afraid of what he is going to say. That's so untrue. I've been around Brig for more than twenty-five years. You *know* what Brig is going to say."

Charlie is right. I am always going to exalt the Lord and tell people what He has done for me and what He can do for others. What He has done for me, He will do for you. Trust Him. Some folks actually confront me about speaking so publicly about how through accepting Christ you can get into heaven. I pretty much respond to them by asking them a question: "So you don't want to hear about how God can save your soul and get your ticket punched to get into heaven?" If they respond negatively to that invitation to go to heaven, I suggest that they will just go to hell. They usually catch the paradox.

What's my advice to people wanting to succeed in life or in network marketing? Same as I have always told them: define your dreams, set your goals, and make a commitment. You must have a dream for which you are willing to fight. Set your goal and commit to reaching that goal within a specific period of time; then, just follow the folks who have gone before you. Do what they have done. Follow the pattern for success. In relational marketing, we're in the people business. People move product; product doesn't move people. So learn to identify people who want more than what they have and are willing to do something about it.

Network marketing is the vehicle to take you to your dreams. We teach that you make friends, and your friends will build the business. Friends do what friends do. After we identify those who want more than they have, we connect with them by teaming up and assisting them in building their businesses. We develop a working relationship that turns into a true friendship, often a friend and associate for life. Success comes to those who start this process and refuse to quit. It doesn't happen overnight, but for anyone who wants to be a part of something bigger than themselves, success is just a decision away.

You can do what we have done. You simply have to dream it, believe it, and decide to achieve it. Can you? Yes. Will you? You are the only one who can make that decision. My questions to you are: Why not you? Why not now?

EPILOGUE

Y OU ARE THE SUM total of all the decisions you have made in life. It is and always will be the choices you make that make you.

That's important, and therein lies the secret to my overcoming and becoming. I raised the bar in my life when I said, "I will no longer permit negative experiences or people to influence me, causing me to decrease in my personhood or character."

Ralph Waldo Emerson wrote, "Sow a thought, reap an action; sow an action, reap a habit; sow a habit, reap a character; sow a character, reap a destiny."

That pattern has proven true in my life. Instead of *being* a character, I developed character. Now, because I choose on a daily basis to move in the direction of improving and growing my character, destiny presents itself. I have become the sum total of all the books I have read and all the people with whom I have chosen to associate. When you are around good people, good things happen. Choosing to be in good environments will cause you to prosper.

I now know that I can help anyone who chooses to become more of what they know in their heart that they can become. I can and will support that person just as others have supported me. I believe that person is *you.* You have a destiny, and it may well be wrapped up in part of mine. I just happen to have a vehicle and a support system to help you identify your destiny and to help you accomplish it.

Do you understand, then, why I get so excited about relational marketing? I chose to be involved in networking because it showed up in my life at a time when I needed something positive to happen for me. I really didn't go searching for a new career. I just made a simple decision to give it a shot, especially since I had no other positive alternatives showing up at that time in my life. As you know from reading my story, I was as low as a person can go.

Who would have guessed that in just a few years I would develop the skills I needed to become one of the most successful networkers on the planet? Who could have known that?

I'll tell you who knew.

God knew. He knew even before I was born. And He believed in me when nobody else did. When He and I connected, He revealed to me His purpose and plan for my life. He let me taste my destiny! I not only found my place in life, I found my purpose and my passion.

Earlier in my life, I had been addicted to things that harmed me, wreaked havoc in my life, and hurt others. I suffered the consequences of choosing the wrong paths, and I left a lot of injured people in the wake of my misery. For that, I will always be sorry.

But my God is the God of second chances—many second chances! I didn't die in the process, so I believe that I survived for a reason. God was not and is not done with me.

Guess what? He's not done with you yet, either!

YOU'VE MADE it this far in my book, so let me sum it all up for you with some of my favorite nuggets of truth:

Dream a dream. Keep it simple. Limit the voices. Go with what shows up. Quit questioning yourself after you've made a decision. Learn to stay fully focused on your goals. Do a little bit every day to reach your goals. Don't compare yourself to others. Give yourself permission and time to succeed. Keep your chin up and your knees down.

Do something, and do it now. Procrastination is the assassination of motivation. Indecision is a decision. Work, work, work like it all depends on you, and pray like it all depends on God. Think in terms of possibilities. Never give up on your dreams.

Get started and don't quit. Winners never quit, and quitters never win.

HELEN KELLER said, "Life is either a daring adventure or nothing. Security does not exist in nature, nor do the children of men as a whole experience it. Avoiding danger is no safer in the long run than exposure."

If I leave you with only one thing after sharing a bit of my story, I would hope that I have somehow encouraged you to at least give yourself a chance to do something great with your life. Don't miss out on what could possibly be the beginning of a great adventure for you and your family. Don't deny yourself the chance to experience the joy so many search for in life.

I've heard it said and I believe that happiness in life is this: having someone to love, something to do, and something to hope for. I couldn't agree more.

When I met folks who sowed into my life with unconditional love, I was led to a point of surrender where I met the One who loved me most. Since that moment in time in August 1979, I have been on a personal mission to pass that love on to countless others whom I've had the honor and privilege of knowing. I have someone to love.

I was introduced to the opportunity of network marketing in January 1979, and my life has never been the same since. I risked trying something way outside of my comfort zone, and guess what? It worked out just peachy. Life has been good, and it's not over yet! I have something to do.

I am on a mission in life to help as many people as I can to succeed and to succeed big. My desire is to help people experience the happiness and joy that I know, and I am able to do so when they are willing to help themselves. I have something to hope for.

Are you willing to help yourself? If so, that's where we get to meet, interact, and develop a relationship. I have the knowledge, ability, and resources to help you do something in an industry that plays no favorites. Any and all can succeed to any level they choose. It's only a decision away.

I've asked you, why not you? why not now? If you were touched by anything in my story, let me ask you another question: Why not this?

Wouldn't it be cool to be mentored personally and professionally by the number-one relational marketer in the world—me! We all market something. I can show you how you can incorporate this into your life. Indecision is a decision, so decide to do something, and do it now. Today is the day you can begin a new chapter in your life.

Please don't deny the world a chance to see the *you* whom God created you to be. I'm offering you an opportunity to be all that you can be with me and others like me who can and will support you in your quest for success.

Blessings on your journey! I wish for you ultimate success. Wear sunglasses, because your future looks bright!

Your friend, associate, and ambassador of goodwill to the world,

Changing my world one person at a time through relational marketing.

Why not you?
Why not this?
Why not now?
Yours is the next great story to be told!

RESOURCES

FOR MORE INFORMATION ABOUT Brig Hart, R3Global, or MonaVie, visit www.brighart.com.

R3Global
6767 Phillips Industrial Boulevard
Jacksonville, FL 32256

Other resources that you may find helpful include:

New Life Network: www.newlifenetwork.org

R3Global.com

Paul Anderson Youth Home
1603 McIntosh Street
Vidalia, GA 30474
(912) 537-7237

Dean Sikes, Spirit of America: www.deansikes.net

Drew Read, *Dangerous Trends Impacting Your Child*

Rex Crain, *Life Lifts*

The MORE Project: www.brighart.com

ACKNOWLEDGMENTS

THERE IS NO WAY I could ever thank all the folks who have contributed to the penning of this book, so I will approach this sensitive matter in this way:

Thanks to all my friends and associates who encouraged me over the years to tell a bit of my story. Thanks to all those who participated in assisting Ken and me in getting it done.

Special thanks to John and Linda Mason for encouraging and helping me over the finish line.

Extra special thanks to my lovely partner for life: Mrs. Lita.

NOTES

1. Ecclesiastes 9:4, NIV.
2. Isaiah 55:11, NKJV.
3. See Matthew 6:21, NIV.
4. John 15:5, NIV.
5. John 16:33, NIV.
6. Romans 8:28, NIV.
7. Matthew 18:19–20, NIV.
8. The U.S. Food and Drug Administration has not yet granted permission to MonaVie to make any medicinal claims concerning their products. At R3Global and Brighart.com we make no claims for the product other than that the natural juice produced by MonaVie's flash-freeze-dried process of nineteen berries gives a person's body the nutrients it needs to heal itself.
9. Matthew 5:39–40, NIV.
10. Proverbs 6:31, NKJV.
11. This information is based on MonaVie's income disclosure statement.
12. Philippians 4:13, NKJV.
13. See 1 Corinthians 3:10–15.
14. Philippians 1:6, NIV.
15. Proverbs 17:22, NIV.
16. Matthew 5:16, NKJV.
17. See John 15:5.
18. See Proverbs 18:21.
19. Proverbs 17:17, NKJV.
20. Proverbs 3:5–6, NIV.
21. Hebrews 10:25, NIV.
22. Romans 8:31, NIV.
23. Proverbs 29:18, KJV.
24. Proverbs 13:17, TLB.
25. Proverbs 22:6, KJV.
26. Mark 12:31, KJV.

27. Luke 6:38, NIV.
28. 2 Corinthians 9:6, NIV.
29. Galatians 6:7, KJV.
30. Luke 12:34, NIV.
31. Proverbs 11:24–25, NIV.
32. Galatians 6:7, NIV.
33. Luke 10:7, KJV.
34. James 1:27, NIV.
35. Zechariah 4:6, NIV.
36. Mark 8:36, KJV.
37. Matthew 25:21, NIV.
38. Jeremiah 29:11, NIV.
39. 3 John 2, KJV.
40. Deuteronomy 28:13, NIV.
41. See Matthew 6:33.
42. Matthew 9:12, NIV.
43. See John 21:15–17.
44. Luke 9:26, NIV.
45. Luke 12:9, KJV.
46. Galatians 5:22–23, NIV.
47. Isaiah 55:11, NIV.
48. Matthew 25:21, NIV.
49. See Luke 5:4–7.